Climate Change as Class War

Climate Change as Class War

Building Socialism on a Warming Planet

Matthew T. Huber

VERSO

London • New York

First published by Verso 2022

1 3 5 7 9 10 8 6 4 2

Verso
UK: 6 Meard Street, London W1F 0EG
US: 388 Atlantic Avenue, Brooklyn, NY 11217
versobooks.com

Verso is the imprint of New Left Books

ISBN-13: 978-1-78873-388-5
ISBN-13: 978-1-78873-389-2 (US EBK)
ISBN-13: 978-1-78873-390-8 (UK EBK)

British Library Cataloguing in Publication Data
A catalogue record for this book is available from the British Library

Library of Congress Cataloging-in-Publication Data
A catalog record for this book is available from the Library of Congress

Typeset by Hewer Text UK Ltd, Edinburgh
Printed and bound by CPI Group (UK) Ltd, Croydon CR0 4YY

For Loretta

Contents

Introduction: Climate Change as Class War

Introduction: We're Still Losing

Most books like this would start by laying out the terrifying science of climate change: the hotter temperatures, Arctic melting, and intensifying droughts. I will not begin like this. If you have this book, chances are you know the situation is dire. And you know we have precious little time. In 2018, the Intergovernmental Panel on Climate Change (IPCC), gave us twelve years (now eight!) to implement "rapid, far-reaching and unprecedented changes in all aspects of society."[1]

You probably also know that, as Bill McKibben constantly points out, we are "losing" the climate fight.[2] And losing badly. After a sudden drop of emissions due to the global health emergency spurred by Covid-19, emissions resumed their march upward in late 2020.[3] A May 2021 report by the International Energy Agency (IEA) not only claimed there should be no new investment in oil and gas or coal power starting immediately, it also observed that fossil fuels still represent 80 percent of total energy supply as of 2020.[4] Another report in June 2021 from a renewable energy group flatly stated, "Since 2009, the [global] share of fossil fuels in final energy consumption has remained the same."[5]

---

1 Intergovernmental Panel on Climate Change, "Summary for Policymakers of IPCC Special Report on Global Warming of 1.5°C approved by governments," October 8, 2018.

2 Bill McKibben, "Winning slowly is the same as losing" *Rolling Stone*, December 1, 2017.

3 Nina Chestney "IEA says global CO2 emissions rising again after nearly 6% fall last year," Reuters, March 2, 2021.

4 International Energy Agency, *Net-Zero by 2050: A Roadmap for the Global Energy Sector* (Paris: International Energy Agency, 2021).

5 "Renewables 2021 Status Report: Key Messages for Decision Makers." ren21.net.

Even though emissions are the only measure of "winning" that matters, many seem to think the tide is turning toward climate action. In 2019, there were massive social protests in the streets, like the youth climate strikes and Fridays for Future, but this momentum was upended by the pandemic. In 2021, due to investor pressure, many fossil fuel firms have announced ambitious new targets—some oil and gas companies even pledged to reach net zero emissions by 2050.[6] Blocs of financial capital have pledged to integrate climate risk into their investment portfolios under the rubric of Environment, Social, and Governance (ESG) investing.[7] After the bleak years of climate denial under the Trump administration, the newly elected president, Joe Biden, has vowed to take a "whole-of-government approach to the climate crisis" and proposed to slash greenhouse emissions by 50 percent below 2005 levels by 2030.[8] Also to much fanfare, the other major emitter, China, announced its own target to reach net zero emissions by 2060.

We should recognize that this talk of targets and pledges projecting out to 2030, 2035, 2050, and 2060 is similar to the talk of the 1990s and early 2000s, when international climate negotiators focused their gaze on 2005 and 2020. What matters is real progress in a rapid and wholesale transition from fossil fuels. And that is simply not happening.

Despite the rhetoric, the Biden administration's main climate policy is an infrastructure bill that falls well short of the fiscal commitment most think is necessary to meet his 2030 target.[9] And, as of this writing, bipartisan negotiations with austerity-minded Republicans and Democrats are whittling it down still further, causing climate activists to beg for the mere *inclusion* of any climate measures. Given

---

6   Myles McCormick, "US producers begin to follow Europe with emissions pledges" *Financial Times*, December 6, 2020.

7   Lizzy Gurdus, "Climate change will be a 'really big' focus for ESG investors in 2021, market analyst says," December 16, 2020. CNBC.com.

8   White House, "Fact Sheet," January 26, 2021, "Fact Sheet," April 22, 2021. Whitehouse.gov.

9   See, Adam Tooze, "America's race to net-zero," *New Statesman*, April 21, 2021.

historical patterns, it is likely that the Democrats, the only US party committed to climate action, will lose their control over Congress in 2022. Despite much media praise around Biden's pledge to "pause" new leases for oil and gas on public lands, the allocation of existing leases under Biden remains similar to levels under Trump: "From the start of February to the end of April, the administration approved 1,179 drilling permits on federal lands, not far from the four-year high of nearly 1,400 approved over a similar three-month period at the end of Trump's term."[10] Those figures are just for public lands; they do not cover the continued extraction of fossil fuels on private lands.

Climate Change as Class War begins from the premise that the climate movement is losing, and seeks how we might not. This is a question of *power*. As Jane McAlevey points out, to build power social movements must first engage in a "power-structure analysis" of "precisely who needs to be defeated, overcome, or persuaded to achieve success."[11] On that front, we need to build power to take on some of the wealthiest corporations in world history. My central argument is that this particular power struggle is a *class struggle* over relations that underpin our social and ecological relationship with nature and the climate itself: ownership and control of production.

Climate Change as Class War argues for both a new "ecological" and Marxist understanding of class. I argue climate change is a class issue in three ways. First, the climate struggle needs to focus on *production*. I argue for a return to the quite orthodox understanding of class as a relationship to the "means of production." This may appear outdated and more relevant to the era of massive industrialization and worker organizing in the late nineteenth and early-to-mid twentieth century. But if we are concerned about climate change and ecological break-down, it remains an issue of industrial production today. In fact, the entire human relationship to the natural world is, at its core, a relationship of production—how we produce the food, energy, housing, and

---

10 Branko Marcetic, "Joe Biden Is Almost as Pro-Drilling as Trump," *Jacobin*, June 3, 2021.

11 Jane McAlevey, *No Shortcuts: Building Power in the New Gilded Age* (Oxford: Oxford University Press, 2016), 4.

other basics of life. It is true that production in twenty-first-century capitalism includes all kinds of so-called immaterial labor, but even these forms of knowledge production have a material basis linked to emissions and the climate crisis (for example, the digital world of the internet relies on the material world of energy-intensive server farms). This production-centered approach means we need to focus our organizing energy against the particular class fraction of the capitalist class that controls the production of energy from fossil fuels and other industrial carbon-intensive industries like steel, cement, and the industry profiled in Chapter 2, nitrogen fertilizer. In Chapter 6, I also examine the production of electricity and the investor-owned private electric utility industry—much of which continues to burn fossil fuels and represents over a quarter of all greenhouse gas emissions in the United States.[12]

Second, a specific class overwhelmingly shapes the climate move-ment: the *professional class*.[13] The most common climate activists include NGO staff, scientists, journalists, think tank analysts, and aspir-ant professionals (students). The professional class is a historically specific class formation that ballooned in the postwar era alongside rapid expansion of higher education alongside mass *deindustrialization* in countries like the United States.[14] Thus, professionals are also defined

---

12 United States Environmental Protection Agency, "Sources of Greenhouse Gas Emissions." epa.gov.

13 I proposed this book in 2017. In the meantime, the concept of the "Professional-Managerial Class" (PMC) has exploded as a central and polarizing topic both between left and liberal politics and within different factions on the left (e.g., the Bernie Sanders–vs.–Elizabeth Warren policy debate of the 2019–20 primary campaign). I will review this debate in Chapter 3, but my general position is that a class politics for our time clearly needs to pay attention to the role of education in creating either divisions within the broadly defined working class or creating separate classes in themselves. (The political and ideological divisions remain regardless of whether we call the PMC a "class" or not.) While I think the debate over class can become pedantic—and not particularly useful politically—I will argue for a conception of the professional class as defined by a specific relationship to production.

14 During the peak of working-class power in the twentieth century, socialist movements were embedded in industrial factory production. The prospect of "seizing" the means of production and transforming capitalist scarcity to socialist abundance seemed viscerally possible. Much of the "proletarian" workforce by definition had directly experienced, or had cultural memories of, their agrarian past (and had little interest in

by their relationship to production—in this case, like the working class, it is separated from production. Unlike the working class, professionals occupy more advantaged segments of the labor market doing what Marxists often call "mental labor," "knowledge work," or "cognitive labor."[15] Yet from an ecological perspective, the knowledge economy is a specific "postindustrial" form of work defined by its temporal and spatial *distance* from industrial mass production. This has two consequences for climate politics: first, professional-class climate politics fixates on its own relatively comfortable consumption as the core driver of climate change (and tends to ignore industrial production). Second, the role of education in class formation leads professional-class climate politics to fixate on the science of the climate crisis and ecological collapse. The professional class centers its politics not on material struggle over resources and power, but on "knowledge," or the belief or denial of climate change itself. It also tends to marshal technocratic knowledge to propose nonconfrontational "smart" policy fixes that brim with logic and good incentives, but fail in terms of mass appeal or clear material benefits. Professional-class climate politics also includes "radical" variants that call for "system change," "climate justice," or "degrowth," but offer little in the way of strategy on how to build the kind of mass movement we need to defeat the fossil fuel industry.

Clearly, for this class the role of education and "credentials" is central to their project of carving out advantages in the labor market, but my argument is more about how educational credentials shape their political outlook. In the United States and much of the Western world, the last few decades have seen increasing partisan polarization

---

going back). In contrast, professional-class climate politics emerged in what Aaron Benanav calls the "postindustrial doldrums" where postmodern thought and ecological crisis have led many to reject industrial modernity *tout court*. These sentiments come out of lived reality completely severed from industrial production, which is either automated or offshored and totally invisible to the professional class. See, Aaron Benanav, *Automation and the Future of Work* (London: Verso, 2020, 56).

15 See, e.g., Nick Dyer-Witheford, "Struggles in the Planet Factory: Class Composition and Global Warming," in jan jagodzinski (ed.) *Interrogating the Anthropocene: Ecology, Aesthetics, Pedagogy, and the Future in Question* (Cham, Switzerland: Palgrave Macmillan, 2018), 75–103; 85–8.

along educational lines (particularly between the college and non–college educated).[16] This has led climate politics to become almost entirely a concern among those in (roughly) the upper third of the educated and credentialed classes. In other words, climate politics primarily appeals to a *minority* of the population (in the United States, only one third of adults have a college degree).[17] This poses a fundamental *democratic* problem for climate politics.

Third, to defeat the entrenched power of the capitalist class, we will need a mass popular movement. I argue only the working class has the capacity to achieve this kind of mass movement. We can define the working class as those separated from the means of production and forced to sell their labor to survive. But we do not often understand this definition as an ecological relationship to the conditions of life. As Stefania Barca puts it, the working class is defined by "a unique and global process of violent separation from their means of subsistence."[18] This separation from the ecological conditions of life forces the working class to survive via the market—a fundamental source of economic insecurity. Furthermore, and unlike the professional class, the working class also tends more toward manual labor and lacks the credentials that create advantages in the labor market and, sometimes, autonomy in the labor process.

Why is the working class central to the climate fight? The power of the working class is rooted in three factors. First, it is the vast majority of the population—meaning any *democratic or majoritarian* approach to climate action must build a working-class coalition. Second, its strategic location at the point of production gives it structural power over the source of capital's profits and social reproduction more generally. Working-class power is most effective in periods of mass

---

16   See, Thomas Piketty, *Capital and Ideology* (Cambridge, MA: Harvard University Press, 2020).

17   Eitan D. Hersh, *Politics Is for Power: How to Move Beyond Political Hobbyism, Take Action, and Make Real Change* (New York: Simon and Schuster, 2020).

18   Stefania Barca, *Forces of Reproduction: Notes for a Counter-Hegemonic Anthropocene* (Cambridge, UK: Cambridge University Press).

strikes and disruption that force elites and capitalists to cede to mass demands.[19] Third, because economic insecurity defines working-class life, they have a fundamental material *interest* in transformations in the relations of production. In recent years, the Green New Deal political program emerged on the premise that these material interests in economic security could help build a popular movement for both decarbonization and economic rights to housing, energy, transport, and other needs. Yet, as I show in Chapter 5, the defeats of Green New Deal candidates like Jeremy Corbyn and Bernie Sanders remind us that such "interests" are not pre-given, but must be organized through durable working-class institutions like political parties, unions, and media infrastructure.

If the planet continues to burn, future historians will no doubt find our society puzzling: we clearly understood the gravity of climate change, but did nothing. Capital, and its associated ideologies, are blocking the changes needed. A clear barrier is simply an ideology of private property. As Andreas Malm observes, "capitalist property has the status of the ultimate sacred realm."[20] This respect for property legally allows private capitalists to continue to extract fossil fuel and sell it for a profit. As of this writing, governments still approve thousands of fossil fuel extractive projects all over the world.[21] It is a great achievement of neoliberal ideology that policymakers today barely imagine the expropriation of fossil fuel property as a conceivable option despite the increasing severity of the crisis.[22] While Marx

19 Adaner Usmani calls this "disruptive capacity." Adaner Usmani, "Democracy and Class Struggle," *American Journal of Sociology*, Vol. 124, no. 3 (2018): 664–704. See also, Tarun Banerjee, Michael Schwartz, and Kevin A. Young, *Levers of Power: How the 1% Rules and What the 99% Can Do About It* (London: Verso, 2020).

20 Andreas Malm, *How to Blow Up a Pipeline* (London: Verso, 2021), 68.

21 As I write this, Extinction Rebellion Cambridge offered a useful thread on Twitter, compiling a list of ongoing and new projects in the works. twitter.com/xr_cambridge/status/1404010271094579203?s=20. (June 13, 2021).

22 However, the idea of nationalizing the fossil fuel industry has finally started to appear in socialist left circles. Peter Gowan, "A Plan to Nationalize Fossil-Fuel Companies," *Peoples Policy Project*, March 21, 2018.

referred to the capitalist class that expropriated the means of production from the working class, capitalists today have expropriated our means of survival, our planetary future;[23] they have expropriated our atmosphere and turned it into their private dumping ground. They are attempting to expropriate our planetary future."[24]

It is equally clear that the climate crisis requires a combination of public investment and central planning to rapidly phase out fossil fuels, but most governments remain committed to private capital and anarchic market competition delivering the energy transition. Such a commitment would have to challenge the private control over investment itself. One can find in history innumerable cases in which private capital refuses to invest in such long-term public investments because of time horizons (like the federal highway system) or lack of profitability (like rural electrification). The reason climate activists have seized on the historical examples of the New Deal and World War II is because these periods elevated public investment and central planning to central planks in a massive program of social restructuring. In Chapter 6, I show how a commitment to public ownership and planning—against the concerns of private property rights and profitability—must be at the core of building a new electricity system (something I call "socialism in one sector"). For example, it is clear a buildout of clean energy would require an entirely new grid based on many more transmission lines—yet private property rights and cost considerations inhibit such a buildout at every step.[25] In 2021, the year the IEA announced that oil and gas companies must make zero new investments to meet climate goals, John Kerry, the Biden administration's climate envoy, asserted, "No government is going to solve this problem . . . the solutions are going to come from the private sector."[26] Treasury Secretary Janet Yellen struck a similar note in

23   Karl Marx, *Capital*, Vol. 1. (London: Penguin, 1990), 929.

24   Ibid., 930.

25   David Roberts, "Transmission week: why we need more big power lines," *Volts. Wtf*, January 25, 2021.

26   Avery Ellfeldt, "Kerry: Markets, not government, will solve climate change," *E&E News*, March 26, 2021.

assessing the massive scale of "green investment" required, saying, "Private capital will need to fill most of that gap."[27] Many policy experts take these assertions as unchangeable facts and design elaborate workarounds that try to nudge private capital in the right direction. Yet all the evidence suggests that volatile markets—and associated booms and busts in clean energy sectors—are not producing the carefully coordinated energy transition that human survival requires.

Finally, the almost religious faith in a market-led transition ensures that all the criteria for clean energy production boil down to the narrow concerns of capital: cost and profitability. But every clean-energy option poses significant cost concerns in comparison to dirty alternatives. So as long as we let "costs" drive the energy system, fossil fuels will continue to win out.

You might have heard that renewable energy is now much cheaper than ever before.[28] However, these cost estimates do not consider that solar and wind energy are intermittent and need backup. The cheapest backup is currently fossil-fuel power plants like natural gas. Geothermal renewable power could provide baseload backup, but it currently still costs too much.[29] What about batteries? They only provide a few hours of backup at most. A viable renewable-powered grid requires something called "long-duration storage," but most of those options are also too costly.[30] Another option is nuclear power, but many market analysts also claim nuclear is "uncompetitive" with cheap natural gas and subsidized renewables.[31]

At a certain point, climate action requires a massive buildout of energy infrastructure that does not satisfy the "profit imperative"; it would mean production for the public good of a stable climate

27   Sarah Ewall-Wice, "Yellen says private sector will need to fill the 'gap' in the transition to a green economy," CBSNews.com, April 21, 2021.

28   Max Roser, "Why did renewables become so cheap so fast? And what can we do to use this global opportunity for green growth?" *Our World in Data*, December 1, 2020.

29   David Roberts, "Geothermal energy is poised for a big breakout," *Vox*, October 21, 2020.

30   David Roberts, "Long-duration storage can help clean up the electricity grid, but only if it's super cheap" *Volts.wtf*, June 9, 2021.

31   Marton Dunai and Geert De Clercq, "Nuclear energy too slow, too expensive to save climate: report," Reuters, September 23, 2019.

regardless of the cost. Once again, this requires challenging the *private control* over energy production itself.

Yet before we get to all of this, we need to clear up something. When confronted with the question of responsibility—the question of *who cooked the planet*—the climate movement is highly confused. Usually the answer points to "all of us." The story of climate responsibility we hear is one of millions of diffuse individual choices—millions of carbon footprints— adding up to a planetary impact. What is wrong with this story?

Who Produced Your Carbon Footprint?

In the summer of 2017, a study published in *Environment and Research Letters* made a big splash in the media.[32] The study set out to determine the "most effective individual actions" to combat climate change. The results were conclusive: have fewer children. Taking an average amongst developed nations, having one less child could save you 58.6 tonnes CO_2-equivalent (tCO2e) emission reductions per year. The next best action, "living car free," paled in comparison, with only 2.4 tCO2e saved per year. The logic behind this wide difference is in the methodology. The study insisted on a full life-cycle analysis of your choice to raise your new child. The problem is, not only will this baby likely emit a whole lot of carbon, but also, if you raise your child well, they will have more babies who will also spew lots of carbon. This is just one example of a disturbing resurgence of neo-Malthusian thinking in relation to climate change.[33]

Underlying this study, and much of our thinking on climate politics, is one basic assumption stated in the first sentence in the abstract: "Current anthropogenic climate change is the result of greenhouse

---

32   Seth Wynes and Kimberly A. Nicholas, "The climate mitigation gap: Education and government recommendations miss the most effective individual actions," *Environmental Research Letters*, Vol. 12, No. 7 (2017).

33   Ojeda, Sasser, and Lunstrum review many such examples including one scholar's proposal to pair carbon pricing with a "baby levy." Diana Ojeda, Jade. S. Sasser, and Elizabeth Lunstrum, "Malthus's specter and the anthropocene" *Gender, Place and Culture*, Vol. 27, no. 3 (2020): 316–332; 320.

gas accumulation in the atmosphere, which records the aggregation of billions of individual decisions."[34] Individuals make choices—to have kids, buy a car, eat meat—and all these choices can be added up to equal the total emissions load in the atmosphere. In this additive view, the atmosphere is a sink of emissions and each particle can be traced to an individual agent. It is hard-wired into the politics of climate change that when we get into a car and turn the ignition the emissions are ours, and ours alone. According to conventional wisdom, this is why solving climate change is so difficult. Responsibility for climate change is fundamentally diffuse. Thus, solving the problem requires mobilizing a colossal revolution in individual behavior. How can we change billions of individual decisions? The key for many is education. The study referenced above actually goes on to blame school textbooks for failing to educate adolescents on the best actions to solve climate change—yet it does not cover sex education, which seems most germane to its recommendations. At its core, their educative political project begins at teaching children the reality of climate change against climate denial. Individuals must first *believe* in climate change, so they can make better and more appropriate choices.

This way of thinking is rooted in a basic quantitative tool called "carbon footprint" accounting.[35] It enables you to input your lifestyle choices—the car you drive, your heating system, how much you fly—and receive a distinct value (for instance, 36,000 lbs. of carbon per year). This allows individuals to engage in various experiments in carbon dieting to try to lower their individual footprints. The data from carbon footprints can lead to a kind of progressive class analysis. In this narrative, climate politics focuses responsibility on a class of rich affluent consumers who are disproportionately responsible. Kevin Ummel, for example, shows that "the top 10 percent of US polluters [households] are responsible for nearly 25 percent of

34   Ibid.
35   This methodology was ultimately rooted in the broader method of ecological footprint analysis. See, Nicky Chambers, Craig Simmons, and Mathis Wackernagel, *Sharing Nature's Interest: Ecological Footprints as an Indicator of Sustainability* (London: Routledge, 1996).

emissions."[36] In this vision, the ultimate villain is a greedy consumer: the prototypical example might be the suburbanite Hummer driver. Scaled up to the globe, it is clear it is the "rich countries" (that is, the countries filled with rich consumers) that bear the most responsibility. In 2015, Oxfam released a report titled *Extreme Carbon Inequality* that found the top 10 percent of people in the world are responsible for 50 percent of emissions, while the bottom 50 percent are responsible for only 10 percent.[37] The abstract announces the project in terms of "comparing the average lifestyle consumption footprints of richer and poorer citizens in a range of countries."[38] Yet again, we are back at the concept of emissions attached to "lifestyle"; the way we live generates emissions that are our own individual responsibility.[39]

What kind of class theory lies behind this "progressive" analysis of carbon inequality between rich and poor consumers? For starters, it equates class with income—and infers that higher-income individuals spend more on carbon-intensive consumption. But, carbon footprint analysis is more deeply rooted in neoclassical economics with its particular theory of power in the economy known as "consumer sovereignty." Essentially, it assumes consumers drive the economy and production with their choices. Kevin Ummel says as much: "The goal is to trace emissions back to the household consumption choices that ultimately led to their production."[40] Since consumers have the

36 Kevin Ummel, "Who Pollutes? A Household-Level Database of America's greenhouse gas footprint—Working Paper 381," Center for Global Development. cgdev.org.

37 Timothy Gore, "Extreme carbon inequality: Why the Paris climate deal must put the poorest, lowest emitting, and most vulnerable people first," Oxfam International, December 2, 2015, mb-extreme-carbon-inequality-021215-en.pdf.

38 Ibid., 1.

39 Even the most radical analyses of climate politics reproduce this imprecise analysis of rich versus poor and focus on differences in consumption. Joel Wainwright and Geoff Mann correctly identify the "capitalist class" as responsible, but also make it about that class's consumption: "within every nation-state, the wealthiest social groups (the richest and most powerful people, in essence the capitalist class) are responsible for most of the consumption and carbon emissions that are causing climate change." Joel Wainwright and Geoff Mann, *Climate Leviathan: A Political Theory of Our Planetary Future* (London: Verso), 73. Since writing this, I am relieved to find one exception: Nick Dyer-Witheford makes this same critique of the Oxfam report in "Struggles in the Planet Factory," 77.

40 Ummel, "Who Pollutes?" 1.

power to drive production decisions, so the analysis goes, we must focus on shaping consumer choices. This is the only conceivable rationale for suggesting, as the Oxfam report does, that individuals have their own distinct "share" of emissions: "Individual consumption is responsible for 64 percent of global emissions, with the remaining 36 percent attributed to consumption by governments, investments in infrastructure and international transport."[41]

The theory of consumer sovereignty assumes that producers are captive to the demands of consumers, indeed that they are simply responding to the latter—rather than what is in fact the case: production constrains consumption choices. Much consumption (like driving) is not a "choice" but a necessity of social reproduction (getting to work). Moreover, when we choose commodities, we can only choose those that are profitable to produce in the first place. A contradiction of "environmentally sustainable" commodities (with lower footprints) is that often they are more expensive. The real question one must ask is: Who do we believe has the real *power* over society's economic resources? Consumer sovereignty theory suggests power is diffuse and scattered among individual consumers. But, in fact, power over the economy is not diffuse, but concentrated in the hands of those who control productive resources.

Thus, it should be no surprise that the industrial capitalist class in control of our energy system has explicitly *promoted* carbon footprint ideology. For example, a recent study found ExxonMobil advertisements systematically "worked to shift responsibility for global warming away from the fossil fuel industry and onto consumers."[42] The article recounts the origins of the carbon footprint concept: "The very notion of a personal 'carbon footprint' . . . was first popularized in 2004–6 by oil firm BP as part of its $100+ million-per-year 'beyond

41   Gore, "Extreme carbon inequality," 3.
42   Geoffrey Supran and Naomi Oreskes, "Rhetoric and frame analysis of ExxonMobil's climate change communications," *One Earth* 4: 696–719; 696. This is an important analysis, but as I explain in Chapter 3, like Oreskes's previous work this analysis lends too much importance to the realms of "rhetoric," "framing," and "knowledge" itself.

petroleum' US media campaign."[43] In October 2019 British Petroleum tweeted: "The first step to reducing your emissions is to know where you stand. Find out your #carbonfootprint with our new calculator & share your pledge today." The tweet includes warm and fuzzy pictures of bikes, light bulbs, and windmills with the slogan, "every pledge matters!"

The equation of carbon footprints with consumption is rooted in deeper history, in which society and politics itself became more oriented around consumption since World War II. Yet even in a "consumer society," consumers still mostly do not own or control productive enterprises. More accurately, we own and control the means of social reproduction.[44] For the middle-class, propertied consumer in the United States, this entails a whole host of often carbon-intensive machines—cars, dishwashers, refrigerators, clothes dryers, central heating and cooling, and the increasingly expansive set of electronic devices that saturate modern life. As I have argued elsewhere, this relative material affluence in the realm of social reproduction was part of a political effort to save capitalism in the wake of the Great Depression of the 1930s.[45] In order to maintain capital's control over production, it became necessary to give sectors of the working class a sense of freedom and material comfort within the realm of social reproduction. Yet since the 1970s, the capitalist class has attacked even these relative scraps of alienating and privatized working-class "comfort." Only some of the dwindling professional classes have clung to its premises of debt-financed higher education, home ownership and what in Chapter 4 I call "privatized provisioning." Since the 1970s, we have also seen massive deindustrialization in those areas of the world where the working class won material gains. In the Global North today, most industrial production is either automated or offshored. In everyday life, all we *see* is the world of

---

43   Ibid., 712.
44   See Tithi Bhattacharya (ed.) *Social Reproduction Theory Remapping Class, Recentering Oppression* (London: Pluto, 2017).
45   Matthew T. Huber, *Lifeblood: Oil, Freedom, and the Forces of Capital* (Minneapolis: University of Minnesota Press, 2013).

consumption. It is unsurprising that we focus carbon responsibility on this realm.

This relative material comfort for some deceives many into thinking it is affluent consumers who are actually in control of the economy and have the power to change it. It is worth exploring, however, the fundamental differences between social reproduction and production under capitalism. For even the richest among us, the goal of social reproduction is to fulfill human needs and, perhaps, enjoy life.[46] This involves a lot of gendered and unpaid work like house cleaning and child care, but it also involves leisure, entertainment, and fun. To put it in Marx's terms, workers exchange the commodity (C) labor power for a wage or income (M) and use that money to purchase the commodities they need to survive (C)—the circuit of C-M-C starts and begins with use values. In the realm of production, and capitalist enterprises more broadly, the goal is altogether different: they start with a sum of money (M), invest it in commodities (C) needed for their enterprise, and hope to emerge with more money at the end of the process (M')—an M-C-M' circuit. Capitalist firms engage in a ruthless competition with one another to generate this profit—often at the expense of workers and the environment. As Marx says repeatedly, accumulation has nothing to do with use value, need, or fun; despite the Ping-Pong tables in Google workplaces, it is about money making more money: "In so far as he is capital personified, his motivating force is not the acquisition and enjoyment of use values, but the acquisition and augmentation of exchange-values. He is fanatically intent on the valorization of value."[47]

Moreover, all the things you consume as commodities must first pass through profit-oriented production first. You derive use value from your car, but it is a private-for-profit corporation who derives profit from consumption of that car. Thus, the emissions coming out of the tailpipe of that car are not purely yours. Any given emission is

---

46 There are important distinctions between needs, wants, and desires that I leave to the side. Marx is clear that the terrain of use value is ultimately about socially constructed and historically situated needs.

47 Karl Marx, *Capital*, Vol. 1 (London: Penguin, 1990), 739.

not the sole product of an individual, but rather is a product of a web of social relations that make the moment of combustion possible. The point is that for everything we consume, there is someone else in the capitalist class who is profiting from our consumption. Every commodity consumed includes two sorts of actors along the commodity chain: users and profiteers. I do not want to say we should completely ignore the choices and agency of consumers, but rather we should pay more attention to the profiteers.

Let us take an example by returning to our hypothetical voracious energy suburbanite. True, it was his choice to buy a fuel-inefficient Hummer; and it is his choice to live in a 6,000-square-foot home that consumes 4500 kwh/month of electricity to cool in the summer. True, he is, no doubt, really an obnoxious and antisocial character . . . but the benefits he derives from these commodities include human use values like comfort, mobility, and a subjective sense of power and self-worth. (Even if he never really overcomes a deep sense of despair and dissatisfaction.) When we look beyond this consumer, we see others—auto companies, oil companies, and for-profit utilities—that derive profits from these commodities.

While we are so used to lambasting consumers, we rarely ask about the carbon footprint of the activities that made these people wealthy in the first place. Let us imagine our obnoxious suburbanite travels in his Hummer to the corporate headquarters of a massive chemical fertilizer company (the industry profiled in Chapter 2), where he is the CEO. Every day, after he thoughtlessly wastes fuel and belches emissions on his journey to work, he very carefully organizes and directs a network of massive carbon-intensive factories whose sole goal is to produce nitrogen commodities for profit. On average, you would need 103,920 American consumers to equal just one of these factories in emissions terms.[48] This person spends eight hours a day managing this industrial capitalist enterprise and only perhaps forty minutes commuting to work—so why do we only pay attention to the latter? Why do we not focus on the activities associated with

---

48 Roughly calculated from my website unequalcarbonfootprints.org.

production and investment when considering this individual's carbon footprint?

I argue that it is because what Marx called the "hidden abode of production" is off-limits to politics in our society. Capitalism separates production (a realm of "work" characterized by despotism and private control) from social reproduction (a realm of "life" characterized by freedom, leisure, and, of course, drudgery and highly gendered work). In climate politics, it often seems that it is only this realm—social reproduction—where our choices and lifestyles must be subject to political concern.

The carbon-footprint approach also internalizes a deeper and more intuitive theory about ecological responsibility. This is a biological theory that points out humans are organisms living in ecosystems much like bears or butterflies. From this standpoint, it is undeniable that each human is responsible for consuming a given set of resources. As some of the earliest ecological footprint practitioners put it, "Every organism, be it bacterium, whale or person, has an impact on the earth."[49] Bears eat fish, humans eat fish tacos, but the ecological consequences are the same on living systems. All the resources we consume require real living ecological spaces of harvest and extraction. This biological theory ignores an important difference. Bears do not access the food they need via money and the commodity form.[50] One class of bears does not enclose the means of fish production and force other bears to work for wages to access fish. Human society is organized on a class basis. When humans consume fish, we consume them as commodities, and there are a whole network of power relations wrapped up in delivering the fish to your plate. In this sense, class needs to mean more than just inequalities between rich and poor consumers. We need a deeper

49   Nicky Chambers, Craig Simmons, and Mathis Wackernagel, *Sharing Nature's Interest: Ecological Footprints as an Indicator of Sustainability* (London: Routledge, 1996), xix.

50   An actual study just came out to confirm this: Sagar A. Pandit, Gauri R. Pradhan, and Carel P. van Schaik, "Why class formation occurs in humans but not among other primates," *Human Nature*, Vol. 31 (2020): 155–73.

theory of class to understand who exactly is responsible for the climate crisis.

The Ecology of Class

We are emerging from a long period where it was impolite to talk about class. In the United States political context, if you brought up class you were accused of waging class warfare.[51] In the wake of the "new social movements" of the 1960s, prominent academic and polit-ical interventions questioned—or "decentered"—the role of class in both analysis and political movements; seeing it as merely one among many on a long list of other "axes" of oppression.[52] While all this discourse directed analysis away from class, there has been a

---

51   My analysis of class in this book will focus mostly on the US context. I understand this is a major drawback for what is of course a *global* problem. While there is no justifiable basis for analyzing class in territorial terms—as if particular classes are only contained within national boundaries—a reason for this analytical focus is the simple fact that US political culture is the largest barrier to climate action globally. As the largest historical emitter, main obstacle to international negotiations, site of the largest political culture of denialism, and corporate home for a huge spectrum of fossil fuel capital, the United States is a core nut to crack if we are ever going to solve climate change. I also will admit my own scholarly (and personal) expertise is based in American studies and US politics. I hope the general argument that we need more class analysis of climate change will inspire others to offer more global or comparative national analyses.

52   Ellen Meiksins Wood's *The Retreat From Class: A New 'True' Socialism* (London: Verso, 1986) recognized this early on. The trend among Marxists of the "New Left" devolved into "Post-Marxism," which abandoned the possibility of working-class self-emancipation. See, most notably, Ernesto Laclau and Chantal Mouffe, *Hegemony and Socialist Strategy: Towards a Radical Democratic Politics* (London: Verso, 1985). Post-Marxism then opened the floodgates for postmodernism and poststructuralism which rejected the "universalist" politics of socialism in favor of a focus on fragmentation, difference, and the multiplicity of social identities. The focus on identity, culture, and discourse also tended to de-emphasize the materiality of class. Even scholars who did theorize class explicitly, rejected traditional Marxist understandings. The poststructuralist feminist J.K. Gibson-Graham offers an "anti-essentialist" (and what I would call flimsy) theorization: "We therefore theorize class as a process without an essence; in other words, class processes have no core or condition of existence that governs their development more closely than any other and to which they can be ultimately reduced." J.K. Gibson-Graham, *The End of Capitalism (As We Knew It)* (Minneapolis, MN: University of Minnesota Press, 1996), 55. On the other hand, Marxist class theory does rely on the essence, core, and condition that human beings must produce and reproduce their material existence.

significant "restoration of class power" to the capitalist class.[53] Over
the last five decades, to quote Warren Buffett, "There's class warfare,
all right . . . but it's my class, the rich class, that's making war, and
we're winning."[54] It seems the construction of class politics as impolite, crude, orthodox, exclusionary, and rigid has underwritten a
massively successful capitalist class victory. Increasingly, analysts are
confronting the centrality of class to explaining our Gilded Age level
of inequality and general political dysfunction. Even one of the foremost advocates of neoliberal free trade and deregulation, Lawrence
Summers, wrote a paper in 2020 along with co-author Anna Stansbury,
suggesting that "declining worker power" is behind many of the
pathologies of the US economy over the last several decades.[55] In the
wake of Trump's election, Brexit, and the clear support for right-wing
populism in old industrial working-class regions throughout Europe,
the concept of "class war" has returned to the lexicon of respectable
analysis.[56]

But, what *is* class? In most circles, class simply means your income
or wealth. You can break up any society into quintiles and have a clear
view of the top, middle, and lower classes, or what Erik Olin Wright
calls the "gradational" concept of class.[57] These measures give us a
clear view of one's consuming power and therefore can help us understand the inequality of carbon footprints described above. Yet, we
know *social class* is more complex than this. An adjunct professor
might make the same income as a fast-food worker. A tenured

---

53 This is how David Harvey defines neoliberalism in *A Brief History of Neoliberalism*
(Oxford: Oxford University Press, 2005), 31.

54 Ben Stein, "In Class Warfare, Guess Which Class Is Winning," *New York Times*,
November 26, 2006.

55 They argue that this factor is more important than rising monopoly corporate
power. So, one could argue their class allegiance remains intact. Anna Stansbury and
Lawrence Summers, "Declining worker power and American economic performance,"
Brookings Papers on Economic Activity (Spring 2020).

56 Just two examples: Michael Lind, *The New Class War: Saving Democracy from the
Managerial Elite* (London: Penguin, 2020); Matthew C. Klein and Michael Pettis, *Trade
Wars Are Class Wars: How Rising Inequality Distorts the Global Economy and Threatens
International Peace* (New Haven: Yale University Press, 2020).

57 Erik Olin Wright, *Understanding Class* (London: Verso, 2015), 33.

professor makes the same as a plumber. Class is also wrapped up in occupation, status, education, and more about what you consume rather than how much you consume.[58] In this view, class is subjective. It is an identity that people perform through their clothing, neighborhood, and way of speaking. Since class *is* an identity, intersectionality became a powerful way to analyze the relations among class, race, gender, sexuality, and many other identity categories.[59]

I argue for a Marxist view of class in this book. This theorization of class focuses less on the subjective aspects of class (although these are still important), and suggests class is an *objective* material relationship to production. As Erik Olin Wright argues, "the central class division in a capitalist society is between those who own and control the means of production in the economy."[60] A Marxist theory also suggests the classes who control production also possess oversized *power* over society as a whole. As Michael Zweig puts it, a class's "most fundamental feature is the different degrees of power each has."[61] For Marxists, class has very little to do with what or how much you consume; it is about how you generate the money that makes consumption possible. Who owns what; who can derive wealth and profit from this ownership; and who owns very little and must work to survive.

I argue for a return to this explicitly Marxist approach to class rooted in production and ownership, precisely because the climate and ecological crisis is fundamentally rooted in these objective,

---

58 This subjective conception of class has many facets such as Pierre Bourdieu's arguments around lived practice and "cultural capital," *Outline of a Theory of Practice* (Cambridge, UK: Cambridge University Press, 1977). Andrew Sayer provides an overview in *The Moral Significance of Class* (Cambridge, UK: Cambridge University Press, 2005).

59 The Combahee River Collective speaks of "interlocking" forms of oppression in the 1970s, but "intersectionality" was coined by Kimberlee Crenshaw. The Combahee River Collective. "The Combahee River Collective Statement" (1977), in *Home Girls, A Black Feminist Anthology*, Barbara Smith (ed.) (New York: Kitchen Table: Women of Color Press, 1983), 264–75. Kimberlee Crenshaw, "Demarginalizing the intersection of race and sex: A Black feminist critique of antidiscrimination doctrine, feminist theory, and antiracist politics" *University of Chicago Legal Forum*: Vol. 1989, No. 1, Article 8 (1989): 139–67.

60 Erik Olin Wright, *Understanding Class* (London: Verso, 2015), 11.

61 Michael Zweig, *The Working Class Majority: America's Best Kept Secret* (Ithaca, NY: Cornell University Press, 2000), 9.

material relations. We can trace nearly all significant emissions and environmental degradation back to for-profit production. In contrast, the lack of control over the basics of life (food, energy, land, housing, etc.) defines working-class life (what I call *proletarian ecology*). As I review in the next chapter, we strangely classify environmental politics today as a "new" and non-class-centered social movement. Yet, a materialist, production-oriented theory of class would situate the ownership and control of land, resources, and "the means of production" at the center of the analysis.[62] While capitalism ensures minoritarian control over production, a working-class ecological politics is an effort to assert democratic control over life's necessities.

It is obviously more fashionable these days to argue that class is wholly rooted in practices of "taste" and "culture," but these mere cultural markers matter little when talking about the parts per million of carbon dioxide in the atmosphere.[63] A more cutting-edge and recent theory of class focuses on the "asset economy" and the ways in which property ownership and financial assets (like stock ownership) are driving class polarization in innumerable ways.[64] While this theory is quite insightful from a political economy perspective, such theories of class, rooted as they are in abstract monetary forms of wealth, are not as relevant to the planetary implications of emissions and global heating. To understand this, we need a class theory somewhat attuned to the material (or use value) side of a capitalist system rooted in production. Put simply, we need to focus on the source of emissions in actual industrial production of real stuff.

The production-centered and ecological theory of class offered

62   Matthew T. Huber, "Reinvigorating Class in Political Ecology: Nitrogen capital and the means of degradation," *Geoforum*, Vol. 85 (2017): 345–52.

63   Pierre Bourdieu, *Distinction: A Social Critique* (New York: Routledge, 1984). For a sharp critique, see Dylan Riley, "Bourdieu's Class Theory," *Catalyst*, Vol. 1, No. 2 (2017): 107–36.

64   Lisa Adkins, Martijn Konings, and Melinda Cooper, *The Asset Economy: Property Ownership and the New Logic of Inequality* (Cambridge, UK: Polity, 2020). Adkins and coauthors explicitly lay this class theory out against Marxist approaches in this article: Lisa Adkins, Melinda Cooper, and Martijn Konings, "Class in the 21st century: Asset inflation and the new logic of inequality," *Environment and Planning A*, Vol. 53, No. 3 (2021): 548–72.

here also stands in contrast to much theorizing around how class relates to other forms of oppression like racism and sexism. Elena Louisa Lange argues much academic theorizing today subscribes to a "trinity formula" centered on race, class, and gender that "reduce the analytical categories of class and the dynamic of capitalist accumulation to a 'subthread' of personal forms of domination."[65] Likewise, Wendy Brown argued in the 1990s, invoking these multiple "axes" of oppression often entails *ignoring* class altogether: "class is invariably named, but rarely theorized or developed in the multiculturalist mantra of 'race, class, gender, sexuality.'"[66] The "trinity formula"—or we could call it the intersectionality approach—fundamentally asserts class and racial or gender domination are *similar types of phenomena* that intersect as distinct variables or identities.

Yet, when we start to think of class as a relationship to production, we see that these forms of oppression are not separate from but often constitute class power. For example, what was plantation slavery but a racialized class system of production? This system generated immense wealth and helped establish the United States as a major global power. As Barbara and Karen Fields remind us, this was not a solely racist institution, "as though the chief business of slavery [was] the production of white supremacy rather than the production of cotton, sugar, rice, and tobacco."[67] Similarly, Melissa Wright's ethnographic work in industrial factories in Mexico and China shows the gendered relations between male bosses and a female proletariat.[68] To be clear, I do not mean all forms of racism or sexism are rooted in class and production. Certainly, there are assorted forms of hate and discrimination

---

65 This draws from Marx's own critique of the political economic 'trinity formula' focused on profit, wages, and rents. Elena Louisa Lange, "The Conformist Rebellion," *Substack*, March 6, 2021.

66 Including sexuality creates the more awkward sounding "quadrinity formula." Wendy Brown, *States of Injury: Power and Freedom in Late Modernity* (Princeton, NJ: Princeton University Press, 1995), 61.

67 Barbara Fields and Karen Fields, *Racecraft: The Soul of Inequality in American Life* (London: Verso, 2012), 117.

68 Melissa Wright, *Disposable Women and Other Myths of Global Capitalism* (New York: Routledge, 2006).

that take place outside production or the private workplace. My point is that a production-rooted theory of class helps us explain how racism, sexism, and other oppression structures class power. These material relations of production are a different sort of thing altogether from the often arbitrary identity categories we ascribe to individuals based on race, gender, citizenship, and even the identity expressions of social class.

Class Structure and Climate Change: A Preliminary Framework

Marxists typically pose a dual theory of class: capitalists seek profit; the working class seeks wages, use values, and social reproduction. Of course, we know that twenty-first-century class relations are much more complex and multifaceted. The first part of the book argues that a small minority of capitalists who own and control the means of production *produce* climate change. A recent study suggests a mere one hundred companies are responsible for 71 percent of emissions since 1988.[69] In this case, it is important to remember that half of total historical emissions since the industrial revolution have come since that year, 1988. I find Andreas Malm's concept of *fossil capital* useful in broad terms to refer to the forms of capital that generate profit *through* emissions, or, as he defines it, "fossil capital is . . . self-expanding value passing through the metamorphosis of fossil fuels into CO_2."[70]

This includes the *extractive capital* that digs up fossil fuels and sell them for profit—coal mining and oil and gas production. Fossil capital also includes *industrial capital*, for whom fossil fuels are a primary input like oil refineries, steel, chemicals, and the case study offered in Chapter 2, the nitrogen fertilizer industry (which is responsible for about 2.5 percent of global GHG emissions).[71] As I explore in Chapter

---

69 Paul Griffin, "The Carbon Majors Database: CDP Carbon Majors Report 2017," *CDP Worldwide*. Carbom-Majors-Report-2017.pdf.

70 Andreas Malm, *Fossil Capital: The Rise of Steam Power and the Roots of Global Warming* (London: Verso, 2016), 290.

71 International Fertilizer Association, "The Role of Fertilizers in Climate-Smart

6, we need to highlight one particular class fraction within the industrial capital called *electricity capital*. This would include the collection
of owners and managers who control investor-owned electric utilities
and independent power producers that generate electricity through
the combustion of fossil fuels (mainly natural gas and coal). Because
of their "natural monopoly" status, utilities are often highly regulated
and subject to public scrutiny. Finally, although this book aims its
analysis on the capitalist culprits who produce climate change, we
should also include a growing set of capitalists associated with "clean
tech," or what we might call *green capital*—renewable energy developers, carbon-offset swindlers, and an emergent field of innovation
based on carbon removal ("negative carbon") and even
geoengineering.[72]

The relationship between ownership, particularly of publicly
traded companies, and corporate governance is a complicated one.
We often hear we live in an "ownership society" where everyone
invests in the stock market and has a 401(k) pension fund. There are
vastly complicated webs of *finance capital*, with ownership stakes in
fossil capital. Indeed, as mentioned above, there are currently massive
fractions of finance capital attempting to direct investment *away* from
these "risky" fossil assets in the name of Environmental, Social,
Governance investments (ESG). A handful of giant asset-manager
firms like BlackRock, Vanguard, and State Street, who themselves
have stakes in most publicly traded firms, have proven effective at
pressuring firms to commit to emission reductions.[73] The reality is

Agriculture," Contribution of the International Fertilizer Association (IFA) to the UN
Climate Change Conference in Marrakesh—COP22/CMP12 (2016), fertilizer.org, "The
Role of Fertilizers in Climate-Smart Agriculture.cdr."

72 On clean tech capital, see Jesse Goldstein, *Planetary Improvement: Cleantech
Entrepreneurship and the Contradictions of Green Capitalism* (Cambridge, MA: MIT Press,
2018). On the various capitalist and noncapitalist strategies for carbon removal, see Holly
Jean Buck, *After Geoengineering: Climate Tragedy, Repair, and Restoration* (London: Verso,
2019).

73 "On the average BlackRock alone controls about 7 percent of every S&P 500
company." Madison Condon, "Climate change's new ally: Big finance," *Boston Review*, July
28, 2020.

that much of the investor class is still "exposed" to investments in fossil capital (including BlackRock and the others). And, in the short term at least, the economic recovery following the initial stages of the ongoing Covid-19 pandemic has rewarded them with skyrocketing stock prices for companies like ExxonMobil, Chevron, and Shell.[74] I want to emphasize the investor-owner class is also a minority of society. In the United States, the richest 10 percent owns 84 percent of stock wealth,[75] and, more importantly, a very small board of directors and CEOs (who often hold the majority of shares, or votes, as well) usually controls corporate governance.[76] Suffice it to say that the CEOs, board of director members, and shareholders with governing stakes in particular companies is a relatively small number of people.[77]

It is clear that, in a capitalist society, it is not just beneficial to own the "means of production," but ownership of wealth and property more generally can yield substantial flows of income. Rent is the concept for income derived simply from ownership (and not production).[78] Capitalism is defined by a massive "rentier class," which can include diverse individuals collecting interest on mass sums of wealth, landlords collecting rents, and corporations whose main revenue comes from a monopoly-level ownership of some key infrastructure or exclusive content. More significant than paltry food stamps or work-contingent welfare, rentiers are the true class of people that collect money without having to work for it.[79] A central

---

74 Jeff Sommer, "Big Oil takes a beating, but its investors are riding high," *New York Times*, June 18, 2021.

75 Rob Wile, "The Richest 10% of Americans Now Own 84% of All Stocks," *Time*, December 19, 2017.

76 *Economist*, "Facebook and the meaning of share ownership," September 30, 2017.

77 See, Zweig, *The Working Class Majority*, for a rudimentary attempt to quantify the capitalist class. When focusing on only the big corporations with 500 employees or more and the super-elite capitalist owners who sit on multiple boards of directors, he comes up with the number 52,000 for the United States—a number he points out could sit comfortably in Yankee Stadium (17).

78 Brett Christophers, *Rentier Capitalism: Who Owns the Economy, and Who Pays for It?* (London: Verso, 2020).

79 This form of what Andrew Sayer calls "unearned income" can be critiqued from the left or the right. For the left critique, see Andrew Sayer, *Why We Can't Afford the Rich*

class in climate politics is the landlord class of rentiers, and I don't mean the landlord who owns the building you live in. I mean the owners of subsurface rights to fossil fuel deposits themselves.[80] In the United States, there are millions of private landowners who receive royalty checks (rents) for oil and gas and other mineral extraction on their lands (some estimate this is as high as 12 million people—a substantial pro–fossil fuel political bloc).[81] For example, this scattered geography of private fossil fuel rentiers provides much public support for hydraulic fracturing over the past decade.[82] Much more centralized and important are what Fernando Coronil called landlord states.[83] For most of the world outside the United States, the state owns subterranean resources like fossil fuels. This creates a whole international bloc of petroleum-exporting states who collectively resist climate action. Saudi Arabia, Nigeria, Venezuela, Russia, and others have geared their entire economies toward collecting rents off the ownership of fossil fuel wealth. While, in the past, these states would lease their oil wealth to international private oil capital, since the oil shocks of the 1970s, many countries have nationalized their oil reserves and managed them under "National Oil Companies" like Saudi Aramco.[84] Oddly enough, this makes states a central part of the fossil fuel capitalist bloc (even as these states are often in conflict with the private oil companies).

(Bristol, UK: Policy Press, 2015). For a libertarian, right-wing attack on rents, see Brink Lindsey, *The Captured Economy: How the Powerful Enrich Themselves, Slow Down Growth, and Increase Inequality* (Oxford: Oxford University Press, 2017).

80   For a variety of reasons, I chose to focus this book on the industrial capitalist class, professional class, and working class, but there could certainly be a whole other part devoted to fossil rentiers.

81   This is the estimate of an advocacy group, the National Association of Royalty Owners. Marie Cusick and Amy Sisk, "Millions own gas and oil under their land. Here's why only some strike it rich," National Public Radio 15, 2018.

82   Gwen Arnold, Benjamin Farrer, and Robert Holahan, "Measuring environmental and economic opinions about hydraulic fracturing: A survey of landowners in active or planned drilling units" *Review of Policy Research*, Vol. 35, No. 2 (2018): 258–79.

83   Fernando Coronil, *The Magical State: Nature, Money, and Modernity in Venezuela* (Chicago: University of Chicago Press, 1997), 8.

84   See, Bernard Mommer, *Global Oil and the Nation State* (Oxford: Oxford University Press, 2002).

Ownership is complicated, and so is "control" of production. There is a "middle class" layer of managers, supervisors, and other infantry enforcing the rule of capital. Kim Moody estimates this managerial class is 14 percent of the US workforce.[85] This managerial class must ultimately answer to their corporate overseers, while maintaining some autonomy in terms of dictating the production process on extractive sites, pipeline projects, and fossil fuel–powered factories. As my conversation with a fertilizer plant manager shows (see Chapter 2), this managerial class often takes on the politics and ideologies of capital. Finally, there are the ever-mentioned small-business owners, often classified as "the petty bourgeoisie." The fossil fuel production complex includes lots of small "independent" oil producers, contractors, housing companies, and retail business that serve the reproduction of fossil capital.

Since the capitalist class is a minority, it relies on these managers and small business owners to bolster its political base. Moody describes the profile of the petty bourgeoisie in the United States:

A 2016 survey by the National Small Business Association tells us 86 percent of small business owners are white, they are twice as likely to be Republicans as Democrats, almost two-thirds consider themselves conservative (78 percent on economic issues), and 92 percent say they regularly vote in national elections. Plus they draw an average salary of $112,000 in 2016, compared to $48,320 for the average annual wage.[86]

Although much of the media focuses on the "white working class" as the new base of the Republican party (from Reagan to Trump), *this* represents the true base of the Republican Party and capital in US politics.[87] The petty bourgeoisie not only own businesses, but perhaps more importantly, they own homes and other real estate property

---

85 Moody, *On New Terrain*, 40.
86 Ibid., 176.
87 For the best take on Trump's base as rooted in the petty bourgeoisie, see Jesse Myerson, "Trumpism: It's Coming From the Suburbs," *The Nation*, May 8, 2017.

(one count claims nearly 80 percent of small business owners own their own home).[88] The phenomenon of widespread home ownership in the United States creates the basis for a much wider ideology of property, ownership, and "entrepreneurial" outlooks on life and work under the rule of capital.[89]

The main opposition to climate change comes not from the working class, but from another fraction within the "middle class": the professional class. In the United States, Moody estimates this class comprises 22 percent of the workforce—a substantial minority.[90] Whether you call them Barbara and John Ehrenreich's "Professional-Managerial Class" (PMC), Nicos Poulantzas's "new petty bourgeoisie," or Erik Olin Wright's "contradictory class locations," the professional class refers to the rapidly expanding rolls of white-collar knowledge workers in the postwar era.[91] For my purposes, the people shaping central policy debates, negotiating climate treaties, and driving the "climate movement" are a loose network of journalists, scientists, legal professionals, government workers, NGO or nonprofit staff, and other college-educated knowledge workers. As stated above, because the entire category of "mental labor" and "knowledge work" is by definition *separated* from material production, professional-class climate politics tends to avoid a politics of production in favor of "science" and reducing consumption. Moreover, the professional class exploded during a simultaneous historical process of deindustrialization. Even if their occupation is not directly involved with understanding environmental or climate issues, the members of the professional class often seek to become more "aware" and "informed" on the nature of the environmental crisis through the consumption of media and other nonfiction accounts of the crisis.

---

88   Ahmad El-Najjar, "Small business in the US by the numbers," Townsquared. townsquared.com/ts/resources/small-business-united-states-numbers.

89   Huber, *Lifeblood*.

90   Moody, *On New Terrain*, 40.

91   Barbara Ehrenreich and John Ehrenreich, "The professional-managerial class," in Pat Walker (ed). *Between Capital and Labor* (Boston: South End Press), 5–45, Nicos Poulantzas, *Classes and Contemporary Capitalism* (London: NLB, 1975), and Erik Olin Wright, "Intellectuals and the Working Class," *Critical Sociology*, Vol. 8, No. 1 (1978): 5–18; 10.

The professional class has some relative degree of material security—whether it be through tenured professorships, public-sector wages and benefits, or highly exclusive professional degrees. Thus, professional class life is defined by significant levels of consumption (often bound up in home and car ownership, the pillars of carbon-intensive social reproduction described above). The overwhelming focus on consumption and carbon footprints as drivers of climate change is rooted in the carbon guilt of the professional class, as I will discuss in Chapter 4.

More than this, however, the professional class reproduces a capitalist ideology of meritocracy that tends to supplement the domination and exploitation of the majority of society (the working class). In his screed against the takeover of the Democratic Party by the professional class, Thomas Frank describes professionals:

> Do well in school, and earn your credential. Earn your credential, and you are admitted into the ranks of the professions. Become a professional, and you receive the respect of the public plus the nice house in the suburbs and the fancy car and all the rest.[92]

The combination of meritocratic ideology, which accords much significance to individual effort, and anxiety over one's relatively comfortable "middle class" consumption, leads the professional class into the delusion that *they* are the ones primarily responsible for climate change. Armed with increasingly sophisticated carbon-footprint accounting tools—again completely erasing profits and production—the professional class agonizes over their status as members of a rich polluter class because of their consumption practices. In a recent podcast for the series *Generation Anthropocene*, the lead researcher on the study blaming babies for their carbon footprints cited earlier describes her horror at her discovery that she was one of the "rich polluters" her own research examined:

---

92 Thomas Frank, *Listen, Liberal: Or, What Ever Happened to the Party of the People?* (New York: Picador, 2016), 31–2.

Wait a minute, it's me! I'm a rich polluter, and all my friends are rich polluters and everyone I went to college and grad school with . . . I am the target audience for this information. It's so bizarre that . . . we are among the most knowledgeable people on this topic and are speaking out about it . . . deeply involved . . . and yet it's possible . . . existing in this avoidance in thinking about what that means for me.[93]

We then learn her grandfather "helped invent industrial factory farming" (the profits from which, I imagine, helped create the conditions for her "rich polluter" lifestyle); still, she focuses on her choice to fly less and eat less meat. Regardless, it is her claim that her friends represent "the most knowledgeable people on this topic" that consolidates this statement as professional-class climate ideology *par excellence*. For the professional class, climate politics is a process of *learning, then knowing, then acting*.

It would be a mistake to imagine the professional class is a monolith in terms of its material comforts. As the Ehrenreichs have argued recently, the professional class is *rapidly proletarianizing*, leading to an increasingly "downwardly mobile" class of highly educated individuals with law degrees or Ph.D.'s who are nevertheless stuck in low-wage overwork or drawing food stamps and rapidly losing faith in the meritocratic creed of the class.[94] Moody explains how teachers and nurses face creeping corporatization of administrative surveillance eroding workplace autonomy. He estimates roughly 36 percent of professionals are proletarianizing.[95] Today, it is the proletarianization of the professional class on the left and the petty bourgeoisie on the right that is "polarizing" politics toward radical alternatives.

In Part II, I attempt to classify three key archetypes of professional-class climate politics. The first is what I call the *science communicators*:

93   Michael Osborne, "Individual Reckoning," *Generation Anthropocene Podcast*, April 18, 2021. genanthro.com/2021/04/18/individual-reckoning.

94   Barbara Ehrenreich and John Ehrenreich, *Death of a Yuppie Dream: The Rise and Fall of the Professional-Managerial Class*, Rosa Luxemburg Stiftung, New York Office, February 2013.

95   Moody, *On New Terrain*, 40.

the scientists and journalists who frame the climate struggle largely in terms of *knowledge,* or belief vs. denial. Obviously, the centrality of education and advanced credentials in shaping professional-class formation supplements their conviction in waging political war against the ultimate sin: climate denial. Second, there are the *policy technocrats*: the academics, legal professionals, government workers, and NGO and think-tank staffers who debate climate policy solutions. The professional class prefers a set of nonconfrontational and technocratic policy tools that aim to solve climate change through capitalist and market relations. Policy technocrats assume we can defeat climate change through "smart" policy—and this is again rooted in the credentialed nature of the class itself.

Third, there are the *anti-system radicals* who tend to understand climate change is rooted in the system of capitalism itself. These professionals include radical academics, journalists, NGO activists, and increasingly those same "downwardly mobile" college-educated workers facing proletarianization and now form the base of, for example, the Democratic Socialists of America (DSA).

I imagine this "type" forms the primary readership of this book, so it is worth discussing them at length. When it comes to climate change, professional-class anti-system radical politics focuses on two core political orientations. First, they demand "system change, not climate change." Yet system-change politics tends to focus more on *aggregate* problems with capitalism as a whole. What is wrong with the capitalist system? Everyone agrees that it is the system's need for "growth," or Gross Domestic Product (GDP), the aggregate statistical estimate of trade in goods and services on a national scale. Naomi Klein has referred to capitalism as a system that requires a "constant drive for endless economic growth."[96] As I review in Chapter 4, a whole movement of "degrowth" has emerged to "challenge the centrality of GDP as an overarching policy objective."[97] But rather than

96   Naomi Klein, *This Changes Everything: Capitalism vs. the Climate* (New York: Simon and Schuster, 2014), 81.
97   "Research & Degrowth: Definition." degrowth.org/definition-2.

calling for less for capital and more for the working class, degrowth politics simply negates this *aggregate* focus on growth with the call for "degrowth", or what Jason Hickel calls "reductions in aggregate throughput."[98] Class struggle does not work on the aggregate—it has to mean more for the many and less for the few. Because these anti-system radicals are themselves from the professional class, they feel anxious about the footprint associated with their relative material comforts. This leads to calls for reductions in consumption on an aggregate level (often targeted to an abstraction called "rich countries," where the bulk of the populations can actually be quite economically insecure). Thus, this professional-class "anti-system radicalism" ends up calling for populations to "live better with less" when they are already trying to live with less, and have been for decades.[99]

Moreover, and in striking contrast to traditional socialist politics that imagines seizing industrial production for human liberation, professional-class radicals propose unappealing anti-industrial solutions. System-change tends to imagine a wholescale *decommissioning* of industrial production in favor of what Lars Lih calls a " 'reactionary utopia' in which economic independence is based on small individual property."[100] The new "system" on offer is small-scale agriculture, artisanal handicrafts, and the localization of resource use. This is all rooted in what Nick Srnicek and Alex Williams call the "folk politics" of everything that appears "grassroots" and "local" against globalizing capital (examples include labor-intensive community gardens and solar micro-grids).[101] This "next system" politics would not confront the class that owns production but *retreat* from them. As Jodi Dean put it, "Goldman Sachs doesn't care if you raise chickens."[102] All of this

98   Jason Hickel, "Degrowth: A theory of radical abundance," *Real-World Economics Review*, No. 87 (2019): 54–68.

99   "Degrowth: Is it time to live better with less?" *CNBC Explains Video Series*, May 20, 2021.

100   Lars Lih, *Lenin Rediscovered: What Is to Be Done in Context* (Chicago: Haymarket, 2006), 47.

101   Nick Srnicek and Alex Williams, *Inventing the Future: Postcapitalism and a World Without Work* (London: Verso, 2015).

102   Quoted in ibid., 25.

"system-change" talk is a classic case of what Frederick Engels calls *utopian* politics. Engels emphasized that utopian socialists tended to imagine an ideal society "attempted to evolve out of the human brain," but they failed to articulate what kind of society is possible given material conditions.[103] Engels's scientific vision of socialism argued the solutions can only be rooted in a materialist understanding of real class antagonisms. This antagonism cannot be resolved through vague calls for "system change," but actually requires conflict and struggle. On balance, anti-system radicalism is also out of touch with the needs and aspirations of the masses of workers today. Lenin's description of socialists detached from the workers' movement applies to many self-styled "eco-socialists" today: "the socialists kept their distance from the worker movement and created teachings that criticized the contemporary capitalist bourgeois social system and demanded the replacement of that system with a higher, socialist system."[104]

The second central plank of radical climate politics is the focus on "climate justice." Climate justice politics is rooted in the correct analysis that climate change is a problem caused by the rich and wealthy, while the poorest and marginalized populations bear the worst effects like rising sea levels, increasing droughts, and deadly heat waves. This basic insight has informed inspiring and important struggles within the climate movement. Yet, like many discussions of justice, the focus is on *distributional effects*, not class, and the relations of production. When targeting the culprits, climate justice advocates often fall into the same carbon footprint ideology that assumes "the rich" are to blame—as in rich *consumers* and "rich countries."

Rich *states* (as opposed to whole populations) do indeed owe massive "climate debt" to the poor states of the world, a debt that should be paid off through building basic human and industrial infrastructure and aiding global decarbonization. (Indeed, the 2010 People's Agreement of Cochabambá, Bolivia, affirms that

---

103   For the latest utopian set of imagined new systems, see "The Next System Project." thenextsystem.org. See also Frederick Engels, *Socialism: Utopian and Scientific* (Chicago: Charles H. Kerr and Co., 1918), 58.
104   Quoted in Lih, *Lenin Rediscovered*, 144.

principle.[105]). But climate justice politics rarely pinpoints the class that owns, controls, and profits from global fossil capital. As a result, climate justice politics often positions the struggle in territorial terms, as a struggle between Global North and South, and not as a global class struggle between capital and an international working class. For example, Jason Hickel and colleagues argue that "high-income countries" engage in an "imperial form of appropriation" from the Global South.[106] Symptomatically, they do not differentiate "income" based on wages versus capital ownership in so-called "high-income countries" (at one point they even narrowly focus on wage differentials between South and North). The authors assume all income—whether it flows to capital or labor—is a form of ecological imperialism.

Further, climate justice politics stands in ambivalent relation to a broader working-class politics this book argues is necessary to *win* the climate struggle. Its core constituency are the "marginalized communities" who directly experience climate disruption, like the increasing streams of migrants deemed climate refugees. This aligns with what I elsewhere called "livelihood environmentalism," which assumes real material environmental struggles will come only from those with direct material relations to land, resources, pollution, or other forms of environmental change.[107] This kind of justice-oriented politics makes no appeal to the masses of working-class people who make their living from the market and face no apparent direct and visible "environmental" threat to their livelihood. For the working class, the main threat to their livelihood is *the market* itself. As Vivek Chibber put it, while much of the left is fixated on the concept of the margins, "the reason the working class is important is because it is not

---

105   "People's Agreement of Cochabamba: Adopted at the World People's Conference on Climate Change and the Rights of Mother Earth, April 22, 2010, Cochabamba, Bolivia." pa-cp.org/peoples-agreement-of-cochabamba.

106   Jason Hickel, Dylan Sullivan, and Huzaifa Zoomkawala, "Plunder in the Post-Colonial Era: Quantifying drain from the Global South through unequal exchange, 1960–2018," *New Political Economy* (early view, March 30, 2021).

107   Matt Huber, "Ecological politics for the working class," *Catalyst*, Vol. 3, No. 1 (2019): 7–45.

marginal . . . The thing about the working class that makes it important is that it is central."[108]

A sober class analysis of the climate justice movement reveals a class coalition between the professional class–based NGOs/academics and the *marginalized* classes not classically defined as the working class under capitalism. Ariel Salleh labels them the "meta-industrial class . . . such as women domestic workers, subsistence farmers, and indigenous peoples, are both inside and outside of the dominant hegemony."[109] In the very long list of members on the Climate Justice Now[110] website, the term "union" appears 25 times, but less than 30 percent are clearly worker trade unions; the vast majority are peasant and farmer unions.

It is important to address specifically those smallholder populations like peasant and indigenous peoples who struggle for perhaps the most important means of production, the land itself. Despite an age of mass proletarianization, one estimate suggests 2 billion people across the planet—475 million households—still practice smallholder agriculture and other subsistence production.[111] Even if they do not fit the Marxist criteria of the proletariat, one might include these peasants and indigenous peoples in the broadly defined working class simply because they must *work* to survive; and, no doubt, many of these households rely on the market for some of their basic goods.

These marginalized classes often experience climate change directly because processes like droughts, floods, and extreme weather immediately affect their subsistence and other forms of land-based production. These mostly rural populations also face climate change–induced displacement from land-based livelihoods and often have no

108   Transcribed from a talk Chibber gave. Vivek Chibber, "Why do socialists talk so much about workers? ABCs of Socialism, Lecture 1." youtube.com.

109   Ariel Salleh, "The meta-industrial class and why we need it," *Democracy & Nature*, Vol. 6, No. 1 (2000): 27–36; 30. The broad definition of the working class reviewed above would *include* these groupings, but it is important to distinguish these populations in the household or informal economy not directly relying on wages for their survival.

110   climatejusticenow.org/cjn-network-members-november-2010.

111   George Rapsomanikis, *The Economic Lives of Smallholder Farmers* (Rome: Food and Agriculture Organization of the United Nations, 2015), 1.

choice but to migrate to cities or across borders in search of cash-generating income. In other words, climate change is now a force of proletarianization. So, for good reason, these "frontline communities" often take center stage in climate justice politics. They also offer "alternative" livelihood relations with nature emphasizing subsistence and the sustainable provision of social needs beloved by anti-system radicals. But again, this particular class base is *limited*. While socialist politics must always assert the right to self-determination of land-based peoples, a majoritarian popular climate politics will not emerge from those directly experiencing its worst effects. In the United States one poll found that 57 percent of Americans do not think climate change will harm them personally.[112] A mass climate politics will need to offer something to those already proletarianized billions who survive not from the land, but from the market. The struggle to survive in the market means climate change seems "abstract" and remote from more immediate material concerns.

This brings us to the real difficulty of how to think about this proletarianized mass majority under capitalism, the working class. From a Marxist perspective, it includes the majority of the population, who own no means of production. As stated above, we do not often highlight the *ecological* basis of this class definition. Under capitalism, the working class lacks access to the means of *life*. Historically, this has meant the working class is a class of people separated from the land as a source of direct livelihood. I argue that this ecological definition of the working class as a class alienated from nature and forced to survive via the market should be central in developing a working-class climate politics.

Although we often talk about the decline in working-class politics since the mid–twentieth century, what is striking about the period since roughly 1980 is the massive *expansion* of the global proletariat torn from the ecological means of subsistence, a process Farshad

---

112 "Yale Climate Opinion Maps—US 2020," *Yale Program on Climate Change Communication*, climatecommunication.yale.edu/visualizations-data/ycom-us.

Araghi calls "global depeasantization."[113] One estimate claims that from 1980 to 2010, the global workforce expanded from 1.2 billion people to 2.9 billion—and will rise to 3.5 billion by 2030.[114] The mass movement of 250 million to 300 million people in China alone from rural livelihoods to formal waged or informal work in cities and industrial districts has been called the largest migration in human history.[115] Many who are "proletarianized" (that is, torn from land-based livelihoods) do not find formal-sector "wage labor" work; they constitute what Mike Davis calls the "informal proletariat."[116] Even if they do not represent Marx's classical idea of wage labor, their separation from the means of production and survival via the market still makes them working class. We also can include in the working class individuals performing unwaged and unpaid forms of care work that are necessary for social reproduction.[117] As Kim Moody puts it:

> The working *class*, as opposed to simply the workforce, of course, is composed not only of its employed members but of nonworking spouses, dependents, relatives, the unemployed and all those who make up the reserve army of labor.[118]

This broad view of the working class is far more ethnically and racially diverse than our standard view of white male factory workers, including low-wage service workers in retail, health care, education, logistics, warehousing, and and other care work.

The key political aspect of defining the working class is its position

113 Farshad A. Araghi, "Global depeasantization, 1945–1990," *The Sociological Quarterly*, Vol. 36, No. 2 (1995): 337–68.

114 Richard Dobbs, Dominic Barton, Anu Madgavkar, Eric Labaye, James Manyika, Charles Roxburgh, Susan Lund, and Siddarth Madhav, *The World at Work: Jobs, Pay, and Skills for 3.5 Billion People*, McKinsey Global Institute (June 2012).

115 John Wagner Givens, "The Greatest Migration: China's Urbanization," *HuffPost*, February 28, 2013.

116 Mike Davis, *Planet of Slums* (London: Verso, 2006), 201.

117 Tithi Bhattacharya (ed.), *Social Reproduction Theory: Remapping Class, Recentering Oppression* (London: Pluto, 2017).

118 Moody, *On New Terrain*, 41.

as the majority of the population. In Moody's schematic picture of the US working class, he estimates it constitutes 63 percent of the employed population, and 75 percent of society if we include those doing unpaid care work. If we truly believe in democracy, the numbers needed to build real social power lie only with the working class. Thus, one of my key arguments in this book is that if we want to build a majoritarian, popular movement around climate change, it must resonate with a broad and diverse working class. More importantly, the working class is also subject to low, stagnating wages and alienating, dangerous work. This poverty and insecurity give the working class a material interest in bettering their lives through transformative change.

What does this all mean for climate politics? The incessant focus on consumers and consumption as the ultimate driver of emissions necessarily leads to what I call a *politics of less*, or what Leigh Phillips calls the "austerity ecology" of much environmentalism.[119] If you believe consumers' affluence is the problem, you necessarily will advocate for things that will lead to less consumption, like a carbon tax that might make energy from fossil fuels costlier. As Phillips points out bluntly, if you really believe we consume too much, you ultimately agree with the neoliberal attack on wages and incomes over the last several decades.[120] Indeed, this austerity politics of less appeals to the professional classes and their carbon guilt. They feel excessive. But make no mistake: a politics of "less" and "limits" has no resonance for the vast majority of people already living precarious and insecure working-class lives. For the working class, steeped as it is in basic material deprivation, we need to assert a *politics of more* that explains how much we have to gain from a climate program.

The focus on consumers ultimately blames working-class consumption as a driver of climate change.[121] But the fact is, in the United

---

119   Leigh Phillips, *Austerity Ecology and the Collapse-Porn Addicts* (London: Zero, 2015).

120   Ibid., 37.

121   For an account of this in relation to food politics, see Elaine Graham-Leigh, *A Diet of Austerity: Class, Food, and Climate Change* (London: Zero, 2015).

States people live impoverished, alienated lives while also consuming energy just to reproduce themselves. This is more a structural necessity than a choice. In fact, new research shows the most recent expansion of poverty is happening in the suburbs.[122] To make a living in impoverished suburbs you might also consume a fair amount of gasoline, electricity, and heating fuel. Politically, it makes no sense to focus on these populations as drivers of climate change. In fact, given the democratic majority position of the working class, it is fundamentally anti-democratic to think we can solve climate change by scolding the consumption of the majority. In the fall of 2018 in France, we saw what happens when climate policies are pushed onto the backs of the working class: the "yellow vest" movement rebelled against the carbon fuel taxes imposed by the neoliberal president, Emmanuel Macron. Protestors articulated the contradictions of these anti–working class climate policies with the slogan, "The politicians care about the end of the world when we have to care about the end of the month."[123] More radically, some protestors *combined* these formulations to highlight the confrontation against the power of capital: "End of the world, end of the month—the same system, the same fight."[124]

Is a working-class politics of climate possible? This is explored in Part III, but a key question is rather old fashioned: What *material interest* does the working class have in climate action? Do workers have *climate interests*? Most scientists would retort that all humans have an interest in saving the planet and making it livable for future generations. Fair enough. But as is often said, climate change is an abstract problem. The weather is getting weirder and there is more and more news of disasters everywhere, but it is difficult to convince the vast majority of people that acting on climate is necessary now. In

---

122 Elizabeth Kneebone and Alan Berube, *Confronting Suburban Poverty in America* (Washington, DC: The Brookings Institution, 2013).

123 Jon Weiner, "Naomi Klein: The Green New Deal Is Changing the Calculus of the Possible," *The Nation*, February 22, 2019.

124 Quoted in Élodie Chédikian, Paul Guillibert, and Davide Gallo Lassere, "The Climate of Roundabouts: The Gilets Jaunes and Environmentalism," *South Atlantic Quarterly*, Vol. 119, No. 4 (2020): 877–87; 886.

order to overcome this, we need to articulate a more standard working-class politics for climate change that appeals to more everyday material concerns.

In the course of writing this book, precisely this kind of working-class climate program emerged under the banner of the Green New Deal proposed by Representative Alexandria Ocasio-Cortez and others. The Green New Deal would attempt to tackle climate change and inequality simultaneously with a job guarantee and expansion of public health care, childcare, and recreation (what is often called "public luxury").[125] Such a program could potentially deliver real material benefits to masses of struggling working-class families in the form of things like *cheaper* energy and public transit, health care, and housing. As Naomi Klein points out, if the calculus puts "end of the month" struggles against "end of the world" struggles, "the brilliance of the Green New Deal framework is that it doesn't ask people to choose."[126] As I explore in Chapter 5, a Green New Deal that focuses on working-class interests has the potential to help build a wider working-class *climate consciousness*. By linking climate solutions to practical improvements in workers' everyday lives, climate politics need not remain so reliant upon masses "learning the truth" of the greenhouse effect or experiencing the effects of climate breakdown. Climate politics will simply mean improvements in one's material life—the ecology that counts for most people.[127]

A working-class climate politics will seek not only to appeal to the material interests of the vast majority of people in a capitalist society; it will also seek to build their *strategic* power in the workplace. This would mean resuscitating a defeated labor and union movement, and

---

125   See, Kate Aronoff, Daniel Aldana Cohen, Allyssa Battistoni, and Thea Riofrancos, *A Planet to Win: Why We Need a Green New Deal* (London: Verso, 2019). For the Green New Deal resolution see: H.Res.109, "Recognizing the duty of the Federal Government to create a Green New Deal." congress.gov/bill/116th-congress/house-resolution/109/text.

126   Weiner, "Naomi Klein: The Green New Deal . . ."

127   Of course, we would prefer if everyone developed deep respect for all of nonhuman nature, but under capitalism mere human survival is an epic struggle for the vast majority.

recovering workers' militant capacity to strike and force elites to concede to radical demands. There appear to be positive signs on this front. The largely teacher-focused strike waves of 2018–19 represented by far the largest strike years since 1986.[128] Major strategic unions like the American Federation of Teachers and the Service Employees International Union have already endorsed the Green New Deal.[129] In 2019, the Massachusetts Teachers Association called for a national teachers' strike for a Green New Deal.[130] In 2020, the Covid-19 pandemic led to massive unemployment and increased worker militancy among so-called "essential workers" in grocery stores, logistics warehouses, and health care.[131] In May 2020, the brutal murder of George Floyd led to the mass anti-racist protests and uprisings centered on #BlackLivesMatter, the largest such uprisings since at least the 1960s, and all during a global pandemic.[132] In 2021, the DSA's eco-socialist working group launched a campaign with unions to pass the Protect the Right to Organize Act (PRO Act), on the premise that a revived labor movement is the key to winning a Green New Deal.

All this rising militancy among the working class over the last two to three years demonstrates that conditions are ripe for the kind of mass disruption from below that has led to transformative political change in the past.[133] Yet the climate crisis is so urgent, we cannot just wait and hope that this happens on its own. As Jane McAlevey advocates, working-class power requires targeting

---

128   US Bureau of Labor Statistics, "25 major work stoppages in 2019 involving 425,500 workers," February 14, 2020.

129   Mindy Isser, "The Green New Deal just won a major union endorsement. What's stopping the AFL-CIO?" *In These Times*, August 12, 2020.

130   "Massachusetts Teachers Union Calls for Strike for the Green New Deal," *Labor Network for Sustainability*. labor4sustainability.org.

131   Steven Greenhouse, "Coronavirus is unleashing righteous worker anger and a new wave of unionism," *Los Angeles Times*, July 28, 2020.

132   Larry Buchanan, "Black Lives Matter May Be the Largest Movement in US History," *New York Times*, July 3, 2020. Workers all over the country went on strike to show solidarity with these movements on July 20, 2020. j20strikeforblacklives.org.

133   Frances Fox Piven and Richard Cloward, *Poor People's Movements: Why They Succeed, How They Fail* (New York: Vintage, 1977).

specific strategic sectors of the economy for union organizing.[134] In Chapter 6, I argue for a focused *sectoral* strategy for climate focused on organizing worker militancy in the electric utility sector. All energy experts agree that electricity is the "linchpin" of any decarbonization strategy: the motto "electrify everything" is actually a two-step process of cleaning up existing electric power generation and expanding it to transport, industrial, and heating sectors.[135] Unsaid in these technological energy discussions is the key fact that the utility sector is one of the most unionized in the US private sector.[136] I suggest that this already existing base of institutional power in the electric sector could be leveraged to force a more rapid decarbonization program.

However, these unions are typically quite conservative. They align with the utility companies themselves, engaging in what Sean Sweeny and John Treat call a nonconfrontational "social dialogue" approach.[137] I argue for employing the "Rank and File Strategy" advocated by Kim Moody and the *Labor Notes* tradition of radical rank-and-file organizing.[138] Only militant worker action from below could forces these utilities to enact transformative change. One member of the International Brotherhood of Electrical Workers (IBEW), the key union representing utility workers, has already proposed the same strategy.[139]

The other key aspect of working-class politics is the concept of solidarity across differences. Traditionally, Marxist approaches emphasize *international working class* solidarity across borders to

---

134   McAlevey, *No Shortcuts*, 203.

135   See, Jesse D. Jenkins, Max Luke, and Samuel Thernstrom, "Getting to zero carbon emissions in the electric power sector," *Joule*, Vol. 2 (2018): 2498–2510; 2498. David Roberts, "The key to tackling climate change: electrify everything," *Vox*, October 27, 2017.

136   US Bureau of Labor Statistics, "Utilities industry has highest union membership rate in private sector in 2017," February 23, 2018.

137   Sean Sweeney and John Treat, "Trade unions and just transition: The search for a transformative politics," *Trade Unions for Energy Democracy: Working Paper No. 11.* (2018): 3, 18–30.

138   Kim Moody, *The Rank and File Strategy* (Solidarity, 2000).

139   Ryan Pollack, "The case for an ecosocialist rank & file strategy in the building trades," *The Trouble*, November 28, 2019.

combat the global rule of capital. It is striking to consider how this is equally important for climate change. Yet classical Marxism not only wanted workers of the world to unite to defeat capital and usher in socialism; it was, in the words of the *Internationale*, a project to "unite the human race!" Marxists argued that the working-class proletariat was the so-called "last class"—the class with the capacity to *abolish class itself* and liberate humanity as a whole from domination. While classical Marxists were intent on abolishing a specific form of human-to-human domination, it is now clear that capital also threatens the nonhuman natural conditions of human survival. We do not need just "international solidarity" but a kind of *species solidarity* where workers in all countries recognize that the very conditions of species survival are at stake, and that survival depends on defeating the small minority of our species who control production. While much of environmental and climate politics looks to humans still tied to the land and local ecological production relations like subsistence economies, it is the global proletariat—the mass majority of humanity, or the "universal class"—that has the capacity to look beyond the local, the parochial, and the community, to see humanity as a whole.

In closing, in advocating a working-class climate politics, *Climate Change as Class War* attempts to assert what Lih calls a "two-front polemical war" against professional-class climate politics.[140] On the one side, there is the climate liberalism that asserts rational appeals to "believe science" will inspire action, or technocratic policies like carbon taxes will logically guide the market without conflict or popular struggle. On the other side, radical climate activists' calls to consume less and start urban gardens simply do not resonate for a beaten-down working class that already consumes too little and has no time to garden. Ultimately a working-class climate politics, following Timothy Mitchell, aims to build an *anti-carbon democracy*—a climate politics rooted in popular appeals to the vast majority of

---

140   Lih, *Lenin Rediscovered*, 144.

society.[141] What is striking is that we have barely tried such an approach, and time is running out.

An Outline of the Book

This book is organized in three parts covering the three major class formations at the core of the analysis: the capitalist, professional, and working classes respectively. Part I focuses on the capitalist class.

In Chapter 1, I argue that many climate policy interventions focus on the realm of market exchange and thus, like Marx's analysis in *Capital*, avoid confronting the core issue of class power: the "hidden abode of production." As I maintain above, while much discussion of carbon responsibility focuses on one's "footprint" rooted in consumption, we should see the core of emissions stemming from *industrial capital*, including fossil fuel production, but also carbon-intensive sectors of manufacturing like cement. After laying out this class analysis of carbon responsibility rooted in production, I explore the odd practice of separating "class" politics from "environmental" politics over the last several decades. This separation has been reified through the "jobs versus environment" debate which further occludes the fact that solving climate or environmental problems is fundamentally one of class struggle.

In Chapter 2, I expand this class perspective through a case study of a particularly carbon-intensive fraction of industrial capital: nitrogen fertilizer production. While almost all ecological approaches to political economy assume that ecological problems are fundamentally separate from issues of production and exploitation, I argue we must also theorize ecology at the heart of Marx's theory of exploitation and surplus value production. Although there are a number of ways to do this, I favor an ecological analysis of *relative surplus value* production,

---

141   Timothy Mitchell, *Carbon Democracy: Political Power in the Age of Oil* (London: Verso, 2011). As I mention in Chapter 5, I've discovered by happy accident that Kate Aronoff proposes a similar use of Mitchell's work under the banner of "postcarbon democracy," *Overheated: How Capitalism Broke the Planet and How We Fight Back* (New York: Bold Type Books, 2021), 241–70.

or increasing labor productivity. Industrial capital first seeks to improve labor productivity through automatic machinery (itself usually reliant on fossil fuel), but also serves to *cheapen* the cost of commodities more generally. The role of industrial nitrogen fertilizer production in cheapening nitrogen inputs and the price of food became central to the cheapening of workers themselves by lowering their cost of reproduction. On the one hand, I show how this process of exploitation and surplus value production produces its own internal ecological effects (including massive levels of carbon emissions). On the other, I show how the logic of capital accumulation makes the industry relatively *indifferent* to the ecological and climate repercussions it causes.

Part II examines professional-class climate politics. In Chapter 3, I dive deeper into a Marxist theorization of the professional class. I focus on how educational credentials create real barriers and segmentations of the labor market, exploding specifically in the post–World War II era. Thus, I argue that education and knowledge are at the core of both the material livelihoods and political ideologies of the professional class framing the ways in which climate politics is seen as a struggle over science and knowledge. First, I show how professional-class climate politics frames the climate struggle as one of belief vs. denial or truth vs. falsehoods. Second, I show how a class of professional technocrats also frame the climate crisis as a "market failure" that can be corrected with nonconfrontational "smart" policy designs and fixes that "correct" for inadequate price signals. I offer a brief case study of the Citizen's Climate Lobby as a prime example of this professional-class approach to climate advocacy.

In Chapter 4, I explore how much of radical climate politics also emerges from the professional class. While the wider postwar suburban boom was a solution to fundamental struggles between capital and the working class in the 1930s, the professional classes also benefited from this suburban regime of privatized provisioning. I hold that a contradiction at the core of professional-class life is the desire for material security based on privatized provisioning, alongside increasing knowledge of the ecological crisis produced through the same system. This contradiction leads to an inward politics rooted in "carbon guilt," which assumes that middle-class consumers are both largely responsible for and central to solutions to the climate crisis. This politics rooted in guilt over consumption (what I have called "lifestyle environmentalism" elsewhere[142]) advocates an austerity *politics of less* that projects their own anxieties about excess onto society as a whole. Yet, while this politics of less appeals to the relative minority of professionals who simultaneously enjoy and feel guilty about their material security, this politics has limited mass appeal to the working class in an increasingly unequal society premised on debt, stagnant wages, and rampant material insecurity. As a prime example, I explore the degrowth movement, whose program demands "less" at the aggregate of society, and whose proponents almost exclusively come from middle-class professional (largely academic) backgrounds.

Part III examines the potential of a working-class climate politics. I first argue for an *ecological* definition of the working class as a class not only separated from the means of production (as is commonly said), but separated from the ecological means of life itself (most notably the land). I suggest we recover the long-discarded notion that the working class has objective "material interests" in accessing the means of *life*—and that capitalism prevents masses of working-class people from meeting the most basic life needs like food, health care, housing, and what Agnes Heller called "radical needs" of love, leisure, creative expression, and freedom.[143] I wager that a climate program which appeals to these basic material interests could construct a much wider *climate class-consciousness* that associates decarbonization with better lives. I show how the politics of the Green New Deal at least represents the potential of appealing to these basic working-class interests in building popular support for climate policy. In contradistinction to professional-class climate politics, this approach does not assume or require that its supporters "know" or even "understand" the truth or scientific intricacies of climate science. This democratic

---

142   Huber, "Ecological politics for the working class."
143   Agnes Heller, *The Theory of Need in Marx* (London: Verso, 1974).

approach is of course a strategy to build popular power through the state—and I end the chapter by exploring the promises and limitations of the most recent effort to harness working-class politics into state power in the United States: the 2020 Bernie Sanders campaign.

If Chapter 5 is rooted in the power of the working class as the vast majority of society, Chapter 6 proposes a more targeted sectoral strategy for building working-class power in the trade union movement. Following Jane McAlevey, in line with the labor movement more broadly, we need to identify *strategic sectors* in the climate struggle.[144] I make the case for the electric utility sector. In contrast, most public-power advocates promote a localist vision of community ownership of distributed renewable energy that fails to explain how we can decarbonize at the necessary speed and scale, one community at a time. I argue that instead we leverage working-class power within the existing centralized utility system to demand a massive public sector–led restructuring of the grid toward *both* clean centralized generation like nuclear and hydro on the one hand, and distributed renewable energy on the other. While democratic socialists and other environmental activists have identified public ownership of electricity as a central goal of the climate struggle, they usually ignore the trade unions as an already existing and organized base of social power.[145]

In Chapter 7, I trace the history and potential current strategies in the electric utility unions within the United States. We cannot assume that the trade union bureaucracy in this sector will deliver these transformations. After a brief historical overview of labor union organizing in the utility sector, I advocate a three-pronged union strategy for the electricity sector: the rank-and-file strategy proposed by Kim Moody and *Labor Notes*, the use of union resources for mass political-education campaigns, and the strategic deployment of strikes and disruption at the point of production.

---

144 McAlevey, *No Shortcuts*, 203.
145 C.M. Lewis, "Opinion: Public utility campaigns have a labor problem," *Strikewave*, July 29, 2021.

The conclusion reflects on the crossroads we face as a species staring at the prospect of planetary ruin. While capitalism, for the first time, tears the vast majority of humanity away from a direct livelihood relationship with the land and ecological systems, it does so through a process of fossil fuel–powered industrialization that is forcing us to re-establish a conscious and sustainable relationship to nature. While much of the environmental left assumes this will be done by re-*localizing* our relationship to food and energy systems, I suggest the opposite: the *planetary* nature of climate change requires we reconstruct our relation to nature at the global scale. While this sounds challenging, capitalism has already in effect produced globalized supply chains and production systems. In Marx's time, and in ours, the goal of all socialists and working-class movements should not be to return to a pre-industrial agrarian communalism, but rather to take social control over what are already socialized production systems. Our species' survival requires a species-wide coordination of production.

1

The Capitalist Class

1

The Hidden Abode of the Climate Crisis: Industrial Capital and Climate Responsibility

> If we are to investigate the class composition of climate change, the first and central proposition must be that capitalism drives climate change, and the class that drives capitalism is the class of capitalists.
>
> —Nick Dyer-Witheford, "Struggles in the Planet Factory: Class Composition and Global Warming," in jan jagodzinski (ed.), *Interrogating the Anthropocene: Ecology, Aesthetics, Pedagogy, and the Future in Question*

Introduction: Climate Inaction for the Working Class

Class politics is already central to the climate struggle . . . if you are on the right. In resisting policy, those resistant to climate action consistently cite the *economic costs* of climate policy—specifically how climate action would lead to job loss, higher energy bills, and pain for working people. Take climate archvillain Charles Koch, who claimed: "I'm very concerned [about climate policy] because the poorest Americans use three times the energy as the percentage of their income as the average American does. This is going to disproportionately hurt the poor."[1] A Heritage Foundation report on President Obama's signature climate policy, the Clean Power Plan, estimated "a loss of $2.5 trillion in GDP and more than 1 million lost jobs."[2] On April 26, 2018, the Republican House members Steve Scalise of

---

1 Matea Gold, "Charles Koch on the 2016 race, climate change, and whether he has too much power," *Washington Post*, August 4, 2015.

2 Nicholas D. Loris, "The Many Problems of the EPA's Clean Power Plan and Climate Regulations: A Primer," *The Heritage Foundation*, July 7, 2015. heritage.org.

Louisiana and David McKinley of West Virginia[3] introduced Congressional Resolution 119, "Expressing the sense of Congress that a carbon tax would be detrimental to the United States economy."[4] The resolution claimed a carbon tax "will mean that families and consumers will pay more for essentials like food, gasoline, and electricity" and "will fall hardest on the poor, the elderly, and those on fixed incomes."[5] Such claims fit nicely within longstanding right-wing populist narratives that environmental policy is simply a ploy of coastal elites to attack your freedom and make your life cost more.

If a consensus on the right channels a class politics of economic costs, the liberal center-left consensus sees climate change as "the largest market failure known to man."[6] Why a market failure? Because the costs of emissions are not accounted for in the price mechanism. Essentially, polluters spew their emissions for free and the rest of us (and the planet) bear the costs of increasing climate change. Al Gore mainstreamed this logic in his 1993 book *Earth in the Balance*: "[we should] find ways to put a price on the environmental consequences of our choices, a price that would be reflected in the marketplace."[7] Bill McKibben explains the market failure in clear terms: "Carbon should not flow unpriced into the atmosphere, any more than you should be allowed to toss your garbage in the street."[8] In the midst of a continual revolt of working-class French

---

3 Readers will note these congressmen represent states almost entirely captured by fossil capital: oil and gas in Louisiana and coal and gas in West Virginia.

4 H.Con.Res. 119: Expressing the sense of Congress that a carbon tax would be detrimental to the United States economy. govtrack.us/congress/bills/115/hconres119/text/ih.

5 Ibid.

6 In the words of Rasmus Helveg, the Danish Minister for Climate, Energy and Building. Clare Saxon Ghauri, "Climate change is the biggest market failure in history and must be tackled to spur growth, finance, and policy leaders agree," *The Climate Group*, September 27, 2014.

7 Al Gore, *Earth in Balance: Ecology and the Human Spirit* (London: Earthscan), 341.

8 To be fair, while McKibben strongly supports carbon pricing he acknowledges in this article it is not enough to solve the problem. Bill McKibben, "Why We Need a Carbon Tax, and Why It Won't Be Enough," *Yale Environment 360*, September 12, 2016. e360.yale.edu.

citizens against carbon-based fuel taxes—the Yellow Vest movement—a team of economists signed a statement in 2019 that sums up this logic perfectly: "By correcting a well-known market failure, a carbon tax will send a powerful price signal that harnesses the invisible hand of the marketplace to steer economic actors toward a low-carbon future."[9] The key to market-based climate policy is this faith in the "invisible hand of the marketplace" as an indirect force that can direct corporations and consumers alike to change their behavior. Even the radical climate activist and leading climate scientist James Hansen has expressly disavowed government action on energy policy in favor of a market-based carbon fee and dividend. He argues, "at present fossil fuels are the dominant energy only because the environmental and social costs are externalized onto society as a whole rather than being internalized into their prices."[10] It is one thing to promote a carbon fee or a carbon tax, but Hansen joined right-wing opponents in criticizing Obama's Clean Power Plan because it uses state power to mandate shifts in the energy sector. "Government shouldn't be making that kind of decision [to choose energy sources]."[11] This sentiment reveals an astonishing faith in the market and price mechanisms.

Underlying the very notion of a "market failure" is the belief that the problem of climate change is one of market exchange. Fossil fuel energy is "too cheap" and clean energy "too expensive." This leads to the conviction that we can correct this failure in the realm of exchange itself; put a price on carbon, perhaps offer subsidized prices for clean energy, and *voila*, consumers will choose clean over fossil fuels. Focusing on the market and exchange also reinforces the sense reviewed above that "all of us" are responsible. Literally every act of exchange can be linked to some

9   "Economists' Statement on Carbon Dividends." https://www.econstatement.org.

10   James E. Hansen, "Environment and Development Challenges: The Imperative of a Carbon Fee and Dividend," in Lucas Bernard and Willi Semmler (eds.), *The Oxford Handbook of the Macroeconomics of Global Warming* (Oxford: Oxford Handbooks Online, 2015).

11   Pamela King, "EPA policy won't solve climate woes—James Hansen," *E&E News*, November 2, 2015.

form of emissions—or carbon footprint. A market failure is the failure of all the diffuse buyers and sellers who interact in the market itself.

Left unsaid in these discussions is what remains hidden through a focus on market exchange. Indeed, from classical liberalism to contemporary neoliberalism, it is the so-called free and voluntary trade between buyers and sellers that remains the ideological core of capitalist hegemony. A critique of this focus on exchange is also the central argument of *Capital* by Karl Marx. Marx sought a theory of capital, understood as the formula M-C-M'. While the classical economists celebrate the *equality* of commodities in exchange, Marx sought an answer for the *inequality* between M and M'; where does this extra value come from? For Marx, the answer required leaving the realm of exchange altogether:

> Let us therefore, in company with the owner of money and the owner of labor-power, leave this noisy sphere, where everything takes place on the surface and in full view of everyone, and follow them into the hidden abode of production, on whose threshold there hangs the notice 'No admittance except on business' ... The sphere of ... commodity exchange ... is in fact a very Eden of the innate rights of man. It is the exclusive realm of Freedom, Equality, Property and Bentham. Freedom because both buyer and seller ... are determined only by their own free will. They contract as free persons, who are equal before the law.[12]

Whereas the realm of exchange presupposes freedom and equality, Marx's venture into the "hidden abode of production" reveals the inherent inequality and antagonism between capital and labor.

Same for the climate. When we focus on the realm of exchange, we assume the climate crisis is a mere aberration of an inherently efficient and rational market system. When we venture into the "hidden abode of production" we see the antagonistic class relations at the root of the climate crisis. Rather than focusing on choices in the

---

12   Marx, *Capital*, Vol. 1, 279–80.

marketplace as consumers, we see a class of producers who control vast flows of energy, resources, and, indeed, emissions—all directed toward one goal: profit (M-C-M'). Only by directing our attention away from the realm of exchange do we see the real cause of the climate crisis: a small minority of owners who control and profit from the production of the energy, food, materials, and infrastructure society needs to function. Only by examining the relations of production—that is, class *power*—do we discover that the climate struggle is not about fixing the price mechanism, but about confronting that small minority of owners. In this chapter, I will detail how the "hidden abode" of industrial production is the core driver of climate change. But first I want to explain how, in our neoliberal era, this abode remains hidden from our politics and vision.

(Neo)Liberalism and the Politics of Exchange

Perhaps the thread connecting classical with "neo" liberalism is the celebration of *exchange* as a pure site of freedom and mutual benefit for individuals and society as a whole. Adam Smith famously asserted there is "a certain propensity in human nature . . . to truck, barter, and exchange one thing for another."[13] The idea of exchange is that individuals will only agree to exchange if it satisfies their mutual interests, wants, and desires. If each individual fulfils this simple maxim—pursue self-interest—all exchanges add up to the betterment of society. The allure of this vision is that any site of exchange is purely based on "freedom" between buyers and sellers.[14] As Milton

---

13 Adam Smith, *An Inquiry Into the Nature and Causes of the Wealth of Nations*, Vol. 1 (London: Alex Murray and Co., 1872), 26.

14 Of course, this imaginary scenario of free buyers and sellers misunderstands the true nature of our capitalist economy. As Elizabeth Anderson points out, liberal economic theory was devised for a society of self-employed producers, each owning their own means of production and selling their wares in the market. As Marx points out, the "free" exchange between capital and labor depends on the unfreedom of a class of workers freed from any means of livelihood of their own. Capital has all the power in this supposedly "free and voluntary" exchange. Elizabeth Anderson, *Private Government: How Employers Rule Our Lives (and Why We Don't Talk About It)* (Princeton, NJ: Princeton University Press, 2017).

Friedman articulates, in an economy based on exchange, "co-opera-tion is strictly individual and voluntary," and the advantage is "it gives people what they want instead of what a particular group thinks they ought to want."[15]

The idolatry of exchange depends upon further assumptions. As Friedman reminds us, the exchange system works "impersonally and without centralized authority."[16] Moreover, the producers of goods and services must also compete with other decentralized producers to capture buyers. Thus, according to these logics, the entire system is driven by the decentralized competitive, entrepreneurial drives of producers and free choices of consumers. This leads to a politics that seeks to *naturalize* the operation of market exchange as self-regulat-ing through these dispersed choices.

Those who celebrate exchange acknowledge that problems can arise. Monopoly power can subvert the role of decentralized compe-tition in shaping prices and markets. Discrimination can prevent exchange for arbitrary and unfair reasons (for example, qualified job applicants). Most significant for the environment and climate is the problem of "externalities"—or when private actors produce costs they do not bear in monetary exchange. Even Milton Friedman recognized the potential dangers of these, what he called "neighbor-hood effects . . . when actions of individuals have effects on other individuals for which it is not feasible to charge or recompense them."[17]

In essence, arising from this ideology is a coherent politics of exchange which is based on a clear goal: for exchange to work the market must be purged of any form of centralized power that is able to control prices or markets through power rather than competitive drive and merit. For the right, centralized power means the state and unions. But for the left it means monopoly power, unfair subsidies for fossil fuels and agribusiness, and entrenched forms of unfair

---

15 Milton Friedman, *Capitalism and Freedom* (Chicago: University of Chicago Press, 1962), 14.

16 Ibid., 15.

17 Ibid., 14.

discrimination. A politics of exchange disdains any kind of *arbitrary power* in the market—special interests that gain resources through theft, monopoly, race, or any other kind of advantage apart from entrepreneurial drive or competitive tenacity. For market exchange to work, and to be fair, it is the dispersed, atomized choices of individuals who must act without more power than any other individual. A politics of exchange is always about re-establishing the conditions of free and fair competition in the market. President Barack Obama was fond of saying repeatedly that American politics is about this conception of fairness: "I believe that this country succeeds when everyone gets a fair shot, when everyone does their fair share, when everyone plays by the same rules."[18] Creating an even playing field means a political project that aims to purify the market of uneven forms of power.

Thus, as I explore in Chapter 3, the politics of exchange ultimately becomes a politics of *correction*—a politics of correcting for externalized costs not visible in the market and correcting for arbitrary or unfair forms of politics and power. The underlying assumption of such a politics is that once market exchange is corrected it can ultimately lead to desired and just outcomes. In contrast to the politics of exchange and correction, a Marxist class politics assumes exchange relations are *already* inherently antagonistic and exploitative. While the politics of exchange assumes the possibility of a society of atomized free and equal buyers and sellers, each getting what they put into the system, a politics of class assumes that capitalism is structured by antagonistic *conflict* between unequal classes. One of the most powerful aspects of Marx's analysis in *Capital* is that he assumes a free, fair, and competitive market. With this assumption, Marx still proves such free and fair exchange is based upon exploitation and domination. As Jonah Birch puts it: "Under capitalism, exploitation occurs mostly through the market. It is the ostensibly noncoercive contractual relationship between workers and employers that masks deeper

---

18   Barack Obama, "Full text of President Obama's economic speech in Osawatomie, Kansas," *Washington Post*, December 6, 2011.

underlying class inequalities."[19] For Marx, however, to truly understand this domination and exploitation we cannot just look at the site of exchange. Only when we venture to the site of production does it become clear that capital and labor are not free and equal players on a market, but highly unequal antagonists fighting for their lives and time. For climate change too, once we venture away from exchange relations and into the hidden abodes of production, we see the *inherent antagonisms* between capital and the climate.

The Ecology of the Hidden Abode

The "hidden abode" of production is literally hidden (with "no admittance except on business"). It is hidden because it is controlled by capitalist private property. Indeed, it is hidden from daily life altogether. It is quite possible for people to carry on their everyday affairs without understanding how and where things are produced. Take a moment to look around you. How many objects in your sightline right now were produced in industrial factories? Now, as you carry on with your day, think of all the objects and infrastructures rooted in industrial production. The pavement you walk on, the bed you sleep on, the table you eat on, the food you eat. As Kim Moody argues, it is conceivable to argue that industrial production is

quite literally, the "foundation" of almost all other economic activity—in the sense that it is the industrial working class that produces (and often runs) the entire infrastructure and "built environment" on which both accumulation and daily life rest: roads, ports, airports, railroads, factories, office buildings, streets, public transit, housing, etc.[20]

In Marx's time, the working class was crowded together in tenements within walking distance from the factory. Now, residential

19   Jonah Birch, "Ending their wars," *Jacobin*, May 28, 2018. jacobinmag.com/2018/05/war-socialists-debs-vietnam-internationalism.
20   Kim Moody, "The industrial working class today: why it still matters—or does it?" *Against the Current*, September-October (1995): 20–6.

and commercial areas are all zoned separately from industrial areas, and more importantly, industrial production itself is dispersed through global supply chains. Since industrial production is hidden from most of us, it escapes our consciousness and political concern. What we *see*—"where everything takes place on the surface and in full view of everyone"—are the sites of exchange, consumption, and the daily process of social reproduction. It is no surprise that, with regard to climate politics, these spaces become political and open to contestation.

The people who cannot hide from production are, of course, the exploited workers who labor in the hidden abode. They appear to engage in a "free" exchange with capital for wages. The core argument of *Capital* is that this appearance of freedom conceals the exploitation at the core of surplus value and profit. Although the worker is free to agree to a given wage rate, capital is free to make the workers produce more value than they receive. Marx illustrates the hidden abode of production is structured by a tension between the abstract forces of value—competition and a relentless focus on time—and the concrete forces of living labor power that can slow down, strike, and struggle. To effectively produce surplus value, capital must *consume* the vital forces of living power by pushing them to work longer and harder. "Capital is dead labour which, vampire-like, lives only by sucking living labor, and lives the more, the more labor it sucks."[21]

When considering industrial production, capital's abstract drive for surplus value also confronts concrete energy as a means of generating heat and work. At the core of modern productive forces, fossil fuel becomes a lever of accumulation. Given capital's inherent drive for accumulation, we can expect an equal drive to consume fossil energy—and expel more emissions in the process. If the quest for surplus value drives the production process, Marx isolates two strategies, both of which can be read through the lens of the climate crisis. First, since workers exchange their labor power for a fixed

---

21   Marx, *Capital*, Vol. 1, 342

value, capital can force workers to work longer and thus produce more value for the capitalist. The extension of the working day is called *absolute surplus value*. This is also fundamentally a question of *energy*—that is, human energy. The human body consumes a given set of food (calories) and has a given set of time and energy for work, leisure, and sleep, and Marx constantly examines capital pushing toward the biological limits of the human body itself.[22] The capitalist project to extend the working day is ultimately one of sapping the life and energy of the worker toward exhaustion.[23] Working-class politics has always struggled to reclaim that time and energy for workers themselves.

Second, individual capitalists can temporarily gain surplus profits by improving labor productivity and underselling the competition below its current value. This inherent drive toward labor productivity has a tendency to *cheapen* commodities, including those necessary to reproduce labor power, like food, energy, and housing. Cheapening the cost of labor power expands the potential for surplus value above the worker's cost of reproduction. While there are a variety of tactics capital can use to improve labor productivity, Marx focuses on the revolutionary role of *machinery* as an "antagonist of human power" in both increasing labor productivity and, often, replacing intransigent labor through automation.[24]

Yet, the secret to machinery—or mechanized industrial power—is an inanimate source of energy to replace human or animal muscular power.[25] The steam era depended upon coal, but today most machinery is driven by electricity, which also relies overwhelmingly on fossil fuels. As labor activist–scholar Paul Hampton puts it, "The process of replacing living labour with machinery—the product of other, past

---

22   See, e.g., Marx, *Capital*, Vol. 1, 341.

23   See, John Bellamy Foster and Paul Burkett, *Marx and the Earth: An Anti-Critique* (Chicago: Haymarket, 2016), 137–64.

24   "According to Gaskell, the steam-engine was from the very first an antagonist of 'human power,' an antagonist that enabled the capitalists to tread underfoot the growing demands of the workers." Marx, *Capital*, Vol. 1, 562.

25   Water power is also an option and did indeed power early industrialization in the UK and US, but it has severe limits to capitalist social relations, as Malm so expertly details.

labour—required an enormous expansion of energy to power such labor processes."[26] Thus, capital's drive for *relative surplus value*—that is to say, its drive to increase *exploitation*—ultimately entails more fossil fuel combustion and an intensification of the climate crisis.

Who Produced the Climate? The Ecology of Industrial Capital

If we take a step back from the pages of Marx and look at the data on emissions, we see that industrial capital—the hidden abode of production—is responsible for the bulk of emissions in capitalist society. Again, this requires venturing away from the site of exchange and examining how industrial capital relates to energy and emissions in production itself. In industrial forms of production, energy consumption is not much of a choice but a structural and even *thermodynamic* necessity of how production is organized. Industrial capital includes all large-scale forms of production (the US Energy Information Agency specifies "mining, manufacturing, agriculture, and construction."[27]) In 2015, the industrial sector consumed more of the world's energy (54.8 percent) than the commercial (7 percent), residential (12.6 percent), and transportation (25.5 percent) sectors *combined* (see Figure 1.1).[28] Even in the so-called "post-industrial" United States, the industrial sector consumes over a third (34 percent) of delivered energy, surpassed only by transportation (39 percent) in a society based upon decentralized suburban housing, automobility, and long-haul trucking.[29]

26 Paul Hampton, *Workers and Trade Unions for Climate Solidarity: Tackling Climate Change in a Neoliberal World* (London: Routledge, 2015), 27; see also Renfrew Christie, "Why does capital need energy?" in Petter Nore and Terisa Turner (eds.), *Oil & Class Struggle* (London: Zed, 1980), 10–25.

27 Energy Information Administration, *International Energy Outlook 2017* (Washington, DC: Government Printing Office), 18.

28 Data taken from Energy Information Agency, 2018. "Table F1. Total world delivered energy consumption by end-use sector and fuel, Reference case, 2015-50." The total (denominator) of these calculations excluded all "electricity related losses" (which constitute 25 percent of the full total).

29 Energy Information Administration, *Annual Energy Outlook 2018*, "Table A2: Energy Consumption by Sector and Source."

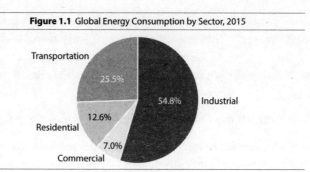

Source: Energy Information Agency, 2018

Given this data, it is not surprising that the industrial sector also leads all others in terms of carbon emissions. The Intergovernmental Panel on Climate Change's 2014 report does a full accounting of emissions (including those from agriculture, forestry, and land-use change) and finds the industrial sector responsible for 21 percent of direct emissions and 11 percent of indirect emissions from electricity consumption.[30] This combined figure of 32 percent leads all others and is rivaled only by agriculture, forestry, and other land uses with 24.87 percent (see Figure 1.2). Moreover, consider how all the other categories—commercial, residential, transportation, even land-use change—fundamentally depend on products from the industrial sector. To follow Moody's insight above, industrial emissions are the *foundation* of all other emissions. There are no transport emissions without industrial systems of mass automobile and trucking production. There are no land-use emissions without massive industrial production of tractors and other earth-moving machinery. Given the critique of carbon-footprint accounting presented earlier, the other key figure is that "all of us" living our consumer lifestyles in the "residential sector" are responsible for a mere 11.5 percent of global emissions. We could also add our contributions to transportation, but this would likely not raise consumption-based emissions to even 15 percent of the total.[31]

---

30   Intergovernmental Panel on Climate Change (IPCC), Working Group III, *Climate Change 2014 Mitigation of Climate Change* (New York: Cambridge University Press, 2014), 9.
31   Ibid., 123.

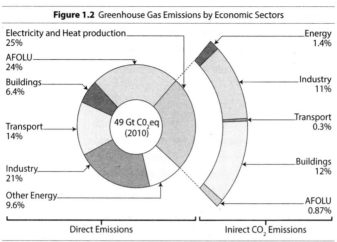

Figure 1.2 Greenhouse Gas Emissions by Economic Sectors

Electricity and Heat production 25%

AFOLU 24%

Buildings 6.4%

Transport 14%

Industry 21%

Other Energy 9.6%

49 Gt CO$_2$eq (2010)

Energy 1.4%

Industry 11%

Transport 0.3%

Buildings 12%

AFOLU 0.87%

Direct Emissions

Inirect CO$_2$ Emissions

Source: Intergovernmental Panel on Climate Change (IPCC), Working Group III, "Climate Change 2014: Mitigation of Climate Change" (New York: Cambridge University Press, 2014)

How do we break down the industrial sector from a climate perspective? First and foremost, the key producers altering the climate are the fossil fuel industry—those enterprises that extract oil, gas, and coal and sell them for profit. Without their production, the mass combustion of fossil fuels would be impossible. As William Carroll and his collaborators show, it is quite possible to map the relationships of power and capitalist ownership shaping this industry.[32] Since the climate movement is quite clear on this class enemy, we should widen our focus to include other detrimental carbon capitalists: the *industrial consumers* of fossil fuel (what I call "industrial fossil capital" in the introductory chapter). Sometimes, we assume that once we extract fossil fuels, they are simply delivered to the masses of consumers for residential consumption. Yet, there are massive, industrial middle spaces where fossil fuel is an input transformed into profit. The most important middle node of fossil fuel consumption is the electric-power sector. Globally, 25.4 percent of all emissions are generated by electric power plants, and 64.3 percent of all that

32   See, William Carroll (ed.), *Regimes of Obstruction: How Corporate Power Blocks Energy Democracy* (Edmonton, Alberta: Athabasca University Press, 2020).

electricity comes from fossil fuels (the remainder coming from
nuclear, hydro, and other renewables).[33] Politically, *electricity capital*
is highly variegated by geography, with most countries allowing some
mixture of publicly owned or highly regulated private for-profit utilities. Because electricity is critical infrastructure to society, it is always
already highly *politicized*. Thus, the climate movement must ultimately put revolutionizing electric infrastructure—thoroughly
remaking the grid—at the core of its demands. (More on this in
Chapter 6.)

But who really consumes all the electricity coming out of these
power plants? By far the industrial sector is the biggest "indirect"
emitter from its consumption of electricity (44 percent of the total
globally).[34] In examining industrial capital's role in climate change
we need to look at the broader industrial manufacturing sector.
Actually, only a handful of industries are responsible for the bulk of
emissions: steel, cement, chemicals, and other energy-intensive
forms of production. As the Intergovernmental Panel on Climate
Change puts it:

> Emissions from industry . . . arise mainly from material processing . . .
> Production of just iron and steel and nonmetallic minerals (predomi-
> nantly cement) results in 44% of all carbon dioxide (CO_2) emis-
> sions . . . from industry. Other emission-intensive sectors are chemi-
> cals (including plastics) and fertilizers, pulp and paper, non-ferrous
> metals (in particular aluminum), food processing . . . and textiles.[35]

A recent article in the *Financial Times* claimed that steel and cement
alone make up 15 to 17 percent of global emissions.[36] All this shows
that production is the core metabolic force causing the climate crisis.

---

33 The emission data is from IPCC, 2014, 9. The global proportions of fossil vs.
renewables is from EIA, 2018 (see footnote 27 above).
34 IPCC, 2014, 9.
35 Ibid., 745–6.
36 Sylvia Pfeifer, "Hydrogen: can the lightest gas turn heavy industry green?"
Financial Times, March 19, 2021.

We could tackle the *core* of the crisis by simply regulating or expropriating the owners of this mere handful of industries (electricity, steel, and cement). So much for "diffuse" responsibility!

Let us take a moment to examine just one industry that analysts estimate is responsible for approximately 7 percent of global carbon emissions: cement.[37] Burning a lot of fossil fuel is not the only reason why cement production generates a lot of carbon. The chemical process of making cement—the calcination of calcium carbonate ($CaCO_3$)—creates carbon dioxide as a waste byproduct, which in turn constitutes between half and a third of emissions. Despite this clear and present climate threat, the cement industry has shown utter disregard for the problem. Since 2000, cement production globally has increased from 1.7 billion to 4.1 billion metric tons—an increase of 241 percent.[38]

Exciting recent advances suggest that the cement industry could employ new material processes and carbon capture and storage to substantially lower emissions—but the freedom of capital stands in the way. "One of [the obstacles to innovation] is a lack of policy incentives to convince cement manufacturers to invest in new technologies."[39]

Another problem: path dependency in the construction industry itself. "The construction of essential infrastructure, like buildings and bridges, carries a great deal of concern about safety and high anxiety toward the introduction of newer, less-proven materials."[40] Clearly, the cement and construction industries will not make these changes on their own.

The massive increase in cement production is largely a story of China, whose cement output rose 416 percent since 2000, and whose global output today constitutes 59 percent of the total (it was only 33

37   Chelsea Harvey, "Cement Producers Are Developing a Plan to Reduce CO_2 Emissions," *E&E News: Climate*, July 9, 2018.
38   See, the US Geological Survey for data on cement, minerals.usgs.gov/minerals/pubs/commodity/cement.
39   Harvey, "Cement producers."
40   Ibid.

percent of the total in 2000).[41] In fact, staggeringly, China consumed the same amount of cement between 2011 and 2013 as the United States consumed in the entire twentieth century.[42]

If class is about production, the core of the analysis should acknowledge the globalization of industry and its associated new international division of labor. These processes have led to the location of much heavy manufacturing in East Asia. Thus, as Joel Wainwright and Geoff Mann put it, citing the work of Minqi Li, China is the "fulcrum of global climate history [. . .] China is the center of world commodity production, but most consumption occurs elsewhere. Who is responsible for the associated emissions?"[43] As I argue in the introduction, this problem of blame is often couched as either the country of China—the Communist Party state, its citizens—or those who consume Chinese products. As Andreas Malm argues, blaming consumers assumes the "western consumer as an absolute sovereign who sends CO_2 packing to other parts of the world."[44] But how can we blame China, which emits so much to produce exports to other parts of the world? This either/or framing—countries or consumers—lets off the hook the capitalists who own, control, and profit from this production. This class is not confined to China or even the Global North; it is a transnational capitalist class located in Hong Kong, China, the United States, Europe, and elsewhere.[45] We should not be tracing the emissions attached to commodities bound for consumers in the Global North, but rather the emissions attached to money-profit flowing to investors all over the world but also concentrated in the Global North. Am I to blame for my iPhone's emissions, or is Terry Ghou, CEO of Foxconn in Taiwan, and Timothy Cook in Cupertino, California?

41   US Geological Survey.

42   Ana Swanson, "How did China use more cement between 2011 and 2013 than the US used in the entire 20th century?" *Independent*, March 25, 2015.

43   Joel Wainwright and Geoff Mann, *Climate Leviathan: A Political Theory of Our Planetary Future* (London: Verso) 39, 122.

44   Malm, *Fossil Capital*, 324.

45   Leslie Sklair, *The Transnational Capitalist Class* (Oxford: Wiley, 2001)

So who are the capitalists profiting from cement? Outside the Chinese market, an estimated 671 companies produce cement around the world.[46] Yet the top 10 companies produce roughly 60 percent of the total output.[47]

And one stands out. In 2013, the world's two largest cement companies, Lafarge (France) and Holcim (Switzerland), merged to form LafargeHolcim, by far the biggest cement company on the planet. This industrial behemoth, which in 2021 changed its name to Holcim Limited, produces 345.2 million metric tons per year, constituting 20 percent of all the cement produced outside China and 8 percent of the global total. On its website, it boasts of a new strategy called "Building for Growth," which "aims to drive profitable growth and simplify the business to deliver resilient returns and attractive value to stakeholders."[48] The company does not seem to see a contradiction between this growth orientation and its stated goal of sustainability, which includes a "mission to cut its net CO_2 emissions per tonne of cement."[49] Of course, if you cut the "emissions per tonne" but keep growing the tonnage you make, you still produce more emissions.

This means that one company—with one CEO (Jan Jenisch) and ten members of the board of directors—is responsible for 0.5 percent of all global emissions. That may not sound like a lot, but let me put it this way: eleven individuals control the operations of a company that released roughly 88.9 million metric tons of carbon in the year 2017. The point is, we could attack a massive source of emissions by focusing on this single company. Even if we wanted to gather the roughly ten capitalists per company who control all the emissions from the cement sector, we're only talking about 6,710 people. In other words, contrary to the narrative of "diffuse" attribution, responsibility for climate change is highly *concentrated*.

The question of cement and China is more complicated, as much

46   Peter Edwards, "Global Cement Top 100 Report 2017–2018," *Global Cement Magazine*, December 4, 2017.

47   Ibid; see also, "China: First in cement," *Global Cement Magazine*, July 23, 2013.

48   "Our Strategy," LafargeHolcim.com.

49   Ibid., lafargeholcim.com/climate.

of the Chinese cement industry is run by "state-owned enterprises." Still, this makes politicizing their actions easier than in a fully capitalist market economy where the freedom of the entrepreneur is sacrosanct. The largest Chinese producer, Annui Conch, produced 217 million metric tons in 2017, an astounding 97 percent increase in output since 2011.[50] If we believe official data this constitutes nearly 10 percent of China's output. The Chinese cement industry is also not confined to China. The second-largest producer, China National Building Materials, is in the process of merging with Sinoma, which is active in major construction projects on Nigeria, Saudi Arabia, and other places all over the world: "Sinoma has about 65 percent of the global cement plant construction market excluding China."[51] As the Chinese Communist Party seems to become more serious about climate change, it *already* has the power to curtail the power and profits of this industry.

On the basis of all this data, the only realistic conclusion is that cement producers must be stopped, severely scaled back, or forced to fundamentally transform their production and material processes. But how could that happen? All this production is undertaken by private enterprises, or by state-owned enterprises that are still profit-oriented, with goals focused on growth and profit.

The only options are abolition, nationalization, or stringent regulation.[52] It is hard to imagine our current world operating *without* cement, so the first option is unlikely. That leaves the other two, making the political task one of direct confrontation and struggle with the class of owners who control the cement industry. How could such a confrontation be successful? Clearly nationalization or stringent regulation implies the existence of a strong concentrated power,

50   "China: first in cement."

51   Eric Ng, "China giants CNBM and Sinoma merge to become world's largest cement maker, eye Silk Road growth," *South China Morning Post*, December 6. 2017.

52   A recent report by CDP highlights what could be the source of such regulation: low-carbon urban planning requiring building materials that come from less carbon-intensive processes. Marco Kisic, Carole Ferguson, Christie Clarke, and James Smyth, *Building Pressure* (CDP: 2018).

a state. As Christian Parenti argues, "Only states have the power to compel such [an energy] transition . . . [but] . . . states will not do this without massive popular pressure from below."[53] What social formation could form the basis for a mass movement "from below"? In Part II, I will show how the climate movement today—made up of professional-class activists and the most marginalized victims of climate change—is too narrowly constructed to constitute a real threat to the power of industrial capital. In Part III, I will argue that the working class not only provides a mass popular base, but also the strategic capacity to disrupt production so that capital and the state feel, as Parenti puts it, "threatened enough" to take action.[54] The focus on the centrality of the working class to the emancipation from capitalism is at the core of socialist politics.

The Severance of Environment From Class Politics at the 'Point of Production'

Given the above, why does an environmental politics focused on class struggle over industrial production not exist? For much of the left, climate and environmental struggle is a "movement" distinct from class-based movements. Tensions between these movements is often constructed as a zero-sum game between "jobs" and "environment." Indeed, trade union leaders have often echoed these divisions.

Yet, from the perspective laid out here, climate change is rooted in class power at the point of production. More broadly, it is difficult to imagine many environmental issues that do not trace back to a private capitalist seeking to turn resources into profit. For example, timber, mining, large-scale agriculture, but also more secondary industrial forms of manufacturing like chemicals and metals production—all these forms of ecological degradation are rooted in capitalist production. And yet, although environmental problems stem from production, their consequences spread far beyond. The degraded climate and

---

53   Christian Parenti, "Why the State Matters," *Jacobin*, October 30, 2015.
54   Ibid.

the environment are clearly *external* to the point of production. As economists like to say, the environment represents a set of uncommodified "ecosystem services" that both underlie the various inputs to production and absorb its waste products and pollutants.[55] More to the point, many movements spring up to protect landscapes, communities, rivers, the atmosphere, and so on. These movements often also *appear* as "outside" or separate from the "point of production." As such, "environmental movements" (including the climate movement) have traditionally been seen as part of the explosion of "new social movements" in the 1960s along with antiwar, civil rights, feminist, queer, and other activism that differentiated themselves from a socialist-labor left.

In 2018, the leading eco-socialist Michael Löwy wrote an article as part of a roundtable discussion on the topic of "Do Red and Green Mix?" Note the very premise of the conversation, namely the separation of the "red" from the "green" (a practice common in eco-socialist and eco-Marxist circles). Löwy suggests, "To realize this vision, however, environmentalists and socialists will need to recognize their common struggle and how that connects with the broader 'movement of movements' seeking a Great Transition."[56] From this perspective, "class" is just one movement alongside "environmentalism," "feminism," "antiwar," "civil rights," and all the rest.

The climate movement also views politics in this way, as perhaps the most famous climate justice organization, 350.org, expressed:

> Climate change is not just an environmental issue, or a social justice issue, or an economic issue—it's all of those at once. It's one of the biggest challenges humanity has ever faced, and we are going to have to work together to solve it. That means bringing people together— not just environmentalists, but students, business owners, faith

55 Nicolás Kosoya and Esteve Corbera, "Payments for ecosystem services as commodity fetishism," *Ecological Economics*, Vol. 69, No. 6 (2010): 1228–36.
56 Michael Löwy, "Why Ecosocialism: For a Red-Green Future," *Great Transition Initiative*. Available online: greattransition.org/publication/why-ecosocialism-red-green-future.

groups, labor unions, universities, and more—and building diverse coalitions that are strong enough to put pressure on governments and stand up to the fossil fuel industry.[57]

This kind of thinking is rampant on the left, the idea that we can build some kind of "diverse coalition"—again the "movement of movements"—that will add up to a societal force with the capacity to "stand up to the fossil fuel industry." While everyone knows it would be good to forge broad coalitions, achieving this unity has proven elusive.

Not only were class and environmental movements viewed as distinct, many on the left concluded that production-centered class politics itself was outmoded, leading to what Ellen Meiksins Wood called the "retreat from class."[58] The strange thing about this retreat is that at the very same moment in the 1970s, the right and capital started organizing on an explicitly *class* basis. As David Harvey recounts in his theorization of neoliberalism as the "restoration of class power," in that decade capital started to organize, win power, and put into practice its agenda of deregulation, tax cuts, and fiscal austerity.[59] The election of Ronald Reagan in 1980 accelerated the process, adding the rollback of environmental regulations and the defunding of critical regulatory agencies; as Interior Secretary James Watt said at the time, "We will use the budget system as an excuse to make major policy decisions."[60] With labor on the defensive, trade union leadership often *aligned* with capital to put "jobs" ahead of environmental safety or regulation.[61]

Meanwhile, the right organized opposition to environmental policies in *class* terms as costing "jobs" or hindering economic

57 "About 350." 350.org/about.

58 Ellen Meiksins Wood, *The Retreat From Class: A New "True" Socialism*, (London: Verso, 1986).

59 David Harvey, *A Brief History of Neoliberalism* (Oxford: Oxford University Press, 1985).

60 Quoted in Daniel Faber, *Capitalizing on Environmental Injustice: The Polluter-Industrial Complex in the Age of Globalization* (Lanham, MD: Rowman and Littlefield, 2008), 128.

61 Erik Loomis, "Why labor and environmental movements split—and how they can come back together," *Environmental Health News*, September 18, 2018.

"competitiveness." This, more than any denial of the science itself, was the primary rationale for George W. Bush to pull out of the Kyoto climate accords and Donald Trump to exit the Paris climate agreement.

The jobs-vs.-environment dilemma has hindered the environmental movement for decades. Ecological politics often focuses on curtailing certain forms of production that employ people. In a capitalist society wherein the majority of people lack secure access to a livelihood, the category of "jobs" is of the utmost moral importance and can eclipse all other concerns. Given the bipartisan evisceration of the welfare state since 1980, can we blame the working class for choosing the only means of survival under neoliberal capitalism (jobs) over abstract notions of "the environment"?

As we explore in Part II, environmental politics also became itself a class project rooted in the rise of the professional class amid deindustrialization and decline. Indeed, much academic theorizing from this professional class has also served to analytically sever class from environmental politics. André Gorz, author of the explicit retreat *Farewell to the Working Class*, suggested elsewhere, "The ecological struggle . . . cannot be subordinated to the political objectives of socialism."[62] From this perspective, the very basics of Marxism must be revised or "greened." Ted Benton advances a vision of environmental politics oriented not toward production itself, but toward the effects of production on external environments and communities. Benton explains:

> The political significance of this in terms of the patterning of conflict along lines of cleavage related to gender, residential location, occupational situation, life-style, and so on needs to be understood, and integrated with the more traditional focus on lines of class cleavage arising "at the point of production." [63]

62 André Gorz, *Ecology as Politics* (Montreal: Black Rose Books, 1980), 20.
63 Ted Benton, "Marxism and natural limits: An ecological critique and reconstruction," *New Left Review* I/178 (November–December 1989): 51–86; 80.

The quarantining of "ecological concerns" as something outside of and distinct from "the point of production" is the key here. The theoretical *severance* of class from environmental politics hinges on a construction of environmental contestation outside production itself. James O'Connor offered the most explicit effort to integrate "new social movements" into Marxist theory. He is quite upfront on the political implications of his argument: "the decline of traditional labor and socialist movements" and the "rise of new social movements as agencies of social transformation" is the starting point of the analysis.[64] Environmental politics, he argues, focus not on traditional socialist concern with production, but rather on the "external conditions of production."[65] The ecological crisis of capitalism was what production did to these ecological conditions. This is conducive to a particular form of environmental politics that simply tries to stop production from the outside to protect a given landscape or river system. The question of *transforming* production is never posed because, as Gorz puts it plainly, "All production is also destruction."[66]

Still today, the most cutting-edge theories of the ecology of capital insist it is not a question of production, the site of traditional class politics. Nancy Fraser reminds us that feminist and ecological Marxism must look "behind Marx's hidden abode" to the unpaid processes of ecological functions and household work that underpin capitalism.[67] Although the critique of dualism is well established, Jason W. Moore suggests his work is new in its attempt to break down what he calls the Cartesian dualism between nature and society.[68] But what is odd is that Moore then creates a dualism of his own, between what he calls "the dialectic of paid and unpaid work."[69] Moore maps this dualism onto the distinction between production and

---

64   James O'Connor, *Natural Causes: Essays in Ecological Marxism* (London: Guilford, 1998), 158.

65   Ibid., 148.

66   Gorz, *Ecology as Politics*, 20.

67   Nancy Fraser, "Behind Marx's Hidden Abode," *New Left Review* 86 (March–April 2014): 55–72.

68   Jason Moore, *Capitalism in the Web of Life* (London: Verso, 2015).

69   Ibid., 64.

reproduction, or "the exploitation of labor power and the appropriation of Cheap Nature."[70] This allows Moore to posit nature alongside
other forms of unpaid work outside the capital relation like the unpaid
household work of women or slaves.[71] Moore creates a separation
between surplus value extraction in the realm of production and the
"unpaid work" of nature outside. Moore presents his own dualism
quite clearly:

> I take paid work (capitalization) to be the domain of the capital-labor
> conflict over shares of value. This is the question of exploitation. I take
> unpaid work to be a struggle over the forms and relations of capital to
> unmonetized social reproduction (as in "domestic labor") and to the
> "work of nature."[72]

This dualism makes it seem as if production and exploitation are
somehow not ecological—and that struggles over "capital-labor" relations in production are separate from environmental forms of
struggle.

These thinkers are correct, in the sense that much of what is
important ecologically is "outside" value and production. In many
ways, they are saying nothing different from the environmental
economists who focus on externalities and ecosystem services. Yet
all this heady theorizing reinforces the idea that class politics is
separate from ecological politics—and a focus on production is
separate from the external world of ecological "conditions." It
neglects one fundamental truth: if you want to change the degradation of ecological conditions, you need a politics aimed at changing
how production is organized.

The "movement of movements" approach is clearly attractive
because of its appeal to a diversity of groups and demands. But it is

---

70   Ibid.

71   He follows the work of Marie Mies, *Patriarchy and Accumulation on a World Scale:
Women in the International Division of Labour* (London: Zed, 1986), 77.

72   Jason Moore, "Cheap food and bad climate: From surplus value to negative value
in the capitalist world-ecology" *Critical Historical Studies*, Vol. 2, No. 1 (2015): 1–43; 6.

time to admit that the approach is not working. In discussion of left strategy, it is increasingly understood that a wider coalition is necessary to build *power*. Naomi Klein has rightly claimed that in order to build "counterpower sufficiently robust to win," we need to begin "strengthening the threads tying together our various issues and movements."[73] She argues repeatedly that we need to "connect the dots" between various struggles.[74]

But we should not see "class" as simply one of the many strands in our "movement of movements"; rather, class politics is a powerful *dot connector*. It aims to tie the threads together to make clear that our movements face a common enemy, the capitalist class, and that our struggles seek common goals based on our common humanity: dignity, freedom, and a livable planet. It is the project of class solidarity to recognize common interests and power through difference. Ellen Meiksins Wood presciently recognized this in 1986:

> Unless class politics becomes the unifying force that binds together all emancipatory struggles, the "new social movements" will remain on the margins of the existing order, at best able to generate periodic and momentary displays of popular support but destined to leave the capitalist order intact.[75]

This is an accurate summation of left politics throughout the neoliberal period.

Conclusion: 'The Demon Core of the Environmental Crisis'

In Connor Kilpatrick's description of the labor environmental politics of Tony Mazzocchi, a union leader with the Oil, Chemical, and Atomic Workers International (OCAW), he explains a different vision of environmentalism: "For Mazzocchi, worker control over

---

73 Naomi Klein, *On Fire: The Burning Case for a Green New Deal* (New York: Simon and Schuster, 2019), 167.

74 Ibid., e.g., 29, 196, 251.

75 Wood, *The Retreat from Class*, 199.

production *was* environmentalism."[76] According to his biographer Les Leopold, "Mazzocchi's conceptual breakthrough was that *pollution always starts in the workplace*, and then moves to the community and natural environment."[77] The environmental effects from production do not necessarily preclude a strategic orientation to the sites of production causing the problems: "As Mazzocchi saw it, those chemicals that poisoned his union's rank and file eventually make their way into communities outside—through the air, soil, and waterways. The factory was therefore the demon core of the environmental crisis."[78] In other words, although the *effects* of production are dispersed but unevenly targeted in poor communities (often of color), the foundation of pollution lies within the "hidden abode" of production. Tony Mazzocchi's production-oriented environmentalism came out of the old-left working-class politics of party building and rank-and-file class-struggle unionism. His ideas increasingly felt like a last gasp of a class-focused left.

Since the effects of pollution are experienced outside of production, community organizing requires some strategic orientation not anchored at the point of production. Yet this does not change the fact that the point of production is still the *source*—and thus the strategic target—of community and environmental organizing energy. Moreover, as I will develop in Part III, workers at the point of production have strategic leverage to impact production, unlike allies within the community or in any other activist circles. Working-class power is not moral but *structural*.[79]

Unfortunately, nearly all environmental and climate activism has allowed capital to strategically leverage their own workers against environmental action under the banner of protecting "jobs." To actually win on these matters, environmental and climate activists must do the hard work of organizing a movement that links working-class

---

76   Conor Kilpatrick, "Victory over the sun," *Jacobin* 26 (2017): 22–7; 24.
77   Les Leopold, *The Man Who Hated Work and Loved Labor: The Life and Times of Tony Mazzocchi* (White River Junction, VT: Chelsea Green, 2007), 246.
78   Ibid., 23.
79   Vivek Chibber, "Why the working class?" *Jacobin*, March 13, 2016.

concerns with the direct, often toxic threats that workers face in production itself. In Part III, we will examine what a climate politics aimed at the "point of production" can look like. But we still need a deeper view into how capital operates within the "hidden abode." Why are carbon emissions not only an unfortunate byproduct or an unintended "externality" of their operations, but also a fundamental and necessary part of the accumulation process?

2

Carbon Exploitation: How the Nitrogen Cycle Became Fossil Capital

Introduction: Inside the Hidden Abode of Nitrogen Capital

Driving up, all I saw were massive white plumes coming out of the nitrogen facility. I later learned this was steam—not a worrisome form of pollution. When I took a tour, I asked the guide to show me where the facility vented carbon dioxide. After several minutes, he finally revealed a single slender vent pipe with a small line of gray exhaust flowing out of it. You could walk around this nitrogen-fueled fertilizer plant for hours and not come across this vent. Yet this single plant, despite its relative invisibility, is in the top forty in emissions of all facilities in the entire country.[1]

I wanted to understand how producing nitrogen was so carbon-intensive—and what the managers and engineers at the plant thought about their carbon problem (if they thought about it at all). Their views were not exactly those of the capitalists who owned the company—the corporate headquarters was nearly one thousand miles away—but they were the ones managing the material flows of natural gas, nitrogen, and ammonia products. The managers were at the locus of fossil capitalism.

The first question might be, why does the production of nitrogen involve so much carbon? The reason is the main input of the entire process: natural gas. The plant manager at the facility joked to me that there are three major aspects of the fertilizer business: "gas, gas, and gas." Plant officials indicated that gas accounts for 85 percent of their

---

1 I received Institutional Review Board approval for this research, and the plant manager's cooperation with this research was premised on me not naming the company in any research products such as this.

operating costs, a figure consistent across the industry. During a PowerPoint presentation, plant engineers boasted of consuming 9 percent of all natural gas consumption in Louisiana, a state brimming with massive natural gas–consuming chemical complexes.

Natural gas is invisible and arrives via what the town's mayor called a "spaghetti network" of pipelines permeating the region. It exits one of those pipelines and flows directly into plant processes. The gas is used primarily as a "feedstock" for the production of hydrogen in a process called "steam reforming." It is also serves as fuel for the generation of heat, necessary for a variety of other plant processes. Both these uses, steam reforming and heat generation, produce carbon dioxide emissions. I learned via public data that this plant emits the highest volumes of greenhouse gases in the entire US chemical sector.

Overall, the fertilizer industry is estimated to contribute 2.5 percent of all global greenhouse-gas (GHG) emissions.[2] In China, which uses coal, not natural gas as its source of hydrogen, the fertilizer sector is responsible for 7 percent of that country's GHG emissions in a country filled with coal powered power plants and steel manufacturing.[3] Clearly, the nitrogen cycle has been amply transformed into fossil capital.[4]

Given its carbon intensity, I was interested in asking plant officials about alternatives to natural gas. They excitedly told me that they had thought about this issue. After all, the 2000s was a period of high natural gas prices; many nitrogen fertilizer companies shuttered their plants due to high costs.[5] But this company boasted of its ability to improve plant efficiency in ways that allowed them to survive the

---

2 International Fertilizer Association, "The Role of Fertilizers in Climate-Smart Agriculture," Contribution of the International Fertilizer Association (IFA) to the UN Climate Change Conference in Marrakesh, COP22/CMP12 (2016). fertilizer.org.

3 Wei-feng Zhanga, et al., "New technologies reduce greenhouse gas emissions from nitrogenous fertilizer in China," *PNAS*, Vol. 110, No. 21 (2013): 8375–80; 8375.

4 Andreas Malm, *Fossil Capital: The Rise of Steam Power and the Roots of Global Warming* (London: Verso, 2016).

5 Wen-yuan Huang, "Impact of rising natural gas prices on US ammonia supply," *Report of the Economic Research Service* (Washington, DC: United States Department of Agriculture, 2007).

price spike. Company officials said they even considered replacing natural gas with a substitute feedstock in the manufacturing process— but their two prime candidates were coal or petcoke, about the dirtiest and most carbon-intensive fuels one could imagine.[6]

It was at this moment that I realized these individuals take a very different approach to carbon responsibility. They did not worry about their carbon footprint, nor did they concern themselves with reforming their behavior to become more responsible consumers in the fight against climate change. These people were not like you and me: they operated according to entirely different logic. If we want to understand the climate crisis, we need to understand how production itself is organized through the logic of capital—and how this abstract logic requires a fundamental *indifference* to the concrete environmental world.

For capital, there is only one goal: to produce surplus value. This is a process (M-C-M') rooted in the abstraction of money growing on itself: "money which begets money."[7] If nitrogen capital can produce surplus value with natural gas or petcoke, that's fine with them. If any kind of capital can continue to produce surplus value in a warming world, or even *because* of a warming world, the planetary crisis simply doesn't matter. Capital is a process of abstract violence to the materiality of the real world.[8]

As I explained last chapter, most ecological approaches to Marxist political economy avoid or exclude a focus on the hidden abode of production. Thus, it should be no surprise that they also have not attempted to integrate ecology into Marx's theory of surplus value.[9] Lately, there has been a resurgence of interest in Marx's theory of value in general, and the relationship between value and nature more

---

6   Using petcoke would be like digging the tar sands bitumen of Alberta and inserting it directly into factory processes.

7   Marx, *Capital*, Vol. 1, 256.

8   See, Derek Sayer, *The Violence of Abstraction: The Analytical Foundations of Historical Materialism* (London: Brill, 1987).

9   For an exception, see John Bellamy Foster and Paul Burkett, *Marx and the Earth: An Anti-Critique* (Chicago: Haymarket, 2016), 137–64.

specifically.[10] This, I would argue, is symptomatic of a neoliberal era through which the realm of exchange—that is, the realm through which capitalist value appears on the surface—dominates our conception of political economy. And, again, many argue that we can solve climate change through this very realm of exchange—leading to a vast scholarship on all the new and bizarre attempts at valuing carbon or other ecosystem services.[11]

Despite the importance of Marx's theory of value, it is not the ultimate destination of his critical theory of capitalism. In *Capital*, the theory of value is more like a springboard to the real substance of his argument: how capital produces *surplus value*. As Frederick Engels noted in his eulogy to Marx: "Marx . . . discovered the special law of motion governing the present-day capitalist mode of production . . . The discovery of surplus value suddenly threw light on the problem, in trying to solve which all previous investigations . . . had been groping in the dark."[12] Marx's theory of value shared the focus on labor of Smith and Ricardo, but no other political economists had fathomed that profit—the entire goal of production—is rooted in the exploitation of labor. Most assumed profit as a fair payment to capital.

Is there an ecology of exploitation? Does capital's drive for surplus value explain the climate crisis? In this analysis of the nitrogen fertilizer industry, I will focus on the industry's drive for *relative surplus value* as a critical aspect in the production of climate change.[13] I will

---

10   See, in particular, Joel Wainwright and Morgan Robertson, "The value of nature to the state," *Annals of the Association of American Geographers*, Vol. 103, No. 4 (2013): 890–905, and the special issue collected by Kelly Kay and Miles Kenney-Lazar, "Value in capitalist natures," *Capitalism, Nature, Socialism*, Vol. 28, No. 1 (2017): 33–8. For my thoughts, see "Value, Nature, and Labor: A Defense of Marx," *Capitalism, Nature, Socialism*, Vol. 28, No. 1 (2017): 39–52.

11   For an overview, see Gareth Bryant, *Carbon Markets in a Climate-Changing Capitalism* (Cambridge, UK: Cambridge University Press, 2019).

12   Frederick Engels, "Frederick Engels' Speech at the Grave of Karl Marx, Highgate Cemetery, London. March 17, 1883." marxists.org/archive/marx/works/1883/death/burial.htm.

13   I am not the first to make this connection. See, Paul Hampton, *Workers and Trade Unions for Climate Solidarity: Tackling Climate Change in a Neoliberal World* (London: Routledge, 2015), 27.

show how the nitrogen industry developed strategies of relative surplus value production that resulted in the *cheapening* of nitrogen inputs for agriculture. This, of course, also allowed farmers to produce food more cheaply—in the end *cheapening* the life and nutrition of the working class itself.

What Is the Source of 'Cheap Nature'?
The Ecology of Relative Surplus Value

As mentioned in the previous chapter, capital can gain relative surplus value through investments in labor productivity. In sum, Marx shows how capitalists who make such investments can generate brief surplus profits by selling their commodities below the social value and capturing more of the market. This process forces other capitalists to adopt these new technologies, and therefore leads to the lowering of their overall value, or *cheapening* of commodities. "Capital therefore has an immanent drive, and a constant tendency, towards increasing the productivity of labor, in order to cheapen commodities and, by cheapening commodities, to cheapen the worker himself."[14] As we can see, this scenario assumes, at least initially, a relatively competitive industry structure where labor saving innovations can effectively capture the market.

For Marx, however, the temporary surplus profits flowing to individual capitalists are not the key to understanding the importance of relative surplus value to capital accumulation. The fact that individual capitalists seek to improve labor productivity creates new horizons of surplus value production for capital as a whole. Marx explains, "with the increase in the productivity of labor, the value of labor-power will fall, and the portion of the working day necessary for the reproduction of that value will be shortened."[15] Cheapening individual commodities leads to cheapening of the commodities needed to reproduce workers themselves. Marx refers to the

---

14   Marx, *Capital*, Vol. 1, 436–7.
15   Ibid., 432.

collection of commodities needed to reproduce the worker as the "value of labor power."[16] As capital drives down the value of labor power, it expands what can be appropriated as surplus value. Politically, this means capitalists, as a class, have an overall interest in cheaper wage goods. For example, in Marx's time, the bourgeoisie was in favor of repealing the Corn Laws in Britain that protected British landed interests and rents through higher prices.[17] They favored "free trade"—and increased food imports—because it would allow them to pay their workers lower wages. This also creates a deeper and more cultural problem where workers themselves often associate their "interests" with access to cheap commodities.

Where is the "ecology" here? Insofar as workers are living, biological animals, the value of labor power includes commodities directly drawn from nature. It is capital's drive for relative surplus value that produces massive gains in labor productivity in the extraction of raw materials like food, energy, and fiber for clothing. One basic economic consequence is that *cheaper* food, energy, clothing, and other necessities allow workers to afford other commodities that can increasingly be seen as central to a desirable standard of living, like smartphones in the Global North. Cheapening leads to more consumption—and thus to more ecological impacts from production and accumulation. While there is much focus on the role of consumption in environmental degradation, the root of these dynamics is in capital's drive for relative surplus value in the mode of production.

As discussed earlier, the most important method of improving labor productivity is the employment of machinery (as in tractors cheapening food production). Since the nineteenth century, the employment of machinery inevitably involves a source of nonhuman energy, usually fossil fuel. Moreover, as capital seeks to develop more mechanized methods of extracting raw materials from nature, it also seeks to displace ecological destruction onto the environment itself in the form of waste and pollution. The process of relative surplus value

---

16 Ibid., 274.
17 Ibid., 404.

creates *cheap commodities*, but, as many environmental economists point out, in ways that create significant costs or externalities to larger ecological systems.

Jason W. Moore argues that capitalism thrives on strategies of producing "cheap nature" as a premise for accumulation (cheap food, cheap energy, etc.).[18] However, his theory leaves out the main mechanism in capitalism that drives the cheapening of all commodities: relative surplus value. Instead, Moore decides to focus on what he calls "unpaid work/energy" as the key driver of nature's cheapness. He not only means the actual unmonetized *work* of nature—things like the work of soil microbes, wetland filtration, carbon sequestration, or what economists awkwardly term "ecosystem services"; he also refers to the manifold forms of *unpaid work* that structures capitalism overall (unpaid child care or slave labor, for example). It is this "unpaid work" that allows commodities to remain cheap. When it comes to "nature," capital stalks the planet looking for new frontiers of freshly exploitable natural resources like forests or mineral deposits. Indeed, it is these "frontier" regions which Moore argues contain reservoirs of unpaid work, since capital has not yet exhausted the soil or other critical ecological elements underpinning these resources.

The problem with this hypothesis: it fails to acknowledge that Marx already had a theory of how the "work" of nature is appropriated: the theory of rent and landed property.[19] Paul Burkett bitingly observes, "Apparently, the critics who condemn Marx for downgrading the productive contribution of limited natural conditions (while ignoring Marx's rent theory) are unaware of these . . . passages in *Capital* that do precisely the opposite."[20] Marx's theory of rent is complex, but at a basic level he borrows Ricardo's theory of differential rent, or what he calls "Differential Rent I." This theory explains how landlords appropriate *surplus profits* flowing from more "fertile" soil or other natural

---

18   Jason Moore, *Capitalism in the Web of Life: Ecology and the Accumulation of Capital* (London: Verso, 2015).

19   See, Karl Marx, *Capital*, Vol. III (London: Penguin, 1981), 751–952.

20   Paul Burkett, *Marx and Nature: A Red and Green Perspective* (Chicago: Haymarket, 2014), 93.

variation in the quality of the land (one example: some oil deposits, like those in the Middle East, are much more productive or easy to produce).[21] Marx suggests that the value of corn, or any commodity coming from the land, is set by the socially necessary labor time it takes to produce on the *least fertile* land. Those producing on more fertile lands see the extra profits due to lower costs of production; these surplus profits are appropriated as rent by landlords.

In other words, if the fertility or productivity of soil or a resource base can be attributed to "extra" work provided by nature, this work is paid, however incompletely, as rent to landlords. As Marx explains, their power to appropriate this rent is due to the power of property itself: "modern form of landed property presupposes the monopoly of disposing of particular portions of the globe as exclusive spheres of their private will to the exclusion of all others."[22] Often, this monopoly power of landed property resides with the state; in most countries, for example, the state is the "landlord" or owner of *all* the subsurface minerals in a given territory.[23]

In contrast to Moore, if parasitical landed property siphons off the work of nature as rent, this does not serve to cheapen natural resources in the slightest. Indeed, the power of landed property to extract rents prevents what are in fact cheap-to-produce resources from becoming cheap commodities. According to Marx, the main force driving the *cheapening* of all commodities (not just natural resources) is not nature or rentiers, but capital and the drive to produce surplus value. Indeed, for Marx, surplus value extracted from living labor is the most important form of "unpaid work"! And, we must look to this hidden abode to understand the roots of cheap nature and the larger ecological and climate crisis. In other words, just as Marx uncovered labor exploitation in surplus value, we can also uncover hidden forms of ecological degradation internal to the production process.

21   David Ricardo, *On the Principles of Political Economy and Taxation* (London: John Murray Albemarle Street, 1821), Chapter 2, "On Rent," 53–75.

22   Ibid., 752.

23   See, Fernando Coronil, *The Magical State: Nature, Money, and Modernity in Venezuela* (Chicago: University of Chicago Press, 1997).

Now, I will show how the nitrogen industry's strategies of relative surplus value production not only inserted an incredibly carbon-intensive form of nitrogen production into agriculture, but also served to *cheapen* food and the bodies of the working class more broadly.

How the Nitrogen Cycle Became Fossil Capital

Nitrogen is a basic building block of life. It forms the base of amino acids, which in turn form the proteins so essential to biological functions. Thus, insofar as all animals rely upon plants, the basis of life is the nitrogen necessary for plant growth.

But while nitrogen is technically *abundant*—79 percent of the atmosphere contains nitrogen gas (N_2)—it is an inert gas that is inaccessible for plant growth. Nitrogen must be *fixed* into nitrogenous compounds, like NH_3 (ammonia), that plants can use. For 99.9 percent of planetary history, the bulk of nitrogen fixation was achieved by microorganisms in the soil and, in marginal amounts, by lightning in the atmosphere.[24] Many of these microorganisms form symbiotic relationships with certain plants, creating higher soil fertility.

Thus, as humans began planting and cultivating specific crops on an annual basis, nitrogen was always a limiting factor. Planting the same crop year after year tends to deplete the nitrogen, and thus the fertility, of a given plot. Historically, the main solution to this was simply to move on to more fertile soil—swidden agriculture often burned forest cover ("slash and burn" cultivation), which aided the fertility of a given plot. Farmers also learned that crop rotation, and particularly the planting of leguminous crops like clover, alfalfa, and peas increased fertility by forming those symbiotic relationships with nitrogen-fixing bacteria. Finally, since the food we eat contains the critical nitrogen compounds of life, our solid waste is itself highly

---

24   G.J. Leigh, *The World's Greatest Fix: A History of Nitrogen and Agriculture* (Oxford: Oxford University Press, 2004), 13.

nitrogenous. Farmers found that animal manure applied to the soil increased its fertility.[25]

Most of these methods of increasing soil fertility relied on "free gifts of nature," or Moore's "unpaid work"—forests, soil microbes, animal digestion, waste. But as more and more land was privatized and the enclosure of the commons made swidden cultivation harder, farmers began to encounter serious problems with soil erosion and infertility. Out of this general soil crisis in nineteenth-century capitalism—Marx described it as a "metabolic rift"—fertilizers were increasingly sold to farmers as a *commodity* input.[26] It began slowly with bone mixtures, fish scraps, and slaughterhouse wastes,[27] but with the rise of the guano trade in the mid–1800s it developed into a global commercial fertilizer industry.[28]

The guano fields—massive piles of bird droppings—on the Chincha Islands off the southern coast of Peru were geographically unique. Lack of rain meant the nitrogen-rich waste was not washed away. However, the process of producing guano as a commodity was an extremely labor-intensive process that relied heavily upon imported Chinese labor. Brett Clark and John Bellamy Foster describe the conditions that were called "worse than slavery":

> The extraction of guano required digging into mounds of excrement that covered rocky islands. The capital outlay for extraction was minimal. The most expensive items were the bags into which guano was loaded. Using picks and shovels, coolies were required to dig through the layers of guano, filling sacks and barrows. Each worker had to load between 80 to 100 barrows, close to five tons, each day. Once the

25   The above paragraph is drawn from Vaclav Smil, *Enriching the Earth: Fritz Haber, Carl Bosch, and the Transformation of World Food Production* (Cambridge, MA: MIT Press, 2001), 1–39.

26   Richard A. Wines, *Fertilizer in America: From Waste Recycling to Resource Exploitation* (Philadelphia: Temple University Press, 1985).

27   Lewis B. Nelson, *History of the US Fertilizer Industry* (Muscle Shoals, AL: Tennessee Valley Authority), 34–45.

28   Gregory Cushman, *Guano and the Opening of the Pacific World: A Global Ecological History* (Cambridge: Cambridge University Press, 2013).

barrows were filled, the workers hauled the guano to a chute to transfer it to the ships. If the workers failed to move five tons during the day, they were physically punished.[29]

Discipline in the guano fields was enforced via coercion and terror: "Infractions by workers were met by severe punishment, such as flogging, whipping, or being suspended for hours in the sun."[30]

Cultivation of the depleted soils of Europe and America quickly came to rely upon the imperial relationship with hyperexploited labor in the Peruvian guano fields. Yet the guano boom lasted only from about 1840 through 1870, as the most easily accessible deposits were rapidly depleted. After 1870, the main source of nitrogen came from sodium nitrate or saltpeter from caliche ore, both found in deposits in the Atacama Desert region of Chile.

The extraction process for saltpeter in the Atacama was only slightly less labor intensive than that for guano in the Chinchas. It involved hand-drilling holes, inserting and detonating explosives, hand-sorting the ores with higher nitrate concentrations exposed by the explosions, boiling that material, drying it into crystalized nitrate, and pouring it into hand-sewn bags.[31] In contrast to the brute manual labor of guano extraction, Chilean nitrates required skilled—but still exploited—labor: "Although poorly paid, the workers were skilled at their jobs and could not be replaced easily by unskilled or untrained workers."[32]

I could go into much more detail, but the key to understanding this geography of nitrogen is *rent*. When natural resources are confined to very few locations, the owners of those deposits can easily charge high rents. This is precisely what happened in Chile, where the government charged exorbitant taxes on nitrate production (70 percent) to

29   Brett Clark and John Bellamy Foster, "Ecological imperialism and the global metabolic rift: unequal exchange and the guano/nitrates trade," *International Journal of Comparative Sociology*, Vol. 50, No. 3–4 (2009): 311–34; 322–3.

30   Ibid., 323.

31   Paul Marr, "Technology, labor, and the collapse of Chile's nitrate industry," *Middle States Geographer*, Vol. 46 (2013): 19–26.

32   Ibid., 21.

create one of the earliest forms of what we call a "rentier state," a term often applied today to those states that rely on oil rents.[33] As resource rents became infused with state power, control of nitrate reserves became a matter of geopolitical and diplomatic strategy and conflict. In 1856, the United States simply declared any guano islands "discovered" by American citizens could be annexed as part of US territory.[34] In 1865–66, Spain seized the guano islands but were fought off by an alliance of Chile, Peru, Boliva, and Ecuador. Then In the 1880s, Chile went to war with Peru and Bolivia in part over control of nitrate fields.

How did the nitrogen cycle shift from a kind of rentier capitalism to a form of *industrial capital* based on surplus value production? In 1898, British scientist Sir William Crookes warned that the scarcity of nitrogen fertilizer meant a "catastrophe little short of starvation for the wheat eaters."[35] Crookes was aware that the "natural" sources of nitrogen were finite and depleting rapidly. He also knew that the atmosphere is 79 percent nitrogen, and believed avoiding mass starvation depended on devising a chemical process to "fix" this atmospheric nitrogen: "It is through the laboratory that starvation may ultimately be turned into plenty."[36]

Breaking the power of nitrate rentiers meant finding a way to "fix" abundant atmospheric nitrogen into a form that could be transformed into fertilizer or munitions (another use for nitrogen). The breakthrough finally took place in 1909 in the laboratories of Fritz Haber and Carl Bosch, where synthesized ammonia (NH_3) was extracted from air. By the 1920s, private chemical capital gained access to the details of this process (specifically the catalysts used) in the United States.[37] The Haber-Bosch process differed markedly from guano and Chilean nitrates not only because it avoided the rentier and land problem—the

33 Ibid., 19.
34 Dylan Matthews, "This 1856 law makes it legal to seize islands for America if they have lots of bird crap," *Vox*, July 31, 2014.
35 Sir William Crookes, *The Wheat Problem: Based on Remarks Made in the Presidential Address to the British Association at Bristol in 1898* (London: Longmans Green, 1898), 44.
36 Ibid., 3.
37 Smil, *Enriching the Earth*, 73–4.

atmosphere is *everywhere*—but also because it was a capital-intensive production process rather than a labor-intensive one. The production of nitrogen no longer required a coercive labor regime, but a capital-intensive regime based on huge investments in enormous boilers, pipes, valves, and compressors.

Once these fixed capital investments are made, the main issue is to find a source of hydrogen to combine with free atmospheric nitrogen to create ammonia (NH_3). Hydrogen, the most abundant element in the universe, is costly to produce because it is only found on earth as compounds with other elements like carbon and oxygen. The process of extricating hydrogen from these compounds is costly in terms of money, energy, and materials. Thus for nitrogen capital, the source of hydrogen becomes a primarily economic question of finding the cheapest method of hydrogen production.

Unfortunately for the climate, the cheapest source of energy and hydrogen feedstock comes from fossil fuels. While one could produce hydrogen from water through a process of electrolysis requiring electricity, chemical firms prefer cheaper hydrocarbons. This is how the nitrogen cycle was subsumed into a form of what Andreas Malm calls fossil capital.[38] The entire process of solving a scarcity of natural sources of nitrogen was premised on a shift from a now-abundant, but inevitably finite, source of hydrogen: fossil fuel. Moreover, as we ramped up the production of synthetic nitrogen drawn from the atmosphere, excess nitrogen overwhelmed the natural nitrogen cycle, which led to nitrous oxide emissions, water pollution, eutrophication, and marine dead zones. Essentially, we overshot the natural nitrogen cycle with synthetic production: "The rate at which nitrogen is being fixed on land today is approximately 300 Mt(N)/yr, roughly double its preindustrial value."[39]

When constructing one of the first synthetic ammonia plants in US history in the 1920s and 1930s, the DuPont corporation laid out

38   Andreas Malm, *Fossil Capital: The Rise of Steam Power and the Roots of Global Warming* (London: Verso, 2016), 290.

39   Robert H. Socolow, "Nitrogen management and the future of food: Lessons from the management of energy and carbon," *PNAS*, Vol. 96, No. 11 (1999): 6001–8; 6002.

its concern for "low-cost hydrogen" from fossil fuel in its own corporate history:

> The manufacture of ammonia by the Haber process implies a source of nitrogen and low cost hydrogen . . . The former is of course available in the air, but the latter is generally associated with carbon or oxygen which it can be extracted only through the expenditure of power. Electrolytic hydrogen is too expensive for use in the United States. The cracking of hydrocarbons or coal produces hydrogen economically.[40]

In 1931, the Shell Chemical Company in California developed a process that used not coal but natural gas as the primary hydrogen feedstock for ammonia synthesis.[41] The process, called "steam reforming," takes methane (CH_4) and combines it with water (H_2O) to create hydrogen gas (H_2). The main waste product of this chemical reaction is carbon dioxide (CO_2). Now, nearly three quarters (72.4 percent) of global ammonia production relies on natural gas, but China still relies on the more carbon-intensive coal feedstock.[42] Natural gas also constitutes the *primary cost* to capital—most firms cite it as 72 to 85 percent of cost.[43] Currently, there is excitement around so-called "green ammonia," which would use abundant, cheap renewable energy to power electrolysis of water to create the needed hydrogen.[44] Yet like everything else in the clean energy world, it is hard to imagine nitrogen capital making a significant shift when "by most estimates, green ammonia will cost two to four times as much to make as conventional ammonia."[45] As if to

---

40   E.P. Bartlett, *The Chemical Division of the DuPont Ammonia Department, 1924–1936* (Wilmington, DE: E.I. du Pont de Nemours & Co., 1949), 9–10.

41   Nelson, *History of the US Fertilizer Industry*, 229.

42   Institute for Industrial Productivity. n.d. Ammonia. ietd.iipnetwork.org/content/ammonia.

43   Wen-yuan Huang, "Impact of rising natural gas prices on US ammonia supply," Report of the Economic Research Service (Washington, DC: United States Department of Agriculture, 2007), 5.

44   Alexander H. Tullo, "Is ammonia the fuel of the future?" *Chemical and Engineering News*, Vol. 99, No. 8 (2021): 20–2.

45   Ibid., 20.

illustrate the point, the firm that owns the facility described in the introduction to this chapter, recently announced a project to install electrolysis plant to produce green ammonia—but the projected production
amounts to 0.25 percent of the facility's total production of nitrogen
products as listed on its website.

Yet, once the elements of this process are in place—the boilers, the
pipes, the water, the gas—capital confronts a problem of how to profit
from it when many other firms have the same materials in place. A
traditional Marxist answer would point to further exploitation of
labor as the ultimate living source of surplus value. But the ammonia
production process requires very little labor at all. The other method
of surplus value production makes labor cheaper *indirectly* through
the production of relative surplus value.

Nitrogen Capital and the Cheapening of Food and Labor in the United States, 1940–70

Just around the time US chemical companies were developing the natural gas–based steam reforming process, war broke out in Europe and
Asia. Nitrogen is not only a critical component in fertilizer; it is also
important for the munitions industry. Fritz Haber's drive to synthesize
ammonia was as much to strengthen the German military in World
War I as it was a solution to soil fertility. Later, as the prospect of US
involvement in World War II became more and more possible, the
Ordnance Department of the Army ordered the construction of ten
new ammonia plants for the war effort and subcontracted the building
to a variety of chemical companies.[46] In effect, this subsidized the most
significant costs involved in nitrogen production—construction
costs—and doubled the number of Haber-based ammonia plants in the
United States from nine to eighteen between 1940 and 1946.[47] Four of
the plants were built to use natural gas; increasingly the feedstock of
choice in the US ammonia industry.[48]

---

46   Nelson, *History of the US Fertilizer Industry*, 325–6.
47   Ibid., 324.
48   Ibid., 325.

As early as 1943, it became clear that the government had a surplus of ammonium nitrate and could shift supplies to farmers for fertilizer. "This was the first time that sizable quantities of the material had become available to American farmers."[49] As the war wound down, the government decided to sell off the plants to private chemical companies, a process it would complete in 1954. Meanwhile, by 1950 some 70 percent of US nitrogen consumption was derived from ammonia synthesis, and farmers were "rapidly learning the economic value of applying large amounts of chemical nitrogen on nonleguminous crops."[50] In trade journals, ammonia industry insiders argued direct sales to farmers played a critical role in industry growth. "When a product carries with it as many benefits as anhydrous ammonia, it is believed that advertising can play a vital role in bringing the facts to the farmer's attention quickly."[51] As Figure 2.1 shows, fertilizer companies aggressively marketed anhydrous ammonia solutions to farmers as opportunities to "grow" their profits (*Agricultural Chemicals*, ads, 1956, Allied). The industry also promoted research studies to show how applying chemical nitrogen boosted profits. An article in the journal *Agricultural Ammonia News* boasted, "Five-year Missouri tests prove: Ammonia boosts profits by $14/acre."[52] Another article, titled "He's sold on NH_3," tells the story of a farmer, Pat Metcalf, who used to average 35 bushels of corn per acre and now sees 86 bushels.[53] "I think that the application of fertilizer was what really made the difference."[54] This was not hyperbole. On average, corn yields were around 36 bushels per acre in 1945–9, and 94 in 1972–3.[55]

---

49   Ibid., 325.

50   Ibid., 323.

51   "Distributor advertising is the quickest way to give farmers facts about ammonia— use of different media discussed by distributors," *Agricultural Ammonia News*, January– March (1955), 10, 56.

52   Miller Carpenter, "Five-year tests prove ammonia boosts profits by $14 per acre," *Agricultural Ammonia News* March–April (1956): 16–20.

53   Ellis Stout, "He's sold on NH_3," *Agricultural Ammonia News* July–August (1957): 11–12.

54   Ibid., 11.

55   Willard W. Cochrane and Mary E. Ryan, *American Farm Policy, 1948–1973* (Minneapolis: University of Minnesota Press, 1976), 3.

Figure 2.1 *Source: Agricultural Chemicals*, March 1956. p. 7

Selling fertilizer to farmers was vital to accumulation in the ammonia industry. Accordingly, in the 1950s the number of ammonia plants expanded from nineteen to fifty-seven.[56] Competition intensified among firms, and prices declined through the World War II and postwar period, until the 1960s.[57] The tremendous expansion of capacity

56 Nelson, *History of the US Fertilizer Industry*, 324.
57 William H. Martin, "Public policy and increased competition in the synthetic ammonia industry," *The Quarterly Journal of Economics*, Vol. 73, No. 3 (1959): 373–92.

in the 1940s and '50s was contingent on millions of farmers shifting to chemical nitrogen inputs. These methods required new machines, new tools, and new rhythms of plowing, planting, and harvesting.[58] It did not take long for industry insiders to worry about the classic problem of overcapacity. An editorial in the trade journal *Agricultural Chemicals* explained, "How long can we keep expanding output before anhydrous ammonia, and as a matter of fact nitrogen in all forms, will be coming out our ears?"[59] Despite this alarm, the journal remained sanguine that "no oversupply should result if it is used by the American farmer at rates that are currently recommended as economically sound."[60]

"Economically sound" rates of application suited the accumulation needs of the industry quite well. The chemical industry had to also look beyond the American farmer toward suburban homeowners and, more important, export markets to solve overcapacity problems.[61] In 1952, the United States exported only 11,000 tons of nitrogen; by 1964, 111,000; and by 1970, 727,000.[62] This parallels the expansion of the "Green Revolution" and its effort to transform peasant agriculture in the Global South toward chemical inputs like anhydrous ammonia.[63]

Ammonia producers not only sought new markets domestically and abroad; they also sought to develop more efficient forms of production—that is, they sought relative surplus value. The real breakthrough came in the early 1960s, when "the M.W. Kellogg Company introduced the jumbo-size, single-train, centrifugal compressor ammonia plants."[64] These plants could produce at much

---

58   Adam Romero, " 'From oil well to farm': Industrial waste, shell oil, and the petrochemical turn (1927-1947)," *Agricultural History*, Vol. 90, No. 1 (2016): 70–93.

59   "Nitrogen: A study of productive capacity," *Agricultural Chemicals* 9 (September 1954): 55–7, 149; 55.

60   Ibid., 149.

61   Paul Robbins, *Lawn People: How Grasses, Weeds, and Chemicals Make Us Who We Are* (Philadelphia, PA: Temple University Press, 2007).

62   US Geological Survey. 2019. "Historical Statistics for Mineral and Material Commodities in the United States" Nitrogen—Supply-Demand Statistics. usgs.gov.

63   Raj Patel, "The long green revolution," *Journal of Peasant Studies*, Vol. 40, No. 1 (2013): 1–63.

64   Nelson, *History of the US Fertilizer Industry*, 333–4.

higher levels than before. Previous plants produced between 25 and 300 tons per day; these produced 600 to 1,500 tons per day.[65] Moreover, the use of a single compressor and increased efficiency through heat capture and recovery created conditions where "ammonia could be produced . . . at one-half the cost" of previous plants.[66]

The first plant came online in 1964, but by 1980, 27 companies operating 43 plants had the same technology and accounted for 71 percent of total US ammonia production.[67] In Marxist terms, these innovations dramatically lowered the "socially necessary labor time" it took to produce ammonia, and that, in turn, lowered the value of ammonia products overall.

In other words, the drive for relative surplus value led to the *cheapening* of nitrogen inputs to agriculture. A historian of agriculture puts it this way: "Rapid expansion in the use of inorganic nitrogen fertilizer in the 1950s and 1960s was not so much a matter of a new, improved input [into agriculture] as large reduction in the cost of manufacturing an old one."[68] The expansion of fertilizer capacity and competition for relative surplus value created declining fertilizer prices in the 1960s before natural gas price spikes in the 1970s complicated matters. Prices for anhydrous ammonia declined 51 percent from $141 per short ton in 1960 to $73 in the fall of 1969.[69] Fertilizer, along with tractors, pesticides, and other industrial inputs, was part of a colossal revolution in labor productivity on American farms. In the early 1920s, it took 122 labor hours per 100 bushels of corn; by the mid-1960s, just seven labor hours were needed.[70] The overall result of this was a rapid decline in employment in the agricultural sector—not

65　Ibid., 332, 334.
66　Ibid., 334.
67　Ibid., 335.
68　Bruce Gardner, *American Agriculture in the Twentieth Century: How It Flourished and What It Cost* (Cambridge, MA: Harvard University Press, 2002), 23.
69　United States Department of Agriculture, Economic Research Service, "Fertilizer Use and Price." ers.usda.gov/data-products/fertilizer-use-and-price.
70　Susan B. Cater, et al., *Historical Statistics of the United States: Millennium Online Edition.* "Table Da1143–71—Labor hours per unit of production and related factors, by commodity: 1800–1986."

just in the United States but in the world. As Aaron Benanav astutely observes:

> In the 1980s, the majority of the world's workers still worked in agriculture; by 2018 that figure had fallen to 28 percent. Thus the major destroyers of livelihoods in the twentieth century was not "silicon capitalism" but nitrogen capitalism.[71]

Key to Marx's theory of relative surplus value is the idea that the cheapening of commodities overall leads to the cheapening of commodities needed to *reproduce* labor power, and thus widen the amount of surplus value that can be extracted from those workers. Obviously, cheap nitrogen inputs meant cheaper inputs for farmers, but this led to the cheapening of perhaps the most important wage good—food. Nitrogen was at the core of what David Goodman and Michael Redclift call the "corn–soya-bean–livestock complex," wherein cheap grain fed cheap meat production.[72] Food prices spiked during and just after World War II, but as Figure 2.2 shows, basic grain commodities declined in price over the postwar period.[73] More importantly, the percentage of overall expenditures on food declined precipitously over the postwar era. A rough average does not capture class inequality, but in 1947, US consumers spent an average of 23 percent of their income on food; in 1970, that share had declined to 13 percent.[74] One reason is, of course, *higher wages*, but it is also worth pointing out that as the proportion spent on food declined, the *amount* of actual food consumed (and wasted) increased dramatically. Figure 2.3 shows the massive expansion of meat consumption during the postwar era.[75]

71   Aaron Benanav, *Automation and the Future of Work* (London: Verso, 2020), 42.

72   David Goodmen and Michael Redclift, *Refashioning Nature: Food, Ecology and Culture* (London: Routledge, 1991), 109.

73   Data from economist David Jacks's website, "Data on 1850–Present." sfu.ca/~djacks/data/boombust/index.html.

74   Our World in Data, "Food expenditure as a share of family disposable income, United States." ourworldindata.org/grapher/food-expenditure-as-share-of-family-disposable-income.

75   United States Department of Agriculture, Economic Research Service, "Per capita availability of chicken higher than that of beef," ers.usda.gov.

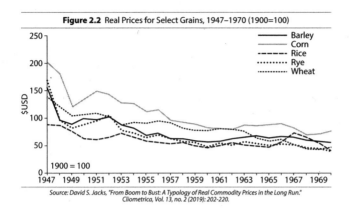

Figure 2.2 Real Prices for Select Grains, 1947–1970 (1900=100)

Source: David S. Jacks, "From Boom to Bust: A Typology of Real Commodity Prices in the Long Run."
Cliometrica, Vol. 13, no. 2 (2019): 202-220.

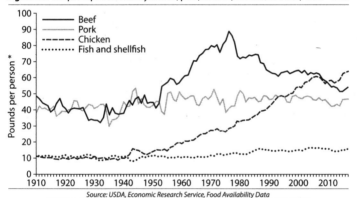

Figure 2.3 U.S. per capita availability of beef, pork, chicken, and fish/shellfish, 1910 – 2017

Source: USDA, Economic Research Service, Food Availability Data
https://www.ers.usda.gov/data-products/chart-gallery/gallery/chart-detail/?chartId=58312
* Calculated on the basis of and edible meat in boneless, trimmed (edible) weight.
Excludes edible offals, bones, viscera, and game from red meat. Includes skin, neck,
and giblets from chicken. Excludes use of chicken for commercially prepared pet food.

Marx also argues that the cheapening of commodities, *cheapens the workers themselves.* The postwar era was defined not only by cheap food in an abstract sense, but also by the rise of processed food increasingly devoid of nutritional content and filled with cheap sweeteners, oils, preservatives, and high levels of sodium and fat.[76] As the postwar era of high wages and union jobs faded away from 1980

---

76   Michael Moss, *Salt Sugar Fat: How the Food Giants Hooked Us* (New York: Random House, 2013).

to the present, the new era was marked by longer working hours and stagnant wages. That led workers to rely more and more on cheap "fast" or other convenient processed food, so as to not interfere with a frantic balancing act between work in the workplace and the work of social reproduction in the increasingly privatized household unit.[77]

Cheap food and cheap workers were less a product of the "unpaid work/energy" of nature and more a product of capital's drive for relative surplus value. One could not really claim agriculture was fully industrialized until the postwar era. In 1940, nearly a quarter of the population still lived and worked on farms; by 1970, the share had declined to less than 5 percent.[78] This drive for improving labor productivity carried over from the farm to "off-farm." As Jack Kloppenburg argued, "The most significant changes in agricultural production . . . is the displacement of production activities off-farm and into circumstances in which fully developed capitalist relations of production can be imposed."[79] What the industrialization of agriculture meant for capital as a whole was much wider horizons of surplus value production. Cheap food and workers created the possibility of huge superprofits for capital as a whole, allowing it to bear the cost of higher wages and collective bargaining for unionized workers in the postwar era.

These transformations have led to the overapplication of cheap nitrogen fertilizer on farms. For the first time in human history, farmers could plant the same crops on the same plots year after year without depleting soil fertility.[80] Now farmers often have an economic incentive to apply too much nitrogen. "Many farmers use extra N fertilizer as a hedge against missing potential high yields in years with exceptionally

77   Julie Guthman, *Weighing In: Food Justice and the Limits of Capitalism* (Berkeley, CA: University of California Press, 2011)

78   Susan B. Carter, et al., *Historical Statistics of the United States*, "Table Da1–13, Farms—number, population, land, and value of property: 1910–1999."

79   Jack Kloppenburg, *First the Seed: The Political Economy of Plant Biotechnology, 1492–2000* (Madison, WI: University of Wisconsin Press, 1988), 31.

80   Romero, "From oil well to farm."

favorable growing conditions."[81] The result is that "of 80 million tons spread onto fields in fertilizer each year, only 17 million tons gets into food. The rest goes missing."[82] This is an astounding level of waste, but it is not just economic waste for the farmers who throw away valuable fertilizer. This lost nitrogen escapes into the atmosphere as nitrous oxide greenhouse gas emissions and circulates into the hydrological system via runoff, leading to eutrophication, or the growth of dense plant life in lakes and rivers that causes mass death from lack of oxygen.

Despite industry pronouncements on teaching farmers to apply nitrogen more efficiently, the uncomfortable fact is nitrogen producers *profit* from these wasteful dynamics—the more nitrogen wasted, the more sold. Most attention on regulation focuses on the overapplication of nitrogen by "wasteful" farmers, but few consider regulating the source of industrial production itself.[83]

These ecological ill effects stem from a *production system* bent on expanding markets and capacity for synthetic ammonia. The expansion of fertilizer production in the postwar period is stunning—from 730,000 tons in 1946 to 19.7 million tons in 1980.[84] Using industry-wide benchmark emissions calculations for natural gas–based ammonia production (1.6 tons per tonne of NH_3), we can calculate emissions rising from just over 1 million metric tons of CO_2 equivalent in 1946 to 28.5 million in 1980; an increase of nearly 2,700 percent.[85] As stated earlier, nitrogen fertilizer today constitutes 2.5 percent of global GHG emissions.[86]

81   G. Phillip Robertson and Peter M. Vitousek, "Nitrogen in agriculture: Balancing the cost of an essential resource," *Annual Review of Environment and Resources*, Vol. 34 (2009): 97–125.

82   Fred Pearce, "The nitrogen fix: Breaking a costly addiction" Yale Environment 360 (2009): e360.yale.edu/features/the_nitrogen_fix_breaking_a_costly_addiction.

83   David R. Kanter and Timothy D. Searchinger, "A technology-forcing approach to reduce nitrogen pollution," *Nature Sustainability*, Vol. 1 (October 2018): 544–52.

84   Nelson, *History of the US Fertilizer Industry*, 324.

85   Institute for Industrial Productivity, n.d. Ammonia. ietd.iipnetwork.org/content/ammonia.

86   International Fertilizer Association, "The Role of Fertilizers in Climate-Smart Agriculture," Contribution of the International Fertilizer Association (IFA) to the UN Climate Change Conference in Marrakesh, COP22/CMP12 (2016).

Resisting 'Carbon Constraints' in the Twenty-First Century

In 2019, researchers at Cornell University and the Environmental Defense Fund published a study that found industrial fertilizer production facilities were leaking one hundred times more methane into the atmosphere than was previously thought.[87] Since these factories are central nodes of natural gas use, much of it leaks along the way—0.34 percent of all gas is lost in this manner, the study shows. That does not sound like a lot until you realize how much natural gas these facilities consume in the first place. This revelation is on top of the known carbon dioxide pollution from ammonia synthesis and the extensive nitrogen pollution from ammonia application on farms. In terms of climate change, all this waste only further cements nitrogen capital's role as a core driver of anthropogenic climate change.

The above historical section is meant to explain how this carbon-intensive industry became embedded within capitalism, the food system, and the reproduction of labor. Fast forward to the twenty-first century, and we see an intransigent industry aware of its carbon problem but unwilling to take significant action to address it. In my research with industry participants, I discovered general indifference and various strategies of displacing responsibility.

The first strategy is to argue that the industry is locked into a fixed technological process of synthesizing ammonia. The Haber-Bosch process is still called this because its basics were discovered by those scientists over 100 years ago. When I attended an industry conference, all the cutting-edge sustainability technology was promoted in the field of fertilizer application on farms, like improving efficiency of nitrogen uptake to prevent loss and pollution. But when conference speakers discussed industrial production, they spoke of a "one-hundred-year-old" technology based on a fixed set of unchangeable

---

87 Xiaochi Zhou, Fletcher H. Passow, Joseph Rudek, Joseph C. von Fisher, Steven P. Hamburg, and John D. Albertson, "Estimation of methane emissions from the US ammonia fertilizer industry using a mobile sensing approach," *Elementa*, Vol. 7, No. 1 (2019): Article 19: 1–12.

chemical equations. A plant manager of a nitrogen facility in Canada laid out the logic in relation to carbon:

> The quagmire we find with greenhouse-gas emissions is the chemistry has been set by the scientists Haber and Bosch just over 100 years ago and there's no change in that chemistry—it is what it is. And so if you're going to make ammonia in this way you're going to generate this amount of CO_2.[88]

Of course, the only thing "set" about the Haber-Bosch process is combining hydrogen with atmospheric nitrogen under conditions of heat and pressure. "This amount of CO_2" is subject to how you produce hydrogen—and the chemistry of emissions is quite different for natural gas, electrolysis of water, or coal. What is really "set" is the most profitable means of producing hydrogen. If an industrial system were directed to other ends, perhaps hydrogen would be produced in cleaner ways. Fact is, we have a carbon-intensive fertilizer industry because a profit-oriented capitalist class owns and controls the means of producing fertilizer.

Second, the industry argues it would be "unfair" for it to be subject to carbon regulation in a global market. The only way industry leaders would agree to what they call "carbon constraints" is if the "global market did it equally." A think tank spokesperson explained this to me:

> The price of fertilizer is dictated by a global price and so those that have a higher cost than others are going to be less competitive than others . . . If we have carbon constraints imposed on us when competitor producers in developing countries don't have similar constraints . . . that un-levels the playing field.[89]

This is precisely how Marx described the capitalist resistance to the regulation of child labor:

> But since capital is by its nature a leveler, since it insists upon equality

---

88 Interview 1, July 16, 2015.
89 Interview 2, July 2, 2015.

in the conditions of exploitation of labor in every sphere of production as its own innate right, the limitation by law of children's labor in one branch of industry results in its limitation in others.[90]

Of course, Marx was talking about national legislation in England, and it is difficult to imagine a "leveled" carbon regulatory playing field for all fertilizer producers everywhere. Thus, the fertilizer industry insists on the "equality in the conditions of exploitation" of the climate—which essentially means free rein to spew carbon dioxide as the normal state of affairs. Industry leaders speak of their global competition with China, the world's largest ammonia producer—a country where production is more carbon-intensive because it relies on coal.

When recent US regulations targeted the power sector, the fertilizer industry was quick to differentiate itself. Ultimately, fertilizer producers compete globally, while electricity generation is a publicly regulated utility whose markets are national or regional. "The power industry is highly regulated and can pass costs [from regulation] onto consumers. We can't."[91]

Third, as the climate crisis intensifies, the industry does not want to appear completely inactive. Thus, it employs a classic "greenwashing" strategy of voluntarist carbon action. The company that controls the plant I visited publicized the sale of "carbon credits" to a major auto company based on nitrous oxide abatement measures taken at one of its seven plants around the country. The company was able to exchange these nitrous oxide reductions for "carbon equivalents" and donate the proceeds to an agricultural education organization, furthering its public relations narrative of "feeding the world." This is the very definition of a climate bait-and-switch. While the fertilizer's role in producing nitrous oxide emissions is most publicized in relation to agricultural application of fertilizers,[92] the majority of emissions from the industrial sector are in the form of carbon dioxide. For

90   Marx, *Capital*, Vol. 1, 520.
91   Ibid.
92   Robertson and Vitousek, "Nitrogen in agriculture."

example, 80 percent of emissions from the plant I visited come in the form of carbon dioxide, and just 20 percent are nitrous oxide from nitric acid production.

All these strategies of displacing responsibility distract us from the continued accumulation of fossil capital in the nitrogen sector—and the continued accumulation of carbon emissions as a result. The ammonia industry is currently experiencing a massive boom due to cheap natural gas produced via hydraulic fracturing ("hydrofracking").[93] Five companies currently control 80 percent of the ammonia market, and profits have surged over the last decade.[94] In fact, while the natural gas extractive industry suffers through low prices, the greatest beneficiary of the hydrofracking boom has been chemical and fertilizer capital, which consumes natural gas as its primary input. Between 2009 and 2019, US nitrogen production rose from 7.7 million metric tons to 12.5 million—an increase of 62 percent.[95] Again, we could roughly calculate emissions to rise with this from 12.3 million tons to 21.3 tons of carbon dioxide equivalent, an increase of nearly 75 percent. New fertilizer plants are now up and running in Iowa and Indiana to produce closer to consumer markets in the US farm belt.[96] All of this has happened while social and political attention to the climate crisis has risen and individual consumers seek to change their behavior in response.

Conclusion

Only as a personification of capital is the capitalist respectable. As such, he shares with the miser an absolute drive towards self-enrichment. But what appears in the miser as the mania of an individual is

---

93   Lucy Cramer and Rhiannon Hoyle, "Here's one industry where the US is already catching China—fertilizers," *Wall Street Journal*, February 12, 2017.

94   David Kanter, "A new way to curb nitrogen pollution: Regulate fertilizer producers, not just farmers," *Salon*, January 20, 2019.

95   US Geological Survey 2019, "Nitrogen Statistics and Information." usgs.gov/centers/nmic/nitrogen-statistics-and-information.

96   Energy Information Administration, "New methanol and fertilizer plants to increase already-growing industrial natural gas use," July 29, 2015. eia.gov/todayinenergy/detail.php?id=22272.

in the capitalist the effect of a social mechanism in which he is merely a cog.[97]

I have spent this part of the book attempting to make clear that climate change requires an antagonistic approach toward *owners of capital* in the "hidden abode" of production. This could lead to a kind of *behavioral* politics that blames the climate crisis on a cabal of greedy capitalist individuals—and that would be as wrongheaded as the effort to blame climate change on the "irresponsible" choices of individual consumers. Marx's analysis of "capital personified" illustrates that the accumulation drive for surplus value by individual capitalists is not a choice, but a structural necessity impelled by what Marx called external "coercive laws of competition."[98] As we see in the case of nitrogen capital, these laws forced the ammonia industry to relentlessly seek gains in labor productivity, which not only cheapened agricultural inputs, but also cheapened the food system and the workers who rely on it. Along with this process of the accumulation of capital, comes the accumulation of carbon dioxide in the atmosphere.

Thus, climate change requires not simply the expropriation of individuals. It requires overcoming the *structural logic* that compels all forms of production under capitalism: the logic of surplus value. This would *free* production from the straitjackets of profits and competition. Only then could production be subjected to what should be the number one priority for species survival: *decarbonization*. Right now, decarbonization only happens if it is profitable.

Yet, as emphasized earlier, the climate movement is clearly nowhere near achieving the revolution in the structuring logics of production. To do so would require a mass social movement with the kind of social power to take on the relatively few who control the productive resources in society. But as currently constituted, the climate movement is overwhelmingly the purview of a minority of the population—the professional class. It is to this class and its role in climate politics we now turn.

---

97   Marx, *Capital*, Vol. 1, 739.
98   Ibid., 433.

II

The Professional Class

3

Credentialed Politics: Knowing the Climate Crisis

Introduction: Knowledge Is Not Power

In the mid-2000s, there was a real sense of momentum in climate politics. In 2006, Al Gore's film *An Inconvenient Truth* was heralded as the *Silent Spring* of our generation; sure to mobilize millions to the climate fight. In the same year, economist Nicholas Stern alarmed the policy world with his *Stern Review on the Economics of Climate Change*, a 700-page report predicting that the costs of climate change could amount to between 5 and 20 percent of GDP.[1] In 2007, the Intergovernmental Panel on Climate Change (IPCC) released its fourth assessment report, laying out the dire science and the rapid changes needed.[2] All of this seemed to be building toward the 2009 international meeting in Copenhagen where many expected the world—and, hopefully, the United States—would finally come together to solve the problem.

The earth itself was also calling for action. In the summer of 2007, the areal extent of Arctic sea ice reached a record low of 4.13 million square miles, 38 percent below the average and shattering the previous record, set in 2005, by 24 percent.[3] The following spring James Hansen and a team of scientists submitted a paper, "Target atmospheric CO_2: Where should humanity aim?" that

---

1 Nicholas Stern, *The Economics of Climate Change: The Stern Review* (Cambridge, UK: Cambridge University Press, 2007).

2 Intergovernmental Panel on Climate Change, *Climate Change 2007: A Synthesis Report* (Geneva, CH: Intergovernmental Panel on Climate Change, 2008).

3 NASA Earth Observatory, "Record Arctic Sea Ice Loss in 2007," earthobservatory. nasa.gov. This record was broken in 2012, hitting 3.389 million square miles or 18 percent below the 2007 level.

declared, "If humanity wishes to preserve a planet similar to that on which civilization developed and to which life on Earth is adapted, paleoclimate evidence and ongoing climate change suggest that CO_2 will need to be reduced from its current 385 ppm to at most 350 ppm."[4]

Given all the momentum and sense of urgency, climate activist Bill McKibben and "a group of university friends" founded the activist organization 350.org, which took Hansen's target of 350 parts per million of CO_2 as a rallying cry for change.[5] McKibben wrote several pieces claiming it was "the most important number on the planet" and organized a massive worldwide day of action for October 24, 2009, to force states to abide by this objective, scientific target.[6] In 2012, his viral article in Rolling Stone, "Global Warming's Terrifying New Math,"[7] focused again on a set of numbers (2° Celsius, 565 giga-tons) and set the stage for his "Do the Math Tour," which "sold out shows in every corner of the country."[8] McKibben used these numbers to lay out the necessary political prescription: The fossil fuel industry will burn every last gigaton of carbon it can access—and it must be stopped.

Yet the reliance on numbers and appeals to scientific objectivity means McKibben and others are always trying to stake out what is *not* political in the climate struggle. In an appearance on Comedy Central's *Colbert Report*, McKibben repeated one of his major talking points: "Science isn't like politics. Chemistry and physics don't bargain that way."[9] Several years later, he described the climate struggle as a battle versus physics. "This negotiation is between people and

4   James Hansen, et al., "Target Atmospheric CO₂: Where Should Humanity Aim?" *The Open Atmospheric Science Journal*, 2 (2008): 217–31; 217.

5   "About 350." 350.org/about. Last accessed May 26, 2020.

6   Bill McKibben "350—the most important number on the planet. We just need to get the politicians to listen to the scientists," *Guardian*, October 23, 2009.

7   Bill McKibben, "Global Warming's Terrifying New Math," *Rolling Stone*, July 19, 2012.

8   "Do the Math." math.350.org. Last accessed May 26, 2020.

9   *The Colbert Report*: "Bill McKibben, August 17, 2009." cc.com/video-clips. Last accessed May 26, 2020.

physics. And therefore it's not really a negotiation. Because physics doesn't negotiate. Physics just does."[10]

McKibben's 350 and others chose to strategically focus on climate politics as a struggle over questions of science and knowledge; for them, it was about what scientists assert are the causes of and solutions to climate change. But in the end, it seems that the critical question at the heart of climate politics is always one of belief or denial in the science.

There are obvious and good reasons for this. We only understand climate change through scientific measurements of greenhouse gases in the atmosphere and increasingly sophisticated models predicting our climate future. That the science has *discovered* the problem of climate change means it will always be at the heart of climate politics. Yet after the seeming momentum of 2007–8, it all went sideways. The global capitalist economy collapsed, the United States reassumed its role as delayer in Copenhagen—and to this day, the climate movement still has not ignited the kind of transformative change needed. In fact, McKibben consistently and correctly points out that we are *losing* the climate fight, and badly.

What are the limits of making climate politics about *knowledge*? In this chapter, I argue that this kind of politics of knowledge appeals to a specific class position: the professional class. I define the professional class broadly as those who marshal degrees, licenses, and other credentials in the market for labor power. Like McKibben and his "group of university friends," the professional class still remains at the core of the climate movement—scientists, journalists, and college students. As I will explore below, the professional class is a product of the historically shifting geographies of capital accumulation where knowledge became an entryway to a secure livelihood amid deindustrialization and declining working-class power. Underpinning the knowledge economy is the centrality of education and credentials in defining one's qualifications for particular kinds of occupations. Yet beyond the labor

---

10   Bill McKibben, "McKibben to Obama: We can't negotiate over the physics of climate change," *Grist.org*, August 31, 2015. grist.org. Last accessed May 26, 2020.

market, the professional class is also reproduced through a socio-cultural milieu that valorizes knowledge in general—keeping up with news, doing your research, and getting the facts straight.

Climate politics is also shaped by a professional world of "policy." As Naomi Klein points out, it was a case of "bad timing" when scientists came to a consensus about the severity of climate change at precisely the same moment when political power shifted toward a free market ideology of deregulation and austerity in the 1980s.[11] Still, for much of this period, professionals in the nonprofit and policy worlds clung to a belief that climate change could be solved through a series of technocratic and market-based solutions. Centrist economist Brad DeLong describes this as a project that aims "to use market means to social democratic ends."[12] For this brand of policy technocrat, the climate struggle is not a power struggle over material production, but a struggle over ideas and logical policy designs. Those in the climate policy community understood that the right had won power and thought they could outsmart them with elegant market-based policies inciting large-scale climate mitigation. They were very wrong.

The Professional Class: Historicizing a Class Formation

Capitalism has always included a specific stratum of intellectuals and other knowledge workers like scientists, lawyers, journalists, accountants, and the like. Much knowledge or mental work is of course central to material production itself, and capital has always sought to stratify mental from manual labor in the division of labor. Marx described such strata as capital's "retinue of lawyers, professors, and smooth tongued orators."[13] In a more general sense, it is important to point out that any "mode of production" can have intellectuals only

11   Naomi Klein, *This Changes Everything: Capitalism vs. the Climate* (New York: Simon and Schuster, 2014).

12   Zach Beauchamp, "A Clinton-era centrist Democrat explains why it's time to give democratic socialists a chance," *Vox*, March 4, 2019.

13   Karl Marx, *The 18th Brumaire of Louis Bonaparte* (22). marxists.org/archive/marx/works/download/pdf/18th-Brumaire.pdf. Last accessed May 26, 2020.

insofar as the necessary *material* forms of production are satisfied. Hal Draper described this as "living space in the economy for unproductive intellectual laborers."[14]

Yet under capitalism, this "living space" is determined not by some aggregate societal surplus, but by revenue paid out of the surplus value that private capital generates. Draper again suggests:

> Contributions to the symphony orchestra, university, church, or opera association come out of the same fund as expenditures for butlers, yachts, private chefs, or fashionable paintings and also ... prison wardens, generals, politicians, lawyers, judges, Boy Scout leaders, or asylum-keepers.[15]

Thus, during periods characterized by high levels of capital accumulation, we might expect to see the expansion of particular kinds of professions not wrapped up in necessary material production or surplus value production.

For the purpose of this argument, I pinpoint the exceptional period of massive capital accumulation in the post–World War II era. Large levels of economic growth and profits not only allowed collective bargaining with unions for high wages, but also relatively high tax rates.[16] In the United States, federal money came in the form of "military Keynesianism" that not only supported the profits of private military contractors, but also research universities.[17] After the 1957 Sputnik crisis, the US government funneled prodigious funds into higher education.[18] The National Defense Education Act of 1958

---

14 Hal Draper, *Karl Marx's Theory of Revolution, Vol. II: The Politics of Social Classes* (New York: Monthly Review Press, 1977), 500.

15 Ibid., 499.

16 Thomas Piketty, *Capital in the Twenty-First Century* (Cambridge, MA: Harvard University Press, 2014).

17 Alex Mintz and Alexander Hicks, "Military Keynesianism in the United States, 1949-1976: Disaggregating Military Expenditures and Their Determination," *American Journal of Sociology*, Vol. 90, No. 2 (1984): 411–17.

18 R.L. Geiger, "The Ten Generations in American Higher Education," in P.G. Altbach, R.O. Berdahl, and P.J. Gumport (eds.), *American Higher Education in the*

aimed to make the United States more competitive with the Soviet
Union through funding scientific research at universities. Beyond
military-based funding, the Higher Education Facilities Act of 1963
and the Higher Education Act of 1965 greatly increased funding for
universities to upgrade their facilities to accommodate increased
enrollments.[19] All this money changed the face of higher education:
"The federal largess, superimposed on mushrooming enrollments
and state support, produced an ephemeral golden age in American
Higher Education."[20]

Between 1945 and 1980, the number of institutions of higher education in the United States nearly doubled from 1,768 to 3,231, an increase
of 83 percent.[21] In 1904, a mere 2.3 percent of those aged 18 to 24
attended such an institution.[22] In 1931, it was still only 7.4 percent. But
by 1950 it had risen to 14.3 percent, and by 1970 to 35.8 percent.[23] The
proportion of the population with a bachelor's degree witnessed a
marked rise from 5.9 percent of those ages 25 to 29 in 1940, to 16.4
percent in 1970, to 22.5 percent in 1980.[24] This expansion of higher
education created an increasingly segmented labor market where a
degree can yield more earning capacity, or what is often called the
"college wage premium."[25] Increasingly specialized, knowledge-based
service work required a college degree, or an advanced graduate degree.[26]

Not all are able to take advantage of this "college wage-premium,"
but the ideology of *meritocracy* circulates strongly among those who

Twenty-First Century: Social, Political, and Economic Challenges (Baltimore, MD: Johns
Hopkins University Press, 1995), 38–70; 60.

19 Ibid.
20 Ibid., 60–1.
21 Susan B. Carter, et al., "Table Bc510-522" In, *Historical Statistics of the United
States: Millennial Online Edition* (Cambridge, UK: Cambridge University Press, 2006).
22 Ibid., "Table Bc523-536."
23 Ibid.
24 National Center for Educational Statistics, "Table 104.20. Percentage of persons 25 to
29 years old with selected levels of educational attainment, by race/ethnicity and sex: Selected
years, 1920 through 2017." nces.ed.gov. Last accessed May 26, 2020.
25 As of this writing college graduates earn a median $617 more per week. The FRED
blog, "Is college still worth it?" Federal Reserve of St. Louis, July 9, 2018 (updated graphs).
26 Roberto M. Unger, *The Knowledge Economy* (London: Verso, 2019).

worked hard, got good grades, and established a "career." Thomas Frank defines the meritocracy of the professional class as "the conviction that the successful deserve their rewards, that the people on top are there because they are the best."[27] Nicos Poultantzas called this new educated class of wage earners the "new petty bourgeoisie," in which the individualized project of a *career* is especially significant: "the new petty bourgeoisie often aspires to 'promotion,' to a 'career,' to 'upward social mobility,' i.e., to becoming bourgeois (the ideological aspects of bourgeois imitation) by way of the 'individual' transfer of the 'best' and 'most capable.' "[28] The subjective associations between working hard and achieving a "good life" are established early in childhood as competition between students over standardized test scores, extracurricular activities, and college admissions saturate the culture of the professional classes. In their classic study *Schooling in Capitalist America*, Samuel Bowles and Herbert Gintis subject the "façade of meritocracy" to critique[29] and suggest schooling's central role is to *legitimate* capitalist inequality. "Through competition, success and defeat in the classroom, students are reconciled to their social position."[30]

Again, the vast majority of society *lacks* these credentials. In the United States, 64.3 percent of the population lacks a bachelor's degree or higher.[31] Yet the educational system can work to convince those without degrees that their status in life is the result of their personal failures in school.[32]

As the professional class expanded, deindustrialization and capital flight hollowed out a swath of good, working-class union jobs requiring little more than a high school degree (if that). While this process

---

27 Thomas Frank, *Listen, Liberal: Or What Ever Happened to the Party of People?* (New York: Picador, 2016), 31.

28 Nicos Poulantzas, *Classes in Contemporary Capitalism* (London: NLB, 1975), 292.

29 Samuel Bowles and Herbert Gintis, *Schooling in Capitalist America: Educational Reform and the Contradictions of Economic Life* (New York: Basic Books, 1976), 103.

30 Ibid., 106.

31 National Center for Educational Statistics, "Table 104.20."

32 Fredrik deBoer, *The Cult of Smart: How Our Broken Education System Perpetuates Social Injustice* (New York: All Points Books, 2020).

began in the postwar era,[33] it accelerated after 1980 as concern over climate change arose.[34] In this "postindustrial society" the centrality of industrial production to the problem of climate change faded into invisibility. Given the ecological and production-centered theorization of class laid out above, the expansion of this "knowledge economy" was increasingly defined by its spatial and temporal separation from the *industrialization* of the nineteenth and early twentieth centuries. Indeed, the whole premise of "mental labor" is the prospect of a "life of the mind" separated from the manual demands of material production. Yet as production simply disappeared from view, so did a politics that retained "the primacy of production, the very foundation of historical materialism."[35] Obviously, this ecological separation from material production will depart from the politics of the industrial working class. During the peak of working-class power in the twentieth century, socialist movements were embedded in industrial factory production. The prospect of "seizing" the means of production and transforming capitalist scarcity into socialist abundance seemed viscerally possible. Much of the "proletarian" workforce had directly experienced or had cultural memories of their agrarian past (and had little interest in going back).

Contrast this with the environmental version of "new social movements" emerging in the 1960s and '70s and populated by the professional classes. For this form of politics, the materiality of production is not something you experience but something more abstract; an object of knowledge or study. The result of such study is usually to show the hidden costs embedded in distant production systems. Once the study was complete, environmental activism often meant organizing to *oppose* specific forms of industrial development from logging to pipeline construction, or to simply advocate for *protecting* specific

---

33   C. Wright Mills, *White Collar: The American Middle Classes* (Oxford: Oxford University Press, 1951).

34   Bennett Harrison and Barry Bluestone, *The Great U-Turn: Corporate Restructuring and the Polarizing of America* (New York: Basic Books, 1990).

35   Ellen Meiksins Wood, *Democracy Against Capitalism: Renewing Historical Materialism* (London: Verso, 1995), 23.

natural spaces from industrial development.[36] The socialist and working-class project of *transforming* industrial production toward human
liberation faded slowly away into what Aaron Benanav calls the
"postindustrial doldrums."[37] But as Part I suggests, transforming
production is *the* project of decarbonization.

Any historical materialist perspective needs to account for these
major changes in the nature of the market for labor power in *class*
terms. In their classic essay on the "professional-managerial class"
(PMC), Barbara and John Ehrenreich rightly point out, "By early in
the sixties, the explosive growth and continued social distinctiveness
of the stratum of educated wage earners had become impossible for
Marxists to ignore."[38] The Ehrenreichs argue that the PMC "must be
understood as comprising a distinct class in monopoly capitalist
society."[39] Although this version of capitalism emerges in the late
nineteenth and early twentieth centuries, it emerges fully in a postwar
era marked by historic levels of profitability and explosive growth in
educated knowledge workers. Since the 1970s, however, the
Ehrenreichs admit that the professional-managerial class has been
substantially eroded through a new form of neoliberal capitalism.[40]

The last several decades have been characterized by what Randy
Martin calls the "decomposition of the professional managerial
class."[41] Kim Moody estimates that out of 30.8 million professionals
in the United States, 11.5 million are "proletarianizing": "growing
numbers of professionals face the contagion of capitalist exploitation along with job standardization and degradation."[42] Moody

36 Robert Gottlieb, *Forcing the Spring: The Transformation of the American
Environmental Movement* (Washington, DC: Island Press, 2005).

37 Aaron Benanav, *Automation and the Future of Work* (London: Verso, 2020), 56.

38 Barbara Ehrenreich and John Ehrenreich, "The professional-managerial class," in
Pat Walker (ed.), *Between Labor and Capital* (Boston: South End Press, 1979), 5–45; 7.

39 Ibid., 9.

40 Barbara Ehrenreich and John Ehrenreich, "Death of a yuppie dream: The rise and
fall of the professional-managerial class," Rosa Luxemburg Stiftung, New York Office,
February 2013.

41 Randy Martin, "Coming up short: Knowledge limits and the decomposition of the
professional managerial class" *International Critical Thought*, Vol. 5, No. 1 (2015): 95–110.

42 Kim Moody, *On New Terrain: How Capital Is Reshaping the Battleground of the*

argues many professionals' "traditional autonomy has been crushed in the vice of measured and monitored standardization and lean just-in-time requirements."[43] Even so, if Moody's estimates are even roughly correct, the secure ranks of the professional class still number something like 20 million people, or roughly 14 percent of the workforce. Those of us deep within climate politics rarely stop to wonder whether most people participating in the debate come from these ranks.

How might we theorize these increasing groups of college-educated workers with some degree of autonomy on the job? As reviewed above, the Marxist perspective on class is less about the ways in which education leads to a higher income or status and more about a social relationship to the means of production. The professional class certainly lacks access to the means of production and to survive must work for a wage—or more accurately, a salary. Thus, many conclude that the professional class can be lumped into the working class.[44] Yet the centrality of credentials mediates their access to the labor market. The Ehrenreichs make much of the ways in which a *profession* shapes a pool of workers' access to the labor market. This includes, among other things, "the existence of a specialized body of knowledge, accessible only by lengthy training."[45] It is important to understand professional degree programs, licensure exams, professional organizations, as institutional means of *class organization* that delimit access to certain occupational categories. Richard Florida notably theorized the "creative class" as one in which knowledge and the mind itself were a critical means of production: "If workers control the means of production today that is because it is inside their own heads; they *are* the means of production."[46] This wrongly follows the meritocracy

---

Class War (Chicagao: Haymarket, 2017), 32.

43   Ibid.

44   See this rather polemical take: David Camfield, "The 'PMC' does not exist and why it matters for socialists," *New Politics*, January 9, 2020.

45   Ehrenreich and Ehrenreich, 1979, 26.

46   Richard Florida, *The Rise of the Creative Class, Revisited* (New York: Basic Books, 2012), 25.

narrative where one's access to the professionalized occupations is due to one's own individual work, talent, and tenacity. The Ehrenreichs' theory pays much more attention to the social relations of power which shape professionalized institutions.

Perhaps most convincingly, Erik Olin Wright refuses to classify such professionals as a class *per se*, but "as occupying a complex contradictory location within class relations."[47] Wright emphasizes that such professionals often have *autonomy* in their labor process unlike the working class, but rely on a wage for survival like the working class. He classifies such workers as "semi-autonomous" and "objectively torn between the antagonistic classes" of capitalist society.[48] At the ideological level, Wright explains how such contradictory class locations can lead to either anti-capitalist (pro–working class) or bourgeois politics. This is clearly the case with professional-class climate politics which contains both bourgeois and radical variants, as explained below. While the professional contradictory class location does not make for a snappy title for this Part II, it is more accurate than referring to the professional *class* in the strict sense.

The Ehrenreichs also point out that Marxists cannot solely understand class as an objective relationship to the means of production. Class is also "characterized by a coherent social and cultural existence; members of a class share a common life style, educational background, kinship networks, consumption patterns, work habits, beliefs."[49] Drawing from the work of Thorstein Veblen, Elizabeth Currid-Halkett offers a theory of what she calls the "aspirational class":

For this new class of people, knowledge is prized independently of economic function . . . The knowledge and cultural capital are used to make informed decisions about what to eat, how to treat the

---

47 See, e.g., Erik Olin Wright, "Intellectuals and the working class," *Critical Sociology*, Vol. 8, No. 1 (1978): 5–18; 5.

48 Ibid., 10.

49 Ehrenreich and Ehrenreich, 1979, 11.

environment, and how to be better parents, more productive workers, and more informed consumers.[50]

This theory ignores the more "objective" aspects of class, but it is worth considering how these sociocultural factors shape the ideological and political aspects of climate politics. The crisis of climate change—and the knowledge metrics of individualized carbon footprints—has led the professional class into a cultural frenzy over "low carbon" lifestyle choices. Yet, it is not just making informed lifestyle choices; an ethic of staying well informed on the latest science of the climate crisis also takes on special importance. As Currid-Halkett puts it, "Reading cultural commentary, being up-to-date on the news . . . are but a number of ways by which to connect with one another irrespective of economic means."[51] For this class, it is easy to see how politics becomes not something rooted in objective material interests and struggle, but rather about knowledge, doing your research, and being informed.[52] While these cultural factors surely depart from a Marxist theorization of class, I insist that they emerge from a *historically specific* relationship to material production in an age of deindustrialization and the "new international division of labor."[53]

---

50   Elizabeth Currid-Halkett, *The Sum of Small Things: A Theory of the Aspirational Class* (Princeton, NJ: Princeton University Press, 2017), 17–18.

51   Currid-Halkett, 2017, 18. This reminds me of a sketch on the show *Portlandia* where two "hipsters" in a coffee shop feverishly ask each other if they've read certain articles from *The New Yorker*, *Mother Jones*, and others, before manically shouting at each other: "Did you read it? Did you read it?" youtube.com. Last accessed May 27, 2020.

52   For an interesting take on politics as a kind of educational hobby, see Eitan Hersh, *Politics Is for Power: How to Move Beyond Political Hobbyism, Take Action, and Make Real Change* (New York: Scribner, 2020).

53   Folker Froebel, Jürgen Heinrichs, and Otto Kreye, *The New International Division of Labour. Structural Unemployment in Industrialised Countries and Industrialisation in Developing Countries* (Cambridge: Cambridge University Press, 1981).

Credentialed Politics

The Ehrenreichs' impetus for theorizing the "professional-managerial class" came from its centrality in shaping the New Left movements of the 1960s and '70s. As they put it: "The rebirth of PMC radicalism in the sixties came at a time when the material position of the class was advancing rapidly. Employment in PMC occupations soared, and salaries rose with them."[54] They describe how the best parts of the New Left certainly contested capitalist control of the economy, but combined this with "moralistic contempt of the working class."[55] The Ehrenreichs cite the famous Port Huron Statement issued by Students for a Democratic Society: "Any new left in America must be, in large measure, a left with real intellectual skills, committed to deliberativeness, honesty, reflection as working tools."[56] Politics, from a professional-class perspective, is a largely *cultural* terrain over knowledge and a coming-to-consensus on ideas.[57] The professional class elevates "intellectual autonomy and public service" alongside credentials and expertise above all else.[58] Moreover, if the university is, in the Ehrenreichs' words, "the historical reproductive apparatus of the PMC,"[59] it also became an epicenter of two kinds of engagement with politics. First, as we will see below, there was an explosion of academic technocrats and other highly educated policy experts who espoused the professional-class commitment to expertise in solving social and environmental problems. Second, the university became a bastion of a new mode of radical political theory, which centered culture over old class lines of struggle.[60]

Yet, as the Ehrenreichs explain, the class antagonisms between the PMC and the working class were never resolved, and by the end of the

54 Ehrenreich and Ehrenreich, 1979, 30.
55 Ibid., 33.
56 Ibid., 32.
57 Vivek Chibber, "Rescuing class from the cultural turn," *Catalyst*, Vol. 1, No. 1 (2017): 27–55.
58 Ibid., 31.
59 Ibid., 33.
60 Ellen Meiksins Wood, *The Retreat From Class: A New 'True' Socialism* (London: Verso, 1986).

'70s the New Left collapsed into "more [of] a subculture than a 'movement.'"[61] As Jean-Christophe Agnew suggests, the professional class's abandonment of old class questions seems even starker as political power continued to shift rightward to capital: "Considering its relative inattention to issues of production, equity, exploitation, cultural politics may seem a singularly inappropriate politics for a time marked by the blatant transfer of wealth between classes."[62] In other words, the capitalist class organized to amass wealth and political power on class terms. Meanwhile, the left, imbued by professional-class values, became convinced that class politics were outmoded, orthodox, and ill-equipped for a new "postindustrial" knowledge economy.

There is perhaps no better example of the ways in which the professional class shaped new forms of politics than the environmental movement. From its beginnings, science was central in shaping environmental movement consciousness and demands. Indeed, it was Rachel Carson, a professional marine biologist, who sparked the movement with her book *Silent Spring* in 1962.[63] The ecology movement placed scientific credentials at the center of ecological politics. In 1972, the *Ecologist* ran a cover story called "A Blueprint for Survival," which claimed a specific politics of authority: "This document has been drawn up by a small team of people, all of whom, in different capacities, are professionally involved in the study of global environmental problems."[64] The Club of Rome's more famous 1972 report on overpopulation, *The Limits to Growth*, enacted the same vision of politics—a struggle over a future adjudicated through scientific models and expertise.[65] As mentioned above, it is not only "intellectual autonomy" but also commitment to "public service" that often characterizes

---

61   Ibid., 42.

62   Jean Christophe-Agnew, "A touch of class," *Democracy*, Vol. 3 (1983): 59–72; 72.

63   Rachel Carson, *Silent Spring* (New York: Mariner, 1962).

64   Various authors, "A blueprint for survival," *The Ecologist*, Vol. 2. No. 1 (January 1972): 1–48; 1.

65   Donella H. Meadows, et al., *The Limits to Growth* (New York: Universe Books, 1974), 11.

professional-class values. This commitment is rooted in the idea that professionals can deploy knowledge toward making the world better.

I offer a very schematic sketch of different types of professionals in the climate political scene who seek to combine expertise and environmental "public service" (see Table 3.1 for a summary).

First, there are the *science communicators* who are either natural scientists themselves like Rachel Carson or James Hansen, or otherwise deeply invested in knowing what the science has discovered, such as science or environmental journalists. These types of people believe that the primary problem in environmental politics is a lack of awareness or an outright denial of scientific knowledge. It argues that if the masses truly *understood* the science, action would follow.

Second, there are the *policy technocrats* whose professional expertise is more likely to be based in law or policy studies and work in think tanks, academia, or professionalized nonprofits. Alongside universities, it is worth highlighting the rise of NGO's—as opposed to unions and parties—as critical centers of activism and politics in the same era where environmental politics arose.[66] These types seek to design "smart" policy solutions to environmental problems. They believe they can use logic and rational policy design to sway politicians and the public toward these policies.

Finally, there are the *anti-system radicals*, whose own exposure to the science of ecological collapse leads to a kind of political radicalization. As I show in Chapter 4, a lot of this radicalization is rooted in guilt over their own complicity in practices of consumption central to professional-class norms. This kind of climate activist is more likely to understand that the cause of environmental problems is systemically rooted in capitalism, but their political response is to look inward through moralistic invocations to consume less, reject industrial society, and advocate micro-alternatives at the local scale. This kind of person might find the only outlet for such radical ideas in academia, or they might eschew a profession entirely in favor of more niche

66   See, Benjamin Y. Fong and Melissa Naschek, "NGOism: The politics of the third sector," *Catalyst*, Vol. 5, No. 1 (2021): 93–131.

knowledge systems like DIY off-the-grid living or studying "perma-culture" agricultural techniques.

Figure 3.1 Professional Class Climate Politics in Three Types

Professional class type	Political Goal	Theory of change
Science communicator	Spreading climate truth/science	Knowledge informs political action/behavior
Policy technocrat	Implementing climate policy	Right-wing policymakers can be won over with smart policy designs channeling market incentives
Anti-system radical	System change, not climate change	Small-scale alternatives and anti-consumerism will erode capitalism

Source: Author

What connects these three highly schematic "types" is the centrality of *knowledge systems* in shaping their political engagements with environmental problems. I want to be clear: my aim is not to discount the importance of knowledge and science in informing politics, but rather to point out the ways in which this politics both evades material conflict and class struggle and appeals only to the minority of society that possesses these educational credentials. Over the course of the next two chapters, I will explore several ways in which these three types shape climate politics.

Denying Politics

At the center of most conversations of climate politics is the question of belief or denial. In the United States, this is indeed a serious problem as nearly the entire Republican Party fails to accept the scientific consensus on climate change.[67] Given the increasing evidence, these

---

67 Polls show a mere 21 percent of Republicans believe climate change should be a federal priority. Ben Geman, "The widening partisan divide on climate change," *Axios*, February 14, 2020.

politicians typically do not deny the existence of climate change as much as its *anthropogenic* (human-based) causes. This is not only a problem for politicians; survey data suggests that as much as 47 percent of the US population believes global warming is *not* caused "mostly by human activities." In some fossil fuel states like Wyoming (62 percent), West Virginia (61 percent), and Utah (53 percent), that number is even higher. Quite stunningly, 33 percent nationally still denies that global warming is even happening.[68]

How did we get here? The most common explanation is offered by Naomi Oreskes and Erik Conway in the book, and now film, *Merchants of Doubt*.[69] It is a quite disturbing story of the fossil fuel industry funding scientists and public relations spokespeople to spread the ideas of climate skepticism. Even though 97 percent of climate scientists agree that climate change is caused by humans, the mere existence of a few skeptical scientists distorts the conversation.[70] It does not help when journalists cover climate change as a "debate" between two sides, the climate believers and skeptics. Oreskes and Conway dub this the "tobacco strategy," because of the tobacco industry's role in spreading uncertainty on the link between cigarettes and cancer. For climate as it was for tobacco, the strategy is a corporate-funded drive to sow doubt and uncertainty around a scientific issue so as to misinform the public and delay action.

The politics of knowledge and professional credentials are central to the story Oreskes and Conway tell. First, they frame this struggle as one over the objectivity of scientific knowledge itself. They describe climate skeptics as betraying the quest for truth: "they were not

---

68   The statistics from the preceding sentences come from Jennifer Marlon, et al., "Yale Climate Opinion Maps 2019," *Yale Program on Climate Communication*. climatecommunication.yale.edu/visualizations-data/ycom-us. Last accessed May 27, 2020.

69   Naomi Oreskes and Erik Conway, *Merchants of Doubt: How a Handful of Scientists Obscured the Truth on Issues From Tobacco Smoke to Global Warming* (New York: Bloomsbury, 2010).

70   Sander L. van der Linden, Anthony A. Leiserowitz, Geoffrey D. Feinberg, and Edward W. Maibach, "The scientific consensus on climate change as a gateway belief: experimental evidence," *PLoS ONE*, Vol. 10, No. 2 (2015): 1–8.

interested in finding facts. They were interested in fighting them."[71] What seems to bother the authors most is that these "scientists"—like noted climate skeptics Frederick Seitz and Fred Singer—dress up their denial in the authority and credentials of scientific expertise. The fossil fuel industry is able to pay for the "science" that conveniently supplements their profits. "They use their scientific credentials to present themselves as authorities."[72] The authors are even more chagrined that Seitz and Singer have no "professional" expertise on the issue whatsoever: "These men had no particular expertise in environmental or health questions . . . these men did almost no original research on any of the issues on which they weighed in."[73] Moreover, Oreskes and Conway charge, journalists betrayed their professional duty to report on the truth of what science has to say: "In all of this, journalists and the public never understood that these were *not* scientific debates taking place in the halls of science among active scientific researchers, but misinformation."[74] All of this serves to patrol the terrain in which one has the proper credentials and knowledge to intervene in climate politics.

I will make two critical points about this kind of argument. First, there is a relentless effort to erect a strict barrier between "science" and "politics" in the climate change struggle. Oreskes and Conway criticize a scientist, Bill Nierenberg, for signing on to a letter criticizing the work of the IPCC. Oresekes and Conway state flatly, "By signing onto Singer's letter, he marked himself . . . as a political actor, not a scientific one."[75] The implication is that because the science is settled on the question of anthropogenic climate change, it should not be subject to politics. There is a core insight here: climate change's existence should not be a "political" debate.

Yet this displaces the actual political issue: *what to do about it.* The response to climate change involves a colossal political struggle

71   Oreskes and Conway, 2010, 5.
72   Ibid., 8.
73   Ibid.
74   Ibid., 7.
75   Ibid., 213.

against some of the most powerful corporations on the planet. The sheer ubiquity of climate skeptic discourse in the 1990s and 2000s was evidence that the skeptics were winning this political struggle. It is another form of denial to suggest that this crisis can be adjudicated purely through truth and science.

Making climate politics purely about science evades the question of power. It allows us to attribute our inaction on climate change as simply due to misinformation rather than *lack of power*. Oreskes and Conway lament that the denialists were able to block climate policies in the 1990s despite this scientific consensus: "Scientifically, global warming was established fact. Politically, global warming was dead."[76] There is a naïve and highly liberal theory of social change lurking in this discussion. Since anthropogenic warming is such a complex biogeochemical process, it assumes political action will be based on informing the public and politicians about the science; the more the public becomes informed, the more likely it will support action. The authors seem to suggest that if the fossil fuel industry had not distorted the science on climate, we would have acted accordingly. It is not clear whether or not this is a naïve pluralist theory that suggests democratic societies act in relation to the prevailing opinion, or if it is a more Weberian bureaucratic theory on how institutions respond to rational information and scientific expertise. Either way, the assumption is that action on climate is a purely scientific-technocratic endeavor where scientists inform the public of science and voters and politicians respond accordingly.

This story of the climate denial machine especially offends professional-class values that assume politics is a rational kind of deliberation. The problem is, politics in a capitalist society does not work this way. Quite apart from the fossil fuel industry's funding the denial machine, industry leaders have spent more energy and resources lobbying politicians and contributing to electoral campaigns—that is, amassing *political power* to advance their agenda of producing fossil

76   Ibid., 215.

fuel for profit.[77] As much as we see fossil fuel capitalists as waging a war on science, they are more accurately organizing political power in the broader terrain of federal and state legislatures and cultural institutions like academia and the media. A scholar of the neoliberal right, Phillip Mirowski, recently made this apt comparison: "the Koch group are unapologetic Leninists—their line is 'we have to take over.' "[78] He contrasts this with more liberal-left groups who presume that "political activity will bubble up from unstructured cadres" and that whoever makes the most convincing "pitch" in the "marketplace of ideas" will win politically.[79] As Jonathan Smucker argues, "right does not equal [political] might."[80]

Yet the grip on power held by the Kochs and other fossil fuel interests shows that no amount of knowledge or information can overcome power itself. It certainly will not be overcome by assuming that climate change is not a political issue or that it can be solved solely through the objective dissemination of scientific knowledge. Mind you, getting the science of climate change out to the public *is* extremely important and will form a terrain upon which the struggle is waged. But, it is only one small aspect of what is ultimately a *material* struggle over how we produce and reproduce society itself.

'Getting the Prices Right'

The struggle of belief vs. denial is the purview of the "science communicator" type sketched out above. While this type is deeply invested in scientific assessments, policy technocrats actually see the climate crisis as a social problem that requires political interventions. But this intervention is not framed in terms of a political struggle against

---

77   For the authoritative account of the Koch Brothers and their political organizing, particularly at the state legislative level, see Jane Mayer, *Dark Money: The Hidden History of the Billionaires Behind the Rise of the Radical Right* (New York: Anchor Books, 2016).

78   Interview with Phillip Mirowski conducted by Alex Doherty, "Why the neoliberals won't let this crisis go to waste," *Jacobin*, May 16, 2020.

79   Ibid.

80   Jonathan Smucker, "The problem of collective action in the United States," *jonathansmucker.org*, July 19, 2012.

vested interests, but rather as a rational set of *policy corrections* to a "market failure." Approaching climate and many other environmental problems as a market failure emerged in precisely the same period when power shifted to capital after the 1970s. Policy technocrats took these political victories as given, and assumed they could solve climate change through outsmarting the market by indirectly nudging the energy system toward the changes needed.

In the early 1970s, the US environmental movement won significant victories with the creation of the Environmental Protection Agency and the passage of the Clean Air Act and Clean Water Act under the conservative tutelage of Richard Nixon.[81] The main legal and regulatory architecture of these interventions assumed *industry* was largely the cause of most environmental problems, and thus, policy required forcing industry to abide by strict environmental standards. That often required large investments in new technology, like scrubbers for power plants. These policy interventions, which essentially federalized environmental protection on a national scale, were successful in producing cleaner air and water throughout the nation.[82]

Later in the decade, something strange happened. The crisis of Keynesianism during the 1970s laid the groundwork for a neoliberal free market critique of all forms of government spending and regulation. Despite the success of environmental regulation, many concluded it was still the wrong way to address environmental problems. While many attribute this shift to the election of Ronald Reagan, geographer Morgan Robertson shows how this shift emerged earlier, during the Jimmy Carter administration.[83] In March 1978, fourteen months after taking office, President Carter issued Executive Order 12044,

---

81 Jeri Friedman, *The Establishment of the Environmental Protection Agency* (New York: Cavendish, 2018).

82 Judith Layzer, *The Environmental Case: Translating Values Into Policy* (Thousand Oaks, CA: Sage, 2016), 32–3.

83 Morgan Robertson, "Flexible nature: Governing with the environment in the development of US neoliberalism," *Annals of the American Association of Geographers*, Vol. 108, No. 6 (2018): 1601–19.

directing "regulatory agencies to find ways to achieve their goals with reduced burden on the private sector."[84] He consistently pushed his administration to explore "alternatives" to regulation, culminating in the "Program on Alternative Regulatory Approaches." This was not an ideological quirk of Carter alone. In a period noted for the massive expansion of money in politics, industry itself was pushing an anti-regulatory policy agenda. Judith Layzer explains how pro-industry forces became influential in the Carter administration: "Industry was resentful and criticized agency staff as ineffective bureaucrats and anti-business zealots."[85]

By the end of the Carter administration and the inauguration of Ronald Reagan, it had become common belief among many politicians and policymakers that strict regulations were inflexible and anti-competitive. In one of his first acts as president, Reagan launched the Presidential Task Force on Regulatory Relief. Vice President George H.W. Bush surveyed industry leaders to learn what regulations were most "burdensome." Daniel Faber describes the response: "The largest number of industry requests for policy changes focused on EPA regulations, particularly in the automobile, chemical, and pesticide industries."[86]

Actually forcing industry into changing environmental behavior came to be equated with Soviet-style rigidity under the term "command and control" environmental policy. Again, this emerged early in the Carter administration. Layzer recounts an EPA booklet that "characterized 'command-and-control' regulation as rigid, wasteful, and sometimes illogical."[87] The charge of illogic is, of course, an affront to professional-class politics. As industry built more *power* over the political system, professional-class technocrats started to believe we could still solve environmental problems through more

84   Ibid., 1606.
85   Judith Layzer, *Open for Business: Conservatives' Opposition to Environmental Regulation* (Cambridge, MA: MIT Press, 2012), 76.
86   Daniel Faber, *Capitalizing on Environmental Injustice: The Polluter-Industrial Complex in the Age of Globalization* (Lanham, MD: Rowman and Littlefield, 2008), 128.
87   Layzer, 2012, 78.

logical policy designs that aimed to achieve the same environmental goals through cheaper and more efficient market means. Before, policy simply forced industry to change, but increasingly, technocrats accepted the austerity-based argument that environmental policy must also be cost-effective.

The question of costs and how to distribute them became central to the field of environmental economics. Again, as Nicholas Stern put it above, climate change and all forms of environmental pollution came to be seen not as a failure of state regulation, but as a market failure. When private market actors pollute they impose a "cost" on society as a whole. Yet this cost is *externalized* from the market price system, so private market actors pollute for free. This idea has deep roots in the history of economic thought. In 1920, Arthur Pigou inspired the concept of "externalities" to explain how private market actors impose costs on third parties.[88] He suggested that private producers whose production had harmful effects on the public could be taxed to offset the costs. Decades later, K. William Kapp's book *The Social Costs of Business Enterprise* argued at length about air and water pollution as paradigmatic cases of social costs.[89] Around the same time, even Milton Friedman acknowledged that the market cannot account for such costs, or what he called "neighborhood effects."[90]

In his 1960 paper "The Problem of Social Cost," University of Chicago economist Ronald Coase argued that it might be preferable to allow social costs to be dealt with through private bargaining and contracts.[91] He is known for expressing frustration that his paper was used to justify using market policy in all cases, but he does make his political leanings clear: "It is my belief that economists, and policy-makers generally, have tended to over-estimate the advantages

---

88   Arthur Pigou, *The Economics of Welfare* (London: Macmillan, 1920).

89   K. William Kapp, *The Social Costs of Business Enterprise* (Nottingham, UK: Spokesmen, 1963).

90   Milton Friedman, *Capitalism and Freedom* (Chicago: University of Chicago Press, 1962), 31.

91   He also suggested there are many cases, including pollution, where this is not appropriate. Ronald Coase, "The problem of social cost," *The Journal of Law & Economics*, Vol. 3 (1960): 1–44.

which come from governmental regulation."[92] He also claims market actors are forced to take account of costs in ways states do not: "The government is able, if it wishes, to avoid the market altogether, which a firm can never do."[93]

The key question for Coase is what are the "transaction costs" for dealing with externalities between private actors and contracts, as compared to the costs of regulation? For private actors to solve a problem of social costs requires meetings, contracts, gathering all the relevant information, and so on. Increasingly, economists began to argue that the most efficient way to communicate the information of "costs" to market actors was through the price system itself.[94] As reviewed in Chapter 1, neoliberals argued that price signals and the system of "exchange" communicated "information" more effectively than any centralized government agency could. Friedrich Hayek argued:

> The more complicated the whole, the more dependent we become on that division of knowledge between individuals whose separate efforts are coordinated by the impersonal mechanism for transmitting the relevant information known by us as the price system.[95]

The price system was constructed as the ultimate source of *knowledge* to inform environmental decision-making. Yet if the prices were wrong, the market failed, and they had to be *corrected*.

Professional-class policy technocrats seized on this idea that environmental problems were due to a lack of information or knowledge in the market and could be corrected with smart policy designs. In 1990, the World Resources Institute published a book called *The Greenhouse Trap*, which argued that solving climate

---

92 Ibid., 18.

93 Ibid., 17.

94 Al Gore, *Earth in the Balance: Ecology and the Human Spirit* (New York: Earthscan, 1993), 348.

95 Friedrich Hayek, *The Road to Serfdom* (Chicago: University of Chicago Press, 1944), 95–6.

change required "making economics environmentally honest" through a "a real, dig-in-our-heels commitment to 'getting the prices right.' "[96] There were two primary ways in which policy experts thought this could be accomplished. First, a Pigovian "carbon tax" or fee on pollution would add the cost of pollution into the prices of energy and other commodities. These prices would communicate the "correct" information to consumers. Another World Resources Report on "Green Fees" explains the logic: "Consumers can respond to new prices by reducing energy use and buying fewer carbon-intensive products."[97]

The second approach actually attempts to re-create emissions as an exchangeable commodity with prices of its own. Known as "cap and trade," these systems create a finite amount (cap) of emission permits—the right to pollute—and allow polluters to trade permits among themselves.[98] In this system the price of carbon is not fixed as a tax, but is subject to the vicissitudes of the market. Again, the theory here hinges on *information*: local polluters are said to be the best informed on their own practices rather than some government entity deciding the level of a carbon tax. A cap-and-trade system is more "cost effective" and allows firms and consumers the flexibility to adjust according to their own local knowledge.

These policies are quite complicated and arcane. They are not meant to attract mass popular support. Their appeal to professional-class technocrats is purely *logical*. They identify a "failure" in the market and correct it through elegantly designed mechanisms that channel incentives in the desired direction. It is on this terrain of logic and policy persuasion that the technocrats expect they can win their preferred policies.

---

96 Francesca Lyman, et al., *The Greenhouse Trap: What We're Doing to the Atmosphere and How We Can Slow Global Warming* (Boston: Beacon Press, 1990), 98.

97 Robert Repetto, Roger C. Dower, Robin Jenkins, and Jacqueline Geoghegan, *Green Fees: How a Tax Shift Can Work for the Environment and the Economy* (Washington, DC: World Resources Institute, 1992), 55.

98 Richard Conniff, "The political history of cap and trade," *Smithsonian Magazine* (August 2009).

Thus, climate policy is not seen as a power struggle, but as a struggle over knowledge. These policies assume the hegemony of free market ideology—that is, they assume the rightward shift of power as a given—and wager that they can still outsmart the market by designing policies that channel it toward desired ends. As quoted above, economist Brad Delong described this as "largely neoliberal, market-oriented, and market-regulation and tuning aimed at social democratic ends."[99] Delong and other liberal centrists believed they could build bipartisan consensus for policies that came out of the neoliberal free market toolkit: "You would then collect a broad political coalition behind what is, indeed, Mitt Romney's health care policy and John McCain's climate policy and George H.W. Bush's foreign policy."[100] We should add that these sensible policies not only aimed to attract right-wing *ideological* support, but also *political* backing from industry itself. President Barack Obama dedicated his energy to cap-and-trade legislation in 2009 lobbied for by US Climate Action Partnership; an industry-environment coalition that included some of the heaviest polluters in the country, like Duke Energy and Caterpillar.[101] The policy game ceded power to carbon-intensive industry from the start.

Costly Politics

Policy technocrats' obsession with internalizing environmental "costs" into the market emerged out of the hegemony of neoliberalism and pro-capitalist free market ideology. In the climate change field, economists, policy scholars, and eventually, under Obama, the Environmental Protection Administration settled on a set of tools and metrics meant to estimate the "social cost of carbon," which "is a measure, in dollars, of the long-term damage done by a ton of carbon

---

99 Beachamp, "A Clinton-era centrist Democrat," Vox March 4, 2019.
100 Ibid.
101 For an incisive account of the folly of such a strategy, see Theda Skocpol, "Naming the problem: What It will take to counter extremism and engage Americans in the fight against global warming" (symposium at Harvard University, February 14, 2013).

dioxide (CO_2) emissions in a given year."[102] These metrics tend to focus on those "costs" that are easily monetized and quantifiable, such as "changes in net agricultural productivity, human health, property damages from increased flood risk, and changes in energy system costs."[103] This metric is meant to inform the entire regulatory infrastructure which measures such "costs" against the benefits of emissions reductions. However, unsurprisingly, the level of the social cost of carbon proved to be highly politicized, depending on who was in power. The Obama administration set it at $45 per ton of carbon dioxide; Trump set it at $1.[104]

I would suggest there is a deeper politics inherent to the category of "costs" beyond these squabbles between Republicans and Democrats. At its core, neoliberal politics is structured through a political ontology of cost. By ontology, I truly mean a way of being that is obsessed with tracking, isolating, and most importantly *cutting* monetary costs. Although the market and competition are constructed as the best mechanism to achieve cost-reduction, these are merely the means to the ends of cost-cutting. Thus, as reviewed above, even if so-called "command and control" regulation was effective in reducing pollution, the main question was transformed into whether or not it was *cost-effective*.

This focus on cost is rooted in the shift to neoliberalism during the 1970s, a decade defined by economic crisis and "stagflation." More than anything, this crisis was experienced as *rising costs* or inflation. Polls indicated that the rising cost of living was the primary concern of the majority of Americans in a decade with no shortage of concerns.[105] In 1971, Nixon set up the Cost of Living Council, whose mission was to tackle rising costs of food, energy, and other key

---

102 Environmental Protection Agency, "The Social Cost of Carbon." 19january2017snapshot.epa.gov/climatechange/social-cost-carbon_.html. Last accessed May 27, 2020.

103 Ibid.

104 Umair Irfan, "Climate change is a global injustice. A new study shows why," *Vox*, September 26, 2018.

105 "Living Costs Are Held Top Problem in US, a Gallup Poll Reports," *New York Times*, July 30, 1978.

commodities by setting mandatory wage and price controls across the economy.

If neoliberalism was, as David Harvey argues, a "class project," this mania over inflation had to be directed toward political ends.[106] Who hates inflation the most? The rich and the financial sector. Inflation, to them, is nothing more than the erosion of the value of accumulated wealth. Moreover, the causes of inflation were universally blamed on what we might call "Left-Keynesian" forces—government spending and unions. In 1975, Alan Greenspan, as a member of the Council of Economic Advisers to the Ford Administration, said in a memo:

> The inflationary environment that prevailed throughout the 1960's and that carried the seeds of eventual recession stemmed from an overly optimistic view of our supply capabilities. Governments strongly committed themselves to ameliorate social inequalities at home and abroad and to achieve an ever-rising standard of living. However morally and socially commendable, these commitments proved to be too ambitious in economic terms—both in what they actually attempted to achieve as well as in the expectations they raised among the public.[107]

Government spending itself was constructed as an overly ambitious cost to society. The logic of belt-tightening spread everywhere, and unions also came to be seen as inflationary. By organizing and achieving an unfair monopoly price on the wages of labor, prices were pushed up. A 1974 pamphlet from the Cost of Living Council featured an illustration of protesters—implicitly union workers—with signs reading, "More Money Now!"[108] The underlying message:

---

106 David Harvey, *A Brief History of Neoliberalism* (Oxford, UK: Oxford University Press, 2007).

107 Alan Greenspan, "The Impact of the 1973–1974 Oil Price Increase on the United States Economy to 1980," US Council of Economic Advisors, Alan Greenspan, Box 48, Folder 1, Gerald Ford Presidential Library, Ann Arbor, Mich.

108 Cost of Living Council, *Inflation: On Prices and Wages and Running Amok* (Washington, DC: Government Printing Office, 1973), 14.

working-class struggles for political power made everything cost too much.

The political focus on the causes of rising costs resulted in a relentless fixation on "cost-cutting" at all levels of society—cuts to household budgets with stagnant wages, cuts to social programs to pay debts, cuts to workforces to raise stock prices, cutting corners in environmental protection, and, of course, cutting costs through automation and through offshoring to low-cost regions. Oddly, in an era of unfathomable wealth accumulation and abundance, society as a whole was forced to accept a logic of belt-tightening.

The logic of cost-cutting infiltrated all policy domains, including environmental policy. In a milieu structured by an ontological fixation on reducing costs at all costs, policy technocrats thought the only way pollution could be stopped was if it was accounted for as "cost." In this ideological context, policy thinkers, and eventually the climate movement itself, came to understand non-monetized environmental destruction—emissions, drought, rising sea levels, and deforestation—as externalized costs to society. The gamble was that once those costs were visible to the market they would be reduced along with all other costs.

As we will see in the next chapter, this idea of imposing new "costs" on the economy also appealed to the professional-class sensibility because members of that class were anxious about their own complicity in mass consumption. Professional-class technocrats *like* the idea of paying more for energy because they like the idea of consuming less. Yet the majority of society was dealing with decades of wage stagnation, austerity, and debt. The right was able to seize on this contradiction by simply equating any and all forms of environmental policy with *costs* to you and your family.[109]

As we saw in Chapter 1, even Charles Koch could claim to be a champion of poor and working-class consumers who would suffer through higher energy costs under the liberal climate policy regime.

---

109 See, Matthew T. Huber, *Lifeblood: Oil, Freedom and the Forces of Capital* (Minneapolis: University of Minnesota Press, 2013), 129–54.

This was not just his own belief. When momentum on climate action seemed possible, the Koch-funded group Americans for Prosperity directed a full frontal attack on all forms of carbon regulation. While most liberal climate activists focused on the group's distortion of climate science, its consistent message focused on the *costs* of climate policy and the limitations on the freedom of consumer choice. In 2008, Americans for Prosperity launched a campaign called the "No Climate Tax Pledge," which urged elected officials to sign a document ensuring, "I will oppose any legislation relating to climate change that includes a net increase in government revenue."[110] The group also sponsored major rallies and events linking high gasoline prices to environmental policy. The group's president said in 2015, "We want the public to know there's a reason these prices are going through the roof: It's because of the environment produced by the regulatory practices of this administration."[111] The irony, of course, was that Obama's policies did next to nothing to prevent a massive *expansion* of oil production in the United States, which ultimately led to lower gasoline prices by the end of his second term—something he bragged about at a public event in 2018.[112]

In sum, the technocratic construction of emissions as a "social cost" to be internalized through the market ultimately led to a politics that implied climate action will impose that cost on the working class and the economy at large. While the logic of getting the prices right and reducing consumption appealed to professionals, it failed to marshal a popular coalition behind it. In perhaps the death knell for these policy initiatives, the liberal and environmentalist state of Washington voted down carbon-tax proposals in both 2016 and 2018 by large margins.[113] Meanwhile during that fall of 2018, working-class

---

110   Howard Gleckman, "What's Up With the 'No Climate Tax' Pledge?" *Forbes*, June 2, 2015.

111   Ben Smith, "A new gas front," *Politico*, June 6, 2011.

112   Tyler Stone, "Obama: Suddenly America Is the Biggest Oil Producer, That Was Me People," *Real Clear Politics*, November 28, 2018.

113   David Roberts, "Washington votes no on a carbon tax—again," *Vox*, November 6, 2018.

commuters in France, calling themselves the Yellow Vest movement, erupted in protest over a particularly regressive fuel tax imposed by President Emmanuel Macron. It seemed as if the "smart" politics of internalizing environmental costs was dead.

'Time to Outsmart Climate Change': The Citizens' Climate Lobby as Professional-Class Politics

I end this chapter with a brief case study of a political organization that epitomizes the policy-technocrat approach to climate politics: the Citizens' Climate Lobby (CCL). Founded in 2007 by real estate capitalist turned climate believer Marshall Saunders, the CCL aims to recruit volunteers to push for carbon pricing—more specifically a "Carbon Fee and Dividend" policy. This policy aims to place a steadily rising fee on carbon—the word "tax" is fastidiously avoided—and redistribute the revenue to individual households as a "dividend." It has 540 active chapters concentrated in the North America, Europe, and Australia, but also in countries like Bangladesh, Zimbabwe, and Panama.[114]

At the core of CCL politics is developing a *smart* politics whose logic can appeal to both the left and the right. In fact, much of its online material includes the slogan, "Time to outsmart climate change," reaffirming the professional-class dictum that politics is ultimately about knowledge and being informed on smart solutions.[115] The CCL's goal is expressly designed to spread the logic through sophisticated communications strategy that involves writing op-eds, calling elected officials, phone banking, and holding public events. As a *New York Times* profile put it, "the organization prepares citizens to be effective lobbyists ... showing them how to make persuasive

114 Information taken from the group's website: citizensclimatelobby.org. Last accessed May 29, 2020.

115 See, Sabine Marx, "Workshop: "Tailoring Communication to Your Audience," CCL Northeast Regional Conference, March 16–18, 2018. documents.grenadine.co. Last accessed May 29, 2020.

arguments about policies to win bipartisan support."[116] At the core of this strategy is the idea that regardless of political ideology, one could be *convinced* of this particular policy on the basis of its logic. Thus the CCL trumpets its conservative supporters such as George Schultz, former Secretary of State under Reagan, and Bob Inglis, the Christian conservative Republican who accepted the truth of climate change, advocated for action, and was swiftly voted out of office by a Tea Party challenger in 2014.[117]

Although the organization champions "diversity" as one of its core values, it is governed completely by the professional class—academics, scientists, legal professionals, and even some actors and artists. Apart from Saunders, whose credentials involve the definitely not low-carbon field of "real estate brokerage specializing in shopping center development and leasing,"[118] the governing board features six people in total, three of whom hold advanced degrees and two of whom are former Republican members of Congress. Two board members also work in finance.[119] The advisory board features 20 individuals; 12 have a Ph.D. That board also includes famed science communicators like James Hansen and Katharine Hayhoe and policy technocrats like economist and carbon tax acolyte Adele Morris, whose Twitter bio once read, "nevertheless she persisted trying to save the planet cost effectively."[120]

The organization claims it is nonpartisan, but its entire strategy cedes politics to the right. It not only frames itself as an alternative to state regulation, it promises to actively stall it. The current legislation in the United States, the Energy Innovation and Carbon Dividend

116   David Bornstein, "Lobbying for the greater good," *New York Times: Opinionator*, May 29, 2013.

117   See Citizens' Climate Lobby "Advisory Board". citizensclimatelobby.org/about-ccl/advisory-board. Last accessed May 29, 2020.

118   Citizens' Climate Lobby "Founder's story": citizensclimateeducation.org/about-cce/the-citizens-climate-story/, last accessed May 29, 2020.

119   See Citizens' Climate Lobby "Governing Board." citizensclimateeducation.org/about-cce/governing-board/, last accessed August 11, 2020.

120   She has since revised this bio; it now states, "Lucky to be working on climate policy solutions." twitter.com/AdeleCMorris.

Act, "pauses the EPA authority to regulate the CO_2 and equivalent emissions covered by the fee."[121] Carbon pricing is itself a right-leaning "free market" solution, but theoretically a carbon fee could raise substantial revenue for government action on climate. However, the dividend aspect of CCL's policy allows it to claim that the policy is "revenue neutral." The group's website pledges: "The fees collected on carbon emissions will be allocated to all Americans to spend any way they choose. The government will not keep any of the fees collected."[122]

In a crisis that many claim will require a World War II–style mobilization of *public investment*,[123] the failure of this policy to raise any revenue for the public sector is a startling conceit. In doing so, the CCL largely accepts the neoliberal premise that money is best spent by consumers, not government.

Furthermore, the faith in the price mechanism also concedes that government regulation should play no role. James Hansen not only sits on the advisory board of CCL, he is one of the loudest proponents of the carbon fee and dividend and advocates it against government involvement. As mentioned earlier, he actively opposed government regulation of carbon emissions under Obama's Clean Power Plan.

The final thing we can note about the CCL is that it has *failed*. Legislation mandating the carbon fee and dividend has not passed; it likely will never pass. In Part III, we will explore a different approach to climate politics, but for now suffice it to say that logical policy design as a tactic to win over the right is a dead end. Instead of moving to the center to find "smart" bipartisan solutions, the other option is to build and expand a real genuine *left* approach to climate solutions rooted in popular power.

---

121   Energy Innovation and Carbon Dividend Act, "How it works." energyinnovationact. org. Last accessed May 29, 2020.

122   Citizens' Climate Lobby, "Energy Innovation and Carbon Dividend Act." citizensclimatelobby.org/energy-innovation-and-carbon-dividend-act. Last accessed May 29, 2020.

123   See, Andrew Bossie and J.W. Mason, "The public role in economic transformation: Lessons from World War II," *Roosevelt Institute*, March 26, 2020.

Conclusion: Climate Careerism

The professional class mobilizes knowledge and credentials in the labor market to secure a stable career. The intensely competitive and tenacious aspects of this experience lead to a sociocultural class formation that valorizes knowledge in all aspects of social life, including politics. The climate movement is currently overrepresented by the professional class, which seeks to deploy knowledge in the climate struggle.

Science communicators act as if climate denial is the major barrier to decarbonization, and not entrenched political and economic power over our energy system. Policy technocrats believe that designing smart policies will ultimately convince those in power to accede to logic. Both of these positions lack a strategic orientation toward power itself and how to build the kind of mass movement that forces those in power to concede to radical demands.

This is what we explore in Part III, but first we must also cover the other aspect of professional-class climate politics that inhibits a mass movement: an inward-looking guilt that blames ones' own consumption for causing the crisis.

4

Carbon Guilt: Privatized Ecologies, Degrowth, and the Politics of Less

Introduction: #Flyless?

It is hard to argue that flying is a pleasurable experience. You are squeezed in every way imaginable: physically into your seat; financially in your bank account; and temporally through cancellations, overbookings, and delays. The airline industry is fundamentally dehumanizing, as you become simply one disposable customer unit in a larger accumulation strategy. In 2017, security officials physically beat a passenger, Dr. David Dao, and dragged him off a United Airlines plane when he refused to give up a seat he had already paid for.[1] The incident revealed the extent to which the industry will go to maintain the unfair practice of overbooking and expelling paid passengers from flights.

Dehumanizing passengers has paid off for the airline industry, which has seen sustained growth in profitability since the financial crisis of 2008.[2] The decline of oil prices in 2014 only buoyed profits more. In 1978, the airline industry was deregulated. This led to more competition and lower prices in some cases, but also ushered in a period of profound volatility in the industry.[3] Low-cost airlines like

---

1   Daniel Victor and Matt Stevens, "United Airlines passenger is dragged from an overbooked flight," *New York Times*, April 10, 2017.

2   Hugo Martin, "US airlines pocketed $15.5 billion last year, including a record $4.6 billion in bag fees," *Los Angeles Times*, May 7, 2018. Of course, these good times have ended. At the time of this writing, the airlines have already received a $25 billion bailout as the Covid-19 pandemic has massively curtailed air travel and revenue for the industry. Alan Rappeport and Niraj Chokshi, "Crippled Airline Industry to Get $25 Billion Bailout, Part of It as Loans," *New York Times*, April 14, 2020.

3   George Williams, *The Airline Industry and the Impact of Deregulation* (London: Routledge, 2017).

Southwest and JetBlue drove down prices; older, more established airlines merged or consolidated, like American buying up TWA and US Air, United merging with Continental, and Delta absorbing Northwest.[4] In 2017, Delta CEO Ed Bastian earned $13 million, or 142 times more than the average Delta employee.[5] The CEO and board of Delta likely generate most of their wealth from their stock in the company itself, as Delta enjoyed a near quintupling of its market capitalization from $7.67 billion in September 2012 to $38.46 billion in January 2020 before the Covid-19 pandemic.[6] This is a company that doesn't merely emit carbon for profit; it literally invested in an oil refinery in 2012.[7]

The airline industry is a major contributor to global carbon emissions—estimates suggest about 2.5 percent.[8] Air travel is essentially a commodity exchange between passengers and these oligopolistic corporations. It is hard to argue that the passengers are the main beneficiaries of this exchange. Yet, in carbon footprint accounting, the passengers are responsible for the emissions. This footprint ideology has led widespread anxiety among the professional classes over the need to "fly less." Climate activists have sworn off air travel and committed to much longer travel times in order to attend important climate meetings, the most famous example being the teenage climate activist Greta Thunberg, who took a sailboat from Europe to New York City for the United Nations Climate Action Summit in September 2019.

This is particularly prevalent in my own academic profession,

---

4 Thomas Pallini, "The past 2 decades saw the number of major airlines in the US cut in half. See how consolidation in the 2000s left customers with fewer options as profits soared," *Business Insider*, March 21, 2020.

5 Jeff Edwards, "Does Doug Parker Get Paid Too Much?" Flyertalk.com, May 4, 2019.

6 "Delta Air Lines Market Cap 2006-2020." macrotrends.net/stocks/charts/DAL/delta-air-lines/market-cap.

7 Clifford Krauss and Niraj Chokshi, "Delta Air Lines Bought an Oil Refinery. It Didn't Go as Planned," *New York Times*, August 12, 2020.

8 Hiroko Tabuchi, " 'Worse Than Anyone Expected': Air Travel Emissions Vastly Outpace Predictions," *New York Times*, September 19, 2019.

where travel to research sites, conferences, and workshops is a standard part of the job. Compared to industrial sectors reviewed in Part 1 like cement and fertilizer, higher education is relatively low carbon— most of its activities like writing, teaching, and research involve very few emissions. Indeed, Alyssa Battistoni argues that any low-carbon society would vastly widen access to higher education: "programs like universal health care and free college that simultaneously expand access to public goods and the scope of the low-carbon economy."[9] This has not stopped a movement among many in the academy to focus on the flying behavior of other academic professionals. Over 2,600 have signed an online petition organized by the "Flying Less" campaign that calls on universities and professional associations to "greatly reduce flying."[10] The campaign has a Frequently Asked Question section that lays out the centrality of flying to the menu of lifestyle changes academics should consider:

> Many university-based academics fly many thousand[s] of miles per year, sufficient to make aviation their single biggest emissions source. We have faculty colleagues who diligently limit their environmental impact in many areas of their lives, but not their flying behavior. For an academic professional who eats comparatively little meat, commutes by public transportation, sets the home thermostat at a reasonable temperature, and drives a fuel-efficient car, unrestrained flying behavior easily may be responsible for a large fraction of his or her total climate change impact.[11]

We are familiar with the logic that individuals have discrete "impacts" associated with the consumption of energy, food, and air travel. The entire political campaign directs its attention toward the consumers of air travel. Left unexamined is the true beneficiary of air travel and the true driver of emissions: the airline industry itself.

---

9   Alyssa Battistoni, "Living not just surviving," *Jacobin*, No. 26 (Summer 2017): 65–71; 71.
10   academicflyingblog.wordpress.com.
11   Ibid., Frequently Asked Questions page. Last accessed June 1, 2020.

There is very little climate activism aimed at regulating or even expropriating this industry for its 2.5 percent contribution to emissions. Nevertheless, academics spend endless hours on trains and other modes of transport to make their already low-carbon jobs even more virtuously low carbon, and even more hours on social media villainizing those who fly as a means of academic survival. Meanwhile, as labor in higher education becomes more and more precarious, the most disadvantaged workers, like graduate students and adjuncts, *need* to fly to improve their chances in a brutally competitive market.

These campaigns advocate behavioral change as either a substitute for or complement to systemic change. In a neoliberal world, individual behavioral change sometimes appears to be the only meaningful option to "do something" about climate change. In a survey of attitudes on flying behavior, Steven Westlake suggests as much:

> In the absence of coordinated government action some people have chosen to stop flying because of aviation's contribution to climate change. This individual stand to give up flying often significantly reduces personal emissions, and also has the potential to send a social signal to others.[12]

Note the "absence of coordinated government action" is *assumed* to be an unchangeable fact, even when it is hard to imagine how the problem of climate change could truly be solved without it. Renowned climate scientist and activist Kevin Anderson argues for more of a complementary view "where vociferous individuals coalesc[e] to form casual collectives that subsequently drive change within larger formal institutions."[13] Both views see individual choices as a form of cultural influence that might add up to bigger change.

12   Steven Westlake, "A counter-narrative to carbon supremacy: Do leaders who give up flying because of climate change influence the attitudes and behaviour of others?" (October 2, 2017). ssrn.com/abstract=3283157.

13   Kevin Anderson, "A succinct account of my view on individual and collective action," kevinanderson.info. Last accessed June 1, 2020.

I do not wish to reject all such efforts to fly less. Certainly, choosing to fly less can spur conversations with others over the crisis of climate change and the large-scale changes needed. But in this chapter, I am more interested in the class basis of an ideology where reducing consumption appears to be the most viable political action to address climate change.

At the heart of the flying less campaign is guilt over one's high carbon lifestyle—what I call carbon guilt. This guilt emerges from a contradiction at the heart of professional-class formation. On the one hand, the entire class project aims to use credentials to achieve the salary and material security of a middle-class lifestyle. On the other hand, professional-class lifestyles relate to massive levels of ecological degradation and waste. This realization creates inward feelings of guilt or complicity as the world burns. But carbon guilt leads one to think it is actually professional, middle-class consumers themselves who are most privileged in a climate changing world. Carbon guilt confuses material privilege—a level of comfort and security—with the *power* to control the material organization of energy production. You might feel privileged to fly on a plane, but the airline industry gains the profit from your privilege.

From the standpoint of carbon guilt—wracked by anxiety over excessive lifestyles—a *politics of less* is intuitively appealing. As ecological footprint scholars put it, "The inescapable conclusion is that we must learn to live a quality life with less."[14] Kevin Anderson also suggests as much, "I see no mathematical alternative but for those of us responsible for the lion's share of emissions to rapidly and deeply reduce our energy consumption."[15] Again, the professional class represents a *minority* of the population, while the majority have experienced the last four decades as increased economic insecurity, stagnating wages, job insecurity, and mounting debt. This politics of less makes little sense to a majority of society already forced to live with less.

---

14 Nicky Chambers, Craig Simmons, and Mathis Wackernagel, *Sharing Nature's Interest: Ecological Footprints as an Indicator of Sustainability* (London: Routledge, 1996), 66.

15 Kevin Anderson, op cit.

In this chapter, I will trace how the postwar explosion of the professional class came alongside a deep critique of affluence and consumerism—a critique that only intensified with the rise of the environmental movement. An ecological politics of less overlapped perfectly with a wider neoliberal focus on austerity that calls on all of us to tighten our belts. I will also review the most prominent professional-class formation expressing the idea of a politics of less: degrowth.

But first, we need to understand how millions of workers came to consume so much in the first place.

The Suburban Solution to Working-Class Power[16]

> If the centralization of population stimulates and develops the property-holding class, it forces the development of the workers yet more rapidly. The workers begin to feel as a class, as a whole; they begin to perceive that, though feeble as individuals, they form a power united . . . The great cities are the birthplaces of labor movements . . .
> —Frederick Engels, *The Condition of the English Working Class*, 1845

In the 1840s, Marx and Engels were prescient about the brewing conflict between capital and labor. Capital's drive for relative surplus value reviewed in Part I has what Engels calls a "centralizing tendency," where massive investments are concentrated in cities. The proletariat was driven into these same cities through the violent dispossession of the peasantry and the destruction of rural artisanal cottage industries. As Andreas Malm shows, coal-fired steam power allowed capital to derive an energy source that was mobile (unlike water power) and could be concentrated in urban centers "where labor is easily procured."[17]

---

16   I borrow this subheading title from Richard Walker's Ph.D. dissertation of a similar name: *The Suburban Solution: Urban Geography and Urban Reform in the Capitalist Development of the United States* (John Hopkins University, 1977).

17   Andreas Malm, *Fossil Capital: The Rise of Steam Power and the Roots of Global Warming* (London: Verso, 2016), 121.

As capital centralizes in cities, so does the working class. It was not only the cooperative nature of factory work that aided working-class organization; it was also the spatial proximity of working-class masses concentrated in urban areas. The tenement houses, pubs, and public spaces like squares and parks all became cauldrons of working-class organization and power. Mike Davis recounts that cities "provided the principal form or shell for the economic, as well political and cultural organization of the working class across craft boundaries."[18] He explains that by 1900, "virtually every industrial city or town in countries where unions were legal had a central building for workers' meetings, union offices, party papers and the like."[19] As Henri Lefebvre argued, the spatial process of urbanization itself became a *revolutionary* force.[20]

By the early twentieth century, it was abundantly clear that the concentrated power of the urbanized working class was a threat to the basic institutions of capitalism. Even in a mainly rural country, "[urban] Russia was the crucible of the 1917 revolution."[21] In the United States of the 1930s, a wave of strikes broke out, and workers and unions demonstrated a capacity to shut down entire cities. Even in the face of brutal and bloody violence, workers organized general strikes in San Francisco and Minneapolis. Battalions of picketers moved via car and truck across the Eastern US, shutting down the entire textile industry from Georgia to Massachusetts. In Flint, Michigan, workers used the sit-down method to prevent General Motors from bringing strikebreakers into the plants, forcing the company to make concessions.[22]

Marked by mass unemployment and deprivation, the crisis of the Great Depression demonstrated the illegitimacy of the capitalist

18   Mike Davis, *Old Gods, New Enigmas*, 83.

19   Ibid., 102.

20   Henri Lefebvre, *The Urban Revolution* (Minneapolis: University of Minnesota Press, 2003)

21   Diane Koenker, "Urbanization and deurbanization in the Russian Revolution and Civil War," *Journal of Modern History*, Vol. 57, No. 3 (1985): 424–50.

22   For detailed descriptions of all these strikes, see Jeremy Brecher, *Strike!* (Oakland, CA: PM Press, 2020).

system. Many assumed that capitalism was finished. In 1934, the *New York Times* ran an editorial titled "Capitalism Is Doomed, Dying or Dead."[23] In the same year, 3,000 people attended a debate in New York City "on whether communism or fascism is preferable in the United States as the new social order to supplant capitalism."[24] The New Deal was a massive state-led project to *disperse* the working-class power that threatened capitalism so acutely. It was not simply a project of "economic recovery"; it was also a highly ideological *anti-urban* project whose goal was to marshal federal resources to build the physical infrastructure and financial incentives for mass suburbanization. New Dealers viewed cities as dirty, unhealthy centers of immorality and dangerous political activity.[25] Giving working-class white urbanites the capacity to move out of the city and live in a privatized single-family home was a way to spur the economy and neutralize working-class power. Politicians like Herbert Hoover understood this function of home ownership long before the 1930s. He argued that "maintaining a high percentage of individual home owners" creates a social mass of people who "have an interest in the advancement of a social system that permits the individual to store the fruits of their labor."[26]

The New Deal put home ownership at the center of its program with the founding of the Federal Housing Administration and Home Owners Loan Corporation. New Deal public works projects also built the highways, bridges, and tunnels that still connect major suburban residential areas to urban business districts. These programs systematically refused to offer mortgages in racialized urban areas ("redlined" as hazardous to lenders). As such, these programs became engines of racial segregation as working-class ethnic whites began fleeing to suburban enclaves.[27] One estimate suggests that "The Federal Housing

23 "Life in It Yet," *New York Times*, December 16, 1934, E4.

24 "Capitalism Is Doomed, Say Fascist and Red," *New York Times*, March 5, 1934, 18.

25 Steven Conn, *Americans Against the City: Anti-Urbanism in the 20th Century* (Oxford: Oxford University Press, 2014), 94–113.

26 Quoted in John Archer, *Architecture and Suburbia: From English Villa to American Dream House, 1690–2000* (Minneapolis: University of Minnesota Press, 2005), 264.

27 Kenneth Jackson, *Crabgrass Frontier: The Suburbanization of the United States* (Oxford UK: Oxford University Press, 1987).

Administration and the Veterans Administration financed more than $120 billion worth of new housing between 1934 and 1962 but less than 2 percent of this real estate was available to nonwhite families."[28] This process of residential segregation also hardened long-existing racial divisions within the working class overall, further eroding working-class power.

With white flight and suburban wealth accumulation, these divisions were more easily mapped through the spatiality of metropolitan regions. Even if Roosevelt had garnered mass support from Blacks through jobs and public housing programs, the Democratic Party New Deal coalition failed to overcome these divisions completely.[29] As Mike Davis argues, a program of Black enfranchisement could have built a mass multiracial working-class majority, but Roosevelt and Truman instead chose to appease the Dixiecrat Southern right wing of the party. Davis explains:

> The entire edifice of Democratic conservatism, as well as the interlinked corporate and Cold War political alliances which it sustained, ultimately rested on the linchpins of Black disenfranchisement and the poll tax.[30]

At precisely the moment when Democrats, led by Lyndon Johnson, finally abandoned this coalition with the passage of Civil and Voting Rights Acts of the mid-1960s, white working-class voters began to abandon the Democrats in favor of an anti–welfare state and anti-tax conservatism.[31]

---

28 George Lipsitz, *The Possessive Investment in Whiteness: How White People Profit From Identity Politics* (Philadelphia: Temple University Press, 2006), 6.

29 See, Touré Reed, *Toward Freedom: The Case Against Race Reductionism* (London: Verso, 2020).

30 Mike Davis, *Prisoners of the American Dream: Politics and Economy in the History of the US Working Class* (London: Verso, 1986), 96.

31 Mary D. Edsall and Thomas B. Edsall, *Chain Reaction: The Impact of Race, Rights, and Taxes on American Politics* (New York: W.W. Norton and Co., 1991).

The Ecological Contradictions of the New Deal

Dispersing working-class power in this manner is a materially energy-intensive project rooted in the contradictions at the heart of the New Deal. On the one hand, it is an outcome of what Mike Davis described as "the highwater mark of the class struggle in modern American history."[32] On the other hand, as many have pointed out, the New Deal was a decidedly not radical project to save capitalism from itself. Although its form of liberalism elevated the public sector to heretofore unseen levels through social security, union rights, financial regulation, housing subsidies, and huge public infrastructure investments, it used this public largesse to finance a geography of *privatism*. Federal housing programs subsidized private single-family homes; federal highway construction provided the connective arteries of a automobility; federal labor law allowed workers to bargain for higher wages that also allowed them to afford things like mortgages, car payments, and a whole suite of electrified consumer durables like dishwashers, refrigerators, and televisions. This all can be called using public investment to allow for the privatization of everyday life.[33]

The New Deal tried to craft a whole geography and way of life that more approximated the myths of the liberal capitalist market as simply an aggregation of individual buyers and sellers. A capitalist market is itself a very strange institution. Although it is highly social and based on global levels of interdependence (think of today's global supply chains involving tens of thousands of workers that provision your daily needs), one can only engage with the market as a private individual. Your bank account is yours and yours alone; you purchase and consume commodities as an atomized market actor. In his discussion of the fetishism of commodities, Marx explained how the money we exchange for commodities conceals the social world we all inhabit:

---

32 Davis, *Prisoners*, 54.
33 I am here conveying arguments I made in *Lifeblood: Oil, Freedom and the Forces of Capital* (Minneapolis: University of Minnesota Press, 2013).

It is however precisely this finished form of the world of commodities—the money form—which conceals the social character of private labor and the social relations between the individual workers, by making those relations appear as relations between material objects, instead of revealing them plainly.[34]

While Marx simply investigates the fetishism of the commodity form itself, the suburban mode of living extends the commodity logic of privatized buyers and sellers to the whole process of social reproduction under capitalism. In the city, workers could more easily understand their sociality and collective power. In the suburbs, what Raymond Williams called "mobile privatization" takes hold: one travels in a private car, to a private workplace, and exchanges private money for commodities.[35]

This privatized experience of life itself yields what Evan McKenzie called an "ideology of hostile privatism."[36] This ideology is convinced that individuals are *on their own* and dependent only on themselves, their life and success a product of their own individual efforts. Living this privatized geography convinces masses that there is no need for public or collective solidarity—or, as Margaret Thatcher once said: "There is no such thing! There are individual men and women and there are families."[37]

This privatized mode of life required almost unimaginably huge public, *material* investment: the building of countless single-family homes, laying concrete and asphalt for highways, massively expanding electric and water utilities, and producing all that gasoline to power the dispersal of single automobiles. The geography of postwar suburban mass consumption is often called "excessive" and "wasteful," so

---

34 Karl Marx, *Capital*, Vol. 1, 168–9.

35 Raymond Williams, *Television: Technology and Cultural Form* (London: Routledge, 1975), 18.

36 Evan McKenzie, *Privatopia: Homeowner Associations and the Rise of Residential Private Government* (New Haven: Yale University Press, 1994), 19.

37 Douglas Keay, "Interview with Margaret Thatcher," *Woman's Own*, September 23, 1987. margaretthatcher.org/document/106689. Last accessed June 2, 2020.

enormous that it required a huge level of material consumption merely for basic everyday social reproduction. Many workers did not consume prodigious amounts of gasoline just for fun, but as a necessity in navigating an increasingly dispersed geography connecting home, work, school, and shopping center.

Think about even the sheer number *of supermarkets* needed to provision commodities to the dispersed masses. The United States, it turns out, has 38,307 supermarkets.[38] It also has 384 metropolitan areas, containing 80 percent of the country's population. If we assume that 80 percent of those stores (roughly 30,000 supermarkets) provision these metropolitan areas, each metropolitan area has an average of 80 supermarkets—each of which is a sprawling 40,000-to-50,000-square-foot building filled with thousands of commodities. Of course, these 80 stores will be located mostly in affluent areas, with huge swaths of the impoverished, mostly urban or rural populations left to fend for themselves in "food deserts." But for the suburban and relatively affluent, the geography of dispersed supermarkets is a necessity. Without it, the logic of privatized living would break down, and too many individuals would need hours, not minutes, to travel for their basic needs.

Crucially, this life of privatized provisioning completely erases the centrality of the "hidden abode" of industrial production underpinning it all (the kind of industrial production at the core of the climate crisis reviewed in Part I). When it is all you see, it makes sense to focus on the role of consumption driving climate change, and this was especially true for the professional class.

Professional Ecologies of Privatized Provisioning

The story of suburbanization is mainly a story of working-class white ethnics moving to relatively modest inner-ring suburbs and living an "American dream" based on single-family home ownership and

---

38 Liam O'Connell, "Number of supermarket stores in the US 2011–2018," Statista.com. Last accessed June 2, 2020.

automobility. Yet the suburbs were also the chosen destination for many in the professional classes like academics, engineers, and tech workers.[39] As reviewed in Chapter 3, meritocracy lies at the core of professional-class politics. Although many professionals revile such a lifestyle, even the most radical professional-class individual ultimately aspires to a "career" that comes with home and other property ownership.

Suburban professional property owners espoused a very specific and peculiar form of politics. Lily Geismar's study of suburban liberals focuses on professional knowledge workers as "the fastest growing occupational sector in the decades after World War II."[40] She argues that a specific form of suburban liberalism centered on an "individualist outlook" that "encouraged white suburbanites to understand their decisions about where to live as individual choices and rights."[41] Overall, she asserts that suburban liberals supported a policy regime that remade the Democratic Party in the 1970s and onward: "The set of policies that took shape at all levels of government magnified the privileging of individual self-interest over collective obligation in postwar liberal ideology and institutions."[42] Much has been made by historians of the role of suburbs in the rise of the New Right in the Republican Party, but Geismar effectively shows how the rightward shift of the Democratic Party also is rooted in a shift in the party's base from working-class urbanites to suburban professionals. This shift in the party base to knowledge workers called "Atari Democrats" marked a move toward those who "focused on government reform and stimulating private sector economic growth, especially high tech industry."[43] Such inward-looking suburban liberalism is often

39 For a fascinating account of engineers and other professionals in the suburbs of Pittsburgh, see Patrick Vitale, *Nuclear Suburbs: Cold War Technoscience and the Pittsburgh Renaissance* (Minneapolis: University of Minnesota Press, 2021).

40 Lily Geismar, *Don't Blame Us: Suburban Liberals and the Transformation of the Democratic Party* (Princeton, NJ: Princeton University Press, 2015), 8.

41 Ibid., 9.

42 Ibid.

43 Ibid., 252.

oblivious to how its "actions perpetuated form[s] of racial and economic privilege and inequality."[44]

This individual-centered perspective shared by suburban professionals also shaped environmental politics.[45] While their class project aims for middle-class security and career success, suburban professionals also live within the ecologically irrational system of *privatized provisioning* emerging out of the New Deal consensus. As examined in the last chapter, the professional class also centers its politics on education and knowing the extent of the environmental and climate crisis. The accumulation of knowledge about the crisis will immediately stand in stark contradiction to the material and energy-intensive nature of the expected professional class mode of life.

It is this cognitive dissonance and apparent hypocrisy of *knowing* the ecological crisis while *living* such a materially intensive lifestyle that produces the ideology of carbon guilt. The practice of everyday life becomes one of material comfort amid stark waste; of material security amid too much "crap." As he is wont to do, Ezra Klein pinpointed the liberal anxiety of professional-class life under climate chaos in these terms: "there is a discordance between the pitch of the rhetoric on climate and the normalcy of the lives many of us live."[46] However, rather than question the politics of privatism inherent in this way of life, the professional class doubles down on a privatized political project of individual behavioral change: lowering your carbon footprint and calling for reduced consumption. As Elizabeth Currid-Halkett argues, the ways this class seeks to marshal knowledge to become an ecologically virtuous and well-informed consumer becomes central to the cultural practices of class distinction and reproduction.[47] In sum, these practices demonstrate at best an

44   Ibid., 9.
45   Adam Rome, *The Bulldozer in the Countryside: Suburban Sprawl and the Rise of American Environmentalism* (Cambridge, UK: Cambridge University Press, 2001).
46   Ezra Klein, "It Seems Odd We Would Just Let the World Burn," *New York Times*, July 15, 2021.
47   Elizabeth Currid-Halkett, *The Sum of Small Things: A Theory of the Aspirational Class* (Princeton, NJ: Princeton University Press, 2017)

ambivalence and at worst an active hostility toward a more collective public-oriented politics. Just as achieving a career is a result of individual merit, the ecologically responsible consumer takes the climate crisis as a matter of individual responsibility. This politics looks toward individuals as responsible to "live better with less."

As the alienation and ecological destruction of suburban lifestyles became more and more apparent throughout the decades, members of the professional class began to see their own way of life as a real problem—a form of what Joe Nevins calls "ecological privilege."[48] This led commentators on both left and right, and ecological politics in particular, to point their critiques toward this suburban "affluent society."

'Anxieties of Affluence'[49]

This affluent mode of privatized mass consumption hit roadblocks in the 1970s. As discussed in Chapter 3, after a few decades of postwar suburban growth, the logic of *cutting costs* infiltrated states, firms, and, in this case, environmentalist households in the '70s. While the politics of capitalism historically railed against the system's inequality and poverty, by the 1970s both the left and right agreed that capitalism faced a new problem: we simply had too much. Rising consumption levels—themselves the product of working-class victories—were now a problem. As mentioned above, Alan Greenspan argued that economic crisis was rooted in overly "ambitious" societal expectations. He went on to suggest that the public must adjust to new "realistic goals" and that "levels of income will be lower and the possible growth in standards of living will be reduced."[50] In 1979, Federal

---

48   Joseph Nevins, "Academic jet-setting in a time of climate destabilization: Ecological privilege and professional geographic travel," *The Professional Geographer*, Vol. 66, No. 2 (2014): 298–310.

49   I borrow this from the title of the book by Daniel Horowitz, *The Anxieties of Affluence: Critiques of American Consumer Culture, 1939–1979* (Amherst, MA: University of Massachusetts Press, 2004).

50   Alan Greenspan, "The Impact of the 1973–1974 Oil Price Increase on the United States Economy to 1980," US Council of Economic Advisors, Alan Greenspan, Box 48, Folder 1, Gerald Ford Presidential Library, Ann Arbor, MI.

Reserve Chair Paul Volcker was blunter: "The standard of living of the average American has to decline . . . I don't think you can escape that."[51] Society had "overshot" reasonable material expectations.

Many on the "New Left" also turned their critique toward the problems of the affluent commodity society. Herbert Marcuse defined "pure domination . . . as administration, and in the overdeveloped areas of mass consumption, the administered life becomes the good life for the whole."[52] Guy Debord asserted that "the diffuse spectacle accompanies the abundance of commodities," and that the commodity has "succeeded in totally colonizing social life."[53] Critical theorist William Leiss asserted that consumer lifestyles did not satisfy fundamental human needs. "This setting promotes a lifestyle that is dependent upon an endlessly rising level of consumption of material goods . . . [in which] individuals are led to misinterpret the nature of their needs."[54] Christopher Lasch lampooned the American "cult of consumption" and directly influenced President Jimmy Carter's so-called malaise speech in which he claimed Americans "tend to worship self-indulgence and consumption."[55] Most agree that Carter's speech admonishing Americans to scale down paved the way for Reagan.[56]

These critiques of affluence came at an odd time, during a decade in which American workers were under attack. As historian Daniel Horowitz explains, "most Americans experienced [the 1970s] as one of economic pain . . . the vast majority of the nation's families experienced diminishing real incomes."[57] Polls reported the rising cost of

51   Steven Rattner, "Volcker Asserts US Must Trim Living Standard," New York Times, October 18, 1979.

52   Herbert Marcuse, One Dimensional Man (Boston: Beacon Press, 1964), 255.

53   Guy Debord, Society of the Spectacle (London: Rebel Press, 1967), 32, 21.

54   William Leiss, Limits to Satisfaction: An Essay on the Problem of Needs and Commodities (Toronto: University of Toronto Press, 1976), x.

55   Christopher Lascsh, The Culture of Narcissism: American Life in An Age of Diminishing Expectations (New York: W. W. Norton & Company, 1979), 32, 73; Jimmy Carter, " 'Crisis of Confidence' Speech," 1979.

56   Daniel Horowitz, Jimmy Carter and the Energy Crisis of the 1970s: The "Crisis of Confidence" Speech of July 15, 1979 (New York: Bedford, 2004).

57   Daniel Horowitz, Anxieties of Affluence: Critiques of American Consumer Culture, 1939–1979 (Amherst, MA: University of Massachusetts Press, 2004).

living was the number one concern for Americans.[58] While the working class struggled to afford the basics, many on both Left and Right told them they already had too much (and the professional class agreed). As the Greenspans and Volckers of the world won out, it became common sense that it was time to "do more with less"; it was time to cut government spending, union benefits, and household budgets alike.

The critique of affluence and "overconsumption" overlapped perfectly with the rise of the environmental movement at the same moment. Much like Greenspan and Volcker, the Club of Rome's 1972 *Limits to Growth* announced a new reality to which society had to adjust: "man is forced to take account of the limited dimensions of his planet."[59] Paul Ehrlich initially trumpeted the crudest Malthusianism in *The Population Bomb*, but in 1974 he and his wife published *The End of Affluence*, arguing that the mass consumer society had overshot its material base.[60] William Catton's influential book *Overshoot* explained that humans had exhausted much of the Earth's carrying capacity and a mass die-off was imminent.[61]

Environmental politics rose and expanded precisely during the period of neoliberal restraint. It subscribed to what Leigh Phillips terms "austerity ecology," a politics of limits, reducing consumption, and lessening our impact, distilled in the slogan "reduce, reuse, recycle."[62] This politics of less, as we will see below with the case of degrowth, is levied against the aggregate of society as whole, or, as new professional radicals became fond of saying, the *system*. The anti-system environmental radical sees an entire human

---

58   Matthew T. Huber, *Lifeblood: Oil, Freedom and the Forces of Capital* (Minneapolis: University of Minnesota Press, 2013), 112.

59   Donella H. Meadows, et al., *The Limits to Growth* (New York: Universe Books, 1974).

60   Paul Ehrlich and Anne Ehrlich, *The End of Affluence: A Blueprint for Your Future* (New York: Ballantine Books, 1974).

61   William Catton, *Overshoot: The Ecological Basis of Revolutionary Change* (Urbana, IL: University of Illinois Press, 1980).

62   Leigh Phillips, *Austerity Ecology and the Collapse Porn Addicts* (London: Zero Books, 2015).

society at odds with the planet and advocates "less" for the system as a whole.

Traditional adherents to labor, socialist, and social democratic politics rejected this vision of antigrowth environmentalism. In a scathing 1976 article in the *New York Times Magazine* headlined "No Growth Has to Mean Less is Less," civil rights and socialist organizer Bayard Rustin lampooned what he called the "antigrowth intelligentsia" and bemoaned a new effort by the "middle-class elite for domination over organized labor and the working class."[63] What Rustin calls "middle class" is of course the ascendant professional class of college-educated masses inundating the New Left. He concludes that "many of those in the vanguard of the environmental movement, themselves members largely of the upper classes, have often sought policies that are clearly detrimental . . . [and] destructive to the needs of those less better off."[64]

One thing that unites these austerity perspectives from Alan Greenspan to *The Limits to Growth* is their professional-class location, isolated from the non–college educated working masses. Given the focus on consuming less, ecological politics turned up its nose at the perceived "excessive" mass consumption of workers, or, to the Ehrenreichs, a politics based in "moralistic contempt of the working class."[65] For example, Rudolf Bahro, of the Green Party in Germany, plainly said: "The working class here [in the West] is the richest lower class in the world . . . I must say that the metropolitan working class is the worst exploiting class in history."[66] You hear exactly the same sentiments today. The German climate justice campaigner Tadzio Müller recently asserted: "The Global North is essentially a global labor aristocracy. The material interests of the vast majority of people

63   Credit to Leigh Phillips for unearthing this text and sharing on social media. Bayard Rustin, "No Growth Has to Mean Less Is Less," *New York Times Magazine*, May 2, 1976.

64   Ibid.

65   Barbara Ehrenreich and John Ehrenreich, "The professional-managerial class," in Pat Walker (ed.), *Between Labor and Capital* (Boston: South End Press, 1979), 5–45; 33.

66   Rudolf Bahro, *From Red to Green: Interviews with the New Left Review* (London: Verso, 1984), 184.

in the Global North are such that they support the continued destruction of the biosphere."[67] Other radical academics argue that the Global
North working class causes the ecological crisis through its "imperial
mode of living":

> The reproduction of the northern working class has benefited not only
> from the institutionalized compromises of class struggle in the global
> North itself, but also the possibility of accessing nature and labor power
> on the global scale and externalizing the socio-ecological costs of
> resource-and-energy-intensive patterns of production and consump-
> tion—a possibility safeguarded by an imperialist world order.[68]

Of course, they ignore how capital has successfully dismantled those
"institutionalized compromises of class struggle," and that it is not the
working class that directly "accesses" nature and labor power but
capitalists in search of profit.

At the core of this professional contempt for the working (and
consuming) masses is a deeper guilt about the professionals' own
complicity in the consumer society and the deep contradictions
between the equation of professional success with a lifestyle of privatized provisioning. This guilt can absolutely lead to dramatic convictions rooted in the "anti-system radicalism" described in Chapter 3.
Yet this radical politics often has more in common with the austerity
politics that has defined the last several decades than they would like
to admit. I will end this chapter with a brief overview of perhaps the
most elaborate ideological expression of this professional-class politics of less from a radical perspective: degrowth.

---

67   Podcast: "#123 Blow up pipelines? Tadzio Müller and Andreas Malm on what next
for the climate movement," *Dissens Podcast*, May 5, 2021. podcast.dissenspodcast
.de/123-climate.
68   Ulrich Brand and Markus Wissen, *The Imperial Mode of Living: Everyday Life and
the Ecological Crisis of Capitalism* (London: Verso, 2021), xx.

'Revolutionary Austerity?' Degrowth and the Politics of Less.

The professional-class politics of less and carbon guilt is obviously concentrated among those academic professionals who study the ecological crisis, a group I am intimately familiar with. While many of these professionals might explore the "science communicator" or "policy technocrat" types discussed in the previous chapter, some identify *systemic* causes of ecological breakdown and seek more apparently radical solutions. The most popular and growing version of this anti-systemic radicalism is the network of researchers and activists advocating degrowth.

Degrowth, it is important to point out, is overwhelmingly a movement of and for the professional class. A journal's recent special issue devoted to degrowth and socialism rightly asserts, "The degrowth movement attracts primarily middle-class, relatively highly educated whites."[69] One of the movement's main proponents, Aaron Vansintjan, states, "Degrowth is mostly an academic movement, focused on challenging mainstream economics."[70] In a moment of honesty, the editors of a recent volume on degrowth and social movements admit, "Self-critical reflection . . . revealed that most of those active in many of the movements are—at least in Germany—well-educated, middle class, and white."[71]

Historically, the degrowth movement (*décroissance* in French) emerged at the same historical moment in the 1970s marked by a larger shift to neoliberal austerity politics. On the left, degrowth researchers credit André Gorz for coining the term in 1972, asking, "Is the earth's balance, for which no-growth—or even degrowth—of material production is a necessary condition, compatible with the

69   Diego Andreucci and Salvatore Engel-Di Mauro, "Capitalism, socialism and the challenge of degrowth: introduction to the symposium," *Capitalism, Nature, Socialism*, Vol. 30, No. 2 (2019): 176–88; 180.

70   Aaron Vansintjan, "Degrowth vs. the Green New Deal," *Briarpatch Magazine*, April 29, 2019.

71   Ibid., 23.

survival of the capitalist system?"[72] Gorz later emphatically argued an eco-socialism must ultimately focus on a politics of less. "The only way to live better is to produce less, to consume less, to work less, to live differently."[73]

More broadly, however, the roots of degrowth overlapped with the rise of the sub-discipline of ecological economics in the 1970s. In 1971, Nicholas Georgescu-Roegen's *The Entropy Law and the Economic Process* held that modern economies fundamentally derived their abundance from a fixed "stock" of fossil fuel energy. The law of entropy dissipation necessitated the exhaustion of that one-time stock and, with it, Georgescu-Roegen posited, the collapse of modern civilization. In what has later been termed "entropy pessimism," he maintains that resource limits will "knell the death bell of the human species."[74] And, like other critics of the time, he believed the driving force of this imminent doom was excess and affluence provided by fossil fuel energy. "Everything man has done during the last two hundred years or so puts him in the position of a fantastic spendthrift."[75] This argument led to a completely new field that sought to apply the law of thermodynamics to economic analysis, bringing an ecological view to the discipline of economics that ignored ecology through its narrow focus on monetary flows and assumed endless growth.[76] The systems ecology of Eugene and Howard T. Odum, which focused on flows of matter and energy as constraining any living system, also played a key role in shaping the field.[77] Additionally, in the early 2000s ecological economics aligned

72   André Gorz, *Nouvel Observateur*, Paris, 397, June 19, 1972. Proceedings from a public debate organized in Paris by the *Club du Nouvel Observateur*, translation by M. Bosquet.

73   André Gorz, *Ecology as Politics* (Montreal: Black Rose Books, 1975), 68–9.

74   Nicholas Georgescu-Roegen, *The Entropy Law and the Economic Process* (Cambridge, MA: Harvard University Press, 1971), 21. See, Auke Hoekstra, "Tomorrow is good: Entropy pessimism and techno wars" *InnovationOrigins.com*, November 18, 2018.

75   Ibid.

76   See, Timothy Mitchell, *Carbon Democracy: Political Power in the Age of Oil* (London: Verso, 2011), 109–43.

77   Howard T. Odum, *Systems Ecology: An Introduction* (New York: Wiley, 1983).

with rebel scholars in the field of petroleum geology to articulate the notion of "peak oil," or the idea that we would soon run out of oil, as an imminent threat to modern capitalism. (This concern has itself dissipated like so much entropy in the deluge of newly fracked crude.)[78] The global energy crisis of the 1970s, and the accompanying discourse of resource scarcity, lent validation to this budding field. Less apocalyptic, Herman Daly and followers resuscitated classical political economy's notion of a "steady-state" or no-growth economy that could provide an answer to the laws of entropy.[79]

Degrowth emerged out of this stew and, like the wider ecology movement itself, saw modern, fossil fuel–powered *affluence* as the prime cause of impending collapse. Joan Martinez-Alier embraced degrowth and brought ecological economic ideas to a left-Marxist audience, maintaining that "economic growth, especially in the high-consumption countries of the North, is not compatible with environmental sustainability."[80] The French economist Serge Latouche has become a leader of the current movement through his landmark 2009 book, *Farewell to Growth*.[81] Interestingly, his earlier work targeted modern consumer society. His 1991 book *In the Wake of the Affluent Society* took aim at what he called the "consumer society's banquet" of modern economies in the global North.[82] The book came out of his experiences in the developing world; he lived two years in Zaire (part of what he calls "Black Africa"), exposing him to lifestyles quite different from those he knew in France.[83] In the text, he argues that the postwar consumer society emerged from an alliance between labor and capital based on the idea that "bosses and workers could be winners together."[84] In this society, "affluence . . . comes at the premise

78   R.W. Bentley, *Introduction to Peak Oil* (London: Springer, 2016).

79   Herman Daly, *Steady-state Economics* (Washington, DC: Island Press, 1991).

80   Joan Martinez-Alier, "Environmental justice and economic degrowth: An alliance between two movements," *Capitalism, Nature, Socialism*, Vol. 23, No. 1 (2012): 51–73; 63–4.

81   Serge Latouche, *Farewell to Growth* (Cambridge, UK: Polity, 2009).

82   Serge Latouche, *In the Wake of the Affluent Society: An Exploration of Post-Development* (London: Zed, 1991), 3.

83   Ibid., 27–8.

84   Ibid., 58.

of the reduction of the worker-citizen to the status of blind servant to the machine," and overall, "the affluent society, consists . . . of a rather illusory reality."[85]

The other important degrowth work is Tim Jackson's *Prosperity Without Growth*, in which he rails against what he calls the "iron cage of consumerism."[86] For Jackson, the materially comfortable consumer is beset by constant stress and dissatisfaction: "Anxious to escape the work and spend cycle, we are suffering from a 'fatigue with the clutter and waste of modern life' and yearn for certain forms of human interaction that have been eroded."[87] This is precisely the anxiety that besets the professional-class consumer worried about their own participation in privatized provisioning.

It is this anxiety around consumer affluence that underlies the very definitions of degrowth, all of which center the idea of *less*. It is even in the word "degrowth"—the prefix "de" indicates less, or as online dictionary defines the prefix: "used to indicate privation, removal, and separation."[88] A recent compilation defines degrowth as "an equitable downscaling of production and consumption that will reduce societies' throughput of energy and raw materials."[89] Latouche claims the goal of degrowth is to "build a society in which we can live better lives whilst working less and consuming less."[90] Giorgos Kallis argues socialism is compatible with degrowth on one condition: "A socialist democracy should ignore growth and reorganize to produce and consume not only differently, but also *less*."[91] A noted degrowth thinker, Jason Hickel, certainly mindful of accusations that degrowth

---

85   Ibid., 100, 102.

86   Tim Jackson, *Prosperity Without Growth: Foundations for the Economy of Tomorrow* (London: Routledge, 2017), 103.

87   Ibid., 125.

88   See, Dictionary.com. dictionary.com/browse/de.

89   Giorgos Kallis, Federico Demaria, and Giacomo D'Alisa, "Introduction: Degrowth," in Giacomo D'Alisa, Giacomo D'Alisa and Giorgos Kallis (eds.), *Degrowth: A Vocabulary for a New Era* (London: Routledge, 2015), 1–18; 3–4.

90   Latouche, *Farewell*, 9.

91   Giorgos Kallis, "Socialism without growth," *Capitalism, Nature, Socialism*, Vol. 30, No. 2 (2019): 189–206; 204.

means austerity, recently wrote an article titled "Degrowth: a theory of radical abundance."[92] He points to many things any socialist would support—shorter working hours, decommodified housing, and a vision of "public wealth"—but still leads with less in his definition of degrowth as "a planned reduction of the material and energy through-put of the global economy." He later acknowledges that "the economy would produce less as a result, yes—but it would also need much less." Naturally, his new book is titled *Less Is More*.[93]

Much of this literature explicitly calls for austerity and restraint. One offshoot is the "voluntary simplicity" movement, which, of course, assumes a particular class position of who can *volunteer* to live with less as opposed to those who *must*. A chapter in a recent degrowth volume on "Simplicity" hedges, "people at the cultural level must be prepared to give up or resist high consumption 'affluent' lifestyles and instead embrace 'simpler' lifestyles of reduced or restrained consumption.[94] Latouche and Kallis both call for a "rediscovered frugality" and "frugal living," which quite nicely align with the belt-tightening mantras of our austerity age.[95] Kallis explicitly calls for austerity, borrowing from what Eurocommunist Enrico Berlinguer calls "revolutionary austerity."[96] Kallis defines this as "private sobriety" and asks, "What is more revolutionary instead than Gandhi's plea to 'live simply so that others may simply live'?"[97] Note the assumption here, in line with footprint ideology, that lifestyle choices shape the life chances of impoverished others (rather than being shaped by the larger power

92 Jason Hickel, "Degrowth: a theory of radical abundance," *Real World Economics Review*, No. 87 (March 19, 2019): 54–68.

93 Jason Hickel, *Less Is More: How Degrowth Will Save the World*, (London: Penguin, 2020).

94 Samuel Alexander, "Simplicity," in Giacomo D'Alisa, Giacomo D'Alisa, and Giorgos Kallis (eds.), *Degrowth: A Vocabulary for a New Era* (London: Routledge, 2015), 133–36; 135.

95 Serge Latouche, "Can the left escape economism?" *Capitalism, Nature, Socialism*, Vol. 23, No. 1 (2012): 74–8; 77–8; Giorgos Kallis, "The left should embrace degrowth," *New Internationalist*, November 5, 2015.

96 Giorgos Kallis, "Degrowth is utopian, and that's a good thing," Unevenearth.org. unevenearth.org. Last accessed June 3, 2020.

97 Ibid.

structures of capitalism). Although he refuses the degrowth label, Troy Vettese argues in the *New Left Review* for "egalitarian eco-austerity" that aims to divide the less stuff equally. The article advocates turning over half the planet to wild nature (an idea he borrows from the sociobiologist E.O. Wilson), universal veganism, and an abstract plan for global per-capita energy rationing.[98] As Rustin warned in his insistence that "less is less," it is clear that this kind of politics will not attract the masses of working-class people in an increasingly unequal economy. Due to wage stagnation, debt, and the evisceration of social services, most have already given up on the idea of "affluence" and live hand-to-mouth, struggling to afford the basics of life.

Other aspects of degrowth politics also express professional-class values. First, there is the focus on the realm of culture and ideas at the basis of the knowledge economy. As opposed to the antagonistic class politics advocated in Part I, degrowth's core target is not a class, but an ideology: growth. Jackson claims that "growth has been the single most important policy goal across the world for most of the last century,"[99] and Kallis says that growth is the "semi-religious totem of modern societies, capitalist and communist alike."[100] Degrowth theorists understand this particular ideology as even more specific to post-World War II Keynesianism and a set of statistical tools used to measure growth and the Gross Domestic Product. In *More: The Politics of Growth in Postwar America*, Robert Collins explains how policymakers "emphasized growth as both an end in itself, and, more important, a vehicle for achieving a striking variety of other, ideological goals as well."[101]

This fixation on the ideology of growth—what Kallis calls the "growth fetish"[102]—obscures material class realities of who precisely

98   Troy Vettese, "To freeze the Thames: Natural geo-engineering and biodiversity," *New Left Review* 111 (May–June 2018): 63–86.

99   Jackson, *Prosperity*, 9.

100   Giorgos Kallis, *In Defense of Degrowth: Opinions and Minifestos* (Open Commons, 2017), 18.

101   Robert M Collins, *More: The Politics of Growth in Postwar America* (Oxford, UK: Oxford University Press, 2000), xi.

102   Kallis, "Socialism without growth," 203.

benefits from growth. The postwar ideology of growth presents a vision of aggregate societal betterment, a rising tide lifting all boats. But this is not how capitalism works. Capitalism does not require aggregate societal growth, but growth *for capital* (M-C-M'). It is private capital that *controls investment*, the profitability of which will determine whether capital grows and, as a byproduct, hires more people. However, private profits are often best achieved at the expense of workers and the environment. It is true that economists have created all manner of statistical tools to track something called "growth," but this does not mean we live in a society where the owners of the means of production collectively devise strategies to grow the economy. Rather, those strategies are usually devised by politicians who claim to enact "growth" policies—but they fundamentally do *not* control most investment. Meanwhile, GDP growth figures just becomes a proxy to give analysts some sense as to whether or not the capitalists who really run the economy are doing things that might create spillover benefits like jobs or tax revenues. As we have seen since the 2008 financial crisis, we can have quite steady growth along-side wage stagnation and declining labor force participation.[103] The mass of the working class is not really benefiting from growth.

Thus, growth ideology creates the myth of a unified aggregate soci-etal "system" of capitalist growth. To be radical was to be against "the system" as a whole. Whether or not one thinks "growth" is essential or ecologically destructive, the politics of growth or degrowth has little to do with antagonistic struggles *within* these systems. The politics is focused on the aggregate—to grow or not to grow. In other words, the politics of the aggregate is very much an ideological product of the "growth fetish" itself. If growth is just a mystifying ideology, degrowth is its negation.

At times, it becomes clear that degrowth advocates are mostly against uttering the word growth. Kallis goes as far as to say that "socialists should not use the word 'growth' for improvements in

---

103 Bureau of Labor Statistics, "Labor Force Participation Rate." data.bls.gov/timeseries/LNS11300000.

things like health or education."[104] But we actually do want to grow health and education. Such a politics is incapable of articulating how some things really do need to grow (such as clean energy), while some need to degrow (such as the military). More to the point, a class politics would articulate a confrontational approach where the capitalist class must degrow so that the working class can see growth in material security and basic human freedom. The politics of degrowth at the aggregate in the name of ecology refuses this kind of antagonistic class politics where some lose but more gain.

Second, degrowth reproduces the professional class's tendency to blame their own consumption for ecological breakdown. Moreover, they tend to *territorialize* responsibility by aiming at "overconsumption" in the Global North. Since GDP is in fact a national statistical construction, degrowth analysis always claims that the fundamental struggle is not between classes, but between *territorial regions*: "rich" or "high income" countries in the Global North versus countries in the Global South. Hickel consistently frames inequality as between the rich countries in the Global North and the poor countries in the Global South.[105] He asserts that degrowth targets focus on "high-income nations with high levels of per capita consumption."[106] A more recent article explains that "the vast majority of ecological breakdown is being driven by excess consumption in the Global North."[107] There is nothing about "excess profits" in the Global North, or capital's disproportionate ownership power over global production networks. Professional-class politics is fixated on, and guilt-ridden over, the role of consumers in driving "the vast majority of ecological breakdown."

In contrast, understanding inequality in class terms cuts across national territories and recognizes the existence of a globally integrated capitalist class, and of a global working class. So while certainly

---

104   Kallis, "Socialism without growth," 191.
105   See, e.g., Jason Hickel, "Forget 'developing' poor countries, it's time to 'de-develop' rich countries," *Guardian*, September 23, 2015.
106   Hickel, "Degrowth: A theory of radical abundance," 57.
107   Jason Hickel, "What does degrowth mean? A few points of clarification," *Globalizations* (early view, 2020): 1-8; 5.

some rich owners need to degrow in "rich countries" like the United States, the vast majority do not; as we shall see in the next chapter, they have material interests in *growth* in the basics of life like health care, food, transit, and more.

A recent survey found that 66 percent of the US population worries about accessing basic health care[108]—pretty bleak for a so-called "labor aristocracy." Degrowth always calls for reductions of energy consumption in so-called "rich countries" like the United States. But if we actually decarbonize energy, the need for *aggregate* reductions in energy consumption is less obvious. How will a working class that often struggles to pay for basic services like heat and electricity respond to such demands? In the United States, one 2018 report estimated, 31 percent struggle to pay their energy bills.[109]

Third, another key material definition of the professional class is their very separation from the means of production—or, more specifically, their separation from the centrality of industrial production in shaping their modern lives of privatized provisioning. Thus, degrowth politics often posit small-scale non-industrial "alternatives" like urban gardens and artisanal production. Such an approach to politics avoids large-scale organization or visions of change more common to working-class or socialist politics. In one essay, Kallis explains the type of alternatives degrowth has on offer: "food production in urban gardens; co-housing and ecocommunes; alternative food networks, producer-consumer cooperatives, and communal kitchens; health care, elder care, and child care cooperatives; open software; and decentralized forms of renewable energy production and distribution."[110] Once again, it strains credulity as to how these small-scale alternatives will attract popular support from the masses of struggling working people without the time to devote to these labor-intensive activities. Kallis does suggest the need for broader social

108   Megan Leonhardt, "66% of Americans fear they won't be able to afford health care this year," CNBC.com, January 5, 2021.

109   Energy Information Administration, "One in three US households faces a challenge in meeting energy needs," September 19, 2018.

110   Giorgos Kallis, *In Defense of Degrowth*, 23.

policies like universal basic income and a job guarantee, but offers no strategy on how to win such programs. A more recent intervention on degrowth and the state from Giacomo D'Alisa and Kallis begins with the alarming premise that degrowth had barely asked the question of how to engage with state power (largely because of ideological affinities with anarchism).[111] In line with much of the New Left focus on culture and knowledge, they suggest that degrowth politics can win state power through "a cultural change of common senses."[112] They argue *participation* in degrowth alternatives will slowly build a new "common sense" and hegemony for degrowth:

> Alternative food networks, open software communities or solidarity practices such as popular health clinics change the common sense of participants and allow them to imagine different knowledge, health care, or education systems. Participants and those who experience these projects become then a potential base for articulating social demands for changing political institutions (e.g. intellectual copyright, or welfare provision) to support their projects.

Under this formulation, simply opening up degrowth alternatives to vaguely defined "participants" will somehow catalyze wider movements for "social demands." That all the participants, including the authors, come from the same minority professional class position does not enter the strategic equation.

A new volume, *Degrowth in Movement(s)*, calls degrowth movements a "mosaic of alternatives as a heterogeneous collective actor,"[113] but the nature and effects of this actor are never delineated. In the introduction, the authors describe the wide range of aligned

111 Giacomo D'Alisa and Giorgos Kallis, "Degrowth and the state," *Ecological Economics*, Vol. 169 (2020): 1-9.

112 Ibid., 7.

113 This is just a fancy way of describing the not particularly successful "movement of movements" approach reviewed in Chapter 1. Corinna Burkhart, Matthias Schmelzer, and Nina Treu, *Degrowth in Movement(s): Exploring Pathways for Transformation* (London: Zero Books, 2020), 9.

movements, "from the anti-globalization or climate justice movements to movements and alternatives such as commons, Buen Vivir,
food sovereignty, non-profit cooperatives, the care revolution, free
software, DIY repair workshops, basic income or transition towns."[114]
I would note the absence of "labor," "working-class party," or "trade
union" among the movements listed here, but the compilation does
devote one chapter to the trade union movement, squeezed between
chapters on transition towns and urban gardening.[115] The thrust of
the trade union chapter focuses on how unions must adapt to a new
politics where "changing one's way of life is of central importance."[116]
The chapter views trade unions simply as one part of the "mosaic,"
insisting that they must be part of a "socio-political player" in "cooperation with civil society actors."[117] Never once do the authors mention
that workers and unions might have their own unique form of social
power that could force societal change, unlike other "actors."

The volume offers no theory of how these movements will themselves build power. All of them aim to present "prefigurative" examples
of a world beyond capitalism but suggest little in the way of strategy for
how to confront and overcome the power of the capitalist class that
currently controls all the things we need to live. In alignment with
other perspectives on "changing the world without taking power," the
authors only highlight the movements' capacity for "criticism of power
and domination" and "resistance" that "start building alternatives in
the cracks of capitalism and power."[118] As such, their strategy mostly
takes aim *not* at production and class owners, but at our *mode of living*,
or lifestyle. They describe their project as one of " 'deprivilegization' of
those who currently live at the expense of others and externalize those
costs in space and time."[119] This simple statement combines the

---

114   Ibid., 11.
115   Ibid., 319–20.
116   Ibid., 322.
117   Ibid., 328, 329.
118   Ibid., 20, 22, 24–5; John Holloway, *Change the World Without Taking Power: The
Meaning of Revolution Today* (New York: Pluto Books, 2002).
119   Ibid., 12.

professional-class commitment to "cost internalization" reviewed in Chapter 3 and a politics of less reviewed in this chapter.

* * *

The main problem: the politics of less is bad strategy. In her own critique of degrowth's need to take class more seriously, Stefania Barca succinctly describes the political "subject" of the degrowth movement as an "ecologically minded global middle class willing to reduce consumerism and work-addiction, and/or to engage in direct action to express its disappointment with economic/environmental policies."[120] Yet, she suggests, if degrowth remains fixed in this class milieu it will fail:

> But this approach will remain politically weak unless it manages to enter into dialogue with a broadly defined global working class including both wage labor and the myriad forms of work that support it— and its organizations.[121]

For advocates of degrowth to win their agenda, they need to challenge the power of capital over investment. Such a movement would have to emerge out of our current society marked by gilded-age levels of inequality, where very few have quite a lot, but the masses struggle to meet their basic needs. It is not clear how a political program whose overarching narrative *leads with less* will appeal to the vast majority of society who already struggle on a daily level. But as this chapter has argued, it is entirely clear that this politics of less *does appeal* to a professional-class fraction guilty about its participation in middle-class lifestyles of privatized provisioning. As Rustin pointedly put it, "One suspects that there is a certain class disdain at work in the anguished cries over materialism."[122] For the professional class, the

---

120   Stefania Barca, "The labor(s) of degrowth," *Capitalism Nature Socialism*, Vol 30, No. 2 (2019): 207–16; 214.

121   Ibid.

122   Rustin, "No growth has to mean less is less."

politics of less speaks directly to anxieties about the contradictions between middle-class "security" and ecological collapse.

Conclusion: The Man and His Donkey

Let me end with an example that beautifully illustrates the strategic dead end of professional-class degrowth politics. Kallis explains the case of François Schneider:

> François Schneider, instigator of the international conferences and founder of the Research & Degrowth thinktank in Paris (now in Barcelona), embodies degrowth's hybridity: a PhD graduate in industrial ecology, he walked for a year with a donkey around France explaining degrowth to passers-by who stopped him bewildered. He lives now in Can Decreix, a bare-basics house on the French-Catalan border, a center of experimentation and education in frugal living.[123]

A Ph.D. with a donkey living in a tiny "bare basics" home! Kallis's observation that passers-by were "bewildered" by this specimen is not surprising. It is hard to imagine most workers, struggling to afford housing and transportation, concluding that donkeys, tiny homes, and "frugal living" are the answer. An image attached to a website describing his journey through France (claiming he marched alongside 500 people by the end) shows a picture of a man extremely familiar to those of us accustomed to professional-class practices of what Pierre Bourdieu called distinction.[124] He wears a very nice waterproof rain jacket and sturdy, well-made hiking boots, and the unshaven stubble and scraggly hair familiar to most graduate programs. No surprise that rural villagers were bewildered by this obviously highly educated professional walking through their town with an ass!

---

123   Giorgos Kallis, *In Defense of Degrowth*, 30.
124   Pierre Bourdieu, *Distinction: A Social Critique of the Judgement of Taste* (London: Routledge, 1984).

This is not a politics that can win. Not only would it "bewilder" most working-class people; it appears actively *antagonistic* to their interests, impelling them to consume less and live in even tinier homes than they currently do. This aligns precisely with the antagonism the Ehrenreichs identified between the PMC and the working class. In the context of the neoliberal assault on the global working class, degrowth and climate politics only appear as yet two more imperatives to "do more with less."

The masses of people without college or advanced professional degrees are likely aware of the ongoing climate crisis, but the standard messages of degrowth and austerity have no resonance with them. To win these masses, we need a new language of climate politics that does not concentrate on less. What would a climate politics of *more*, aligned with the material interests of the working class, look like?

III

The Working Class

5
Proletarian Ecology: Working-Class Interests and the Struggle for a Green New Deal

Introduction: "that Green New Deal thing"

Rhiana Gunn-Wright: If people like a policy, they understand how it works, they rely on it, it becomes very difficult to [repeal] . . .

Jason Bordoff (host): It may be harder to make that point for environmental protection because the ways in which it comes and goes are less visible to people.

Rhiana Gunn-Wright: Yes, but if you're connecting it to jobs and other things that people understand and realize that this is part of that Green New Deal thing, I want that to pass; it's bringing in jobs and now I have different health care, and they understand its packaged together.

—from the February 9, 2019, episode of the podcast *Columbia Energy Exchange*, "The Green New Deal: Rhianna Gunn-Wright."

Introduction

Gunn-Wright was one of the key architects of the Green New Deal for the left policy think tank New Consensus.[1] In this podcast exchange with Jason Bordoff, the director of the Center on Global Energy Policy, Gunn-Wright suggests a key strategy of the Green New Deal is to appeal to basic material interests in building popular support.

This exchange stuck with me because it hits at a longstanding problem of environmental and climate politics. Bordoff's core assumption is that environmental politics are "less visible to people." This is an entrenched idea that assumes climate change is an "abstract" global

---

1   newconsensus.com.

biogeochemical process, with dispersed effects in space and time—and that reducing emissions would somehow go unrecognized. People would not notice the *lack* of catastrophic floods, hurricanes, and fires should we succeed with a mass decarbonization program.

Because of this disjuncture between lived experience and environmental gains, many assume the key way to build support is through environmental education and awareness. On the fiftieth anniversary of Earth Day, Michael Moore and Jeff Gibbs released the highly controversial film *Planet of the Humans*. At the climax of the film, Gibbs rehearses one of the oldest tropes in environmental politics: "I truly believe that the path to change comes from awareness; that awareness alone can begin to create the transformation." If people understood the extent of our planetary ruin in scientific terms, they would undoubtedly take action. I spent Part II explaining the pitfalls inherent in the professional-class focus on *knowledge* as the terrain of climate struggle. I will spend this chapter elaborating Gunn-Wright's wager that climate politics should appeal to people's basic material interests.

Notice that Gunn-Wright implies that the *appeal* of a Green New Deal will not be complicated; it won't even require an explanation of the greenhouse effect. It will be intuitively appealing simply as "that Green New Deal thing." Imagine "that thing" hiring your uncle to build new transmission lines . . . "that thing" delivering housing as a human right . . . "that thing," which does *not* mean higher cost energy, delivering cheaper or even free electricity for all.

I argue that this kind of climate strategy requires resurrecting the long-discarded notion that the working class has objective material interests. Although we typically ascribe working-class interests in a purely "economic" register (workers want higher wages and more benefits), my goal is to extend the notion of material interests into a broader ecological framework. As Geoff Mann says, the very notion of "interest" is oriented toward *the future*, like the climate problem itself: "To have an interest is precisely to be concerned with something to come."[2]

---

2 Geoff Mann, *Our Daily Bread: Wages, Workers, and the Political Economy of the American West* (Chapel Hill, NC: University of North Carolina Press, 2007), 152.

The challenge is to convince masses of people that they have a material interest in restructuring production to make possible a livable planetary future. Humanity as a whole appears to possess an "interest" in solving climate change. German Green Party intellectual Rudolf Bahro, for instance, argued that green politics means constructing a universal "species interest."[3] Others have argued ecological interest-formation will emerge from the concrete nature of struggles over the environment itself. Bue Rübner Hansen argues that "[under] conditions of atmospheric suffocation"—ecological interests could emerge around a "universal right to breathe."[4] Stefania Barca recounts a story of communist activists in Italy trying to mobilize workers at a dangerous industrial plant by using a "class ecology" approach, "centered on industrial pollution as the most compelling and politically relevant aspect of the environmental crisis and on working-class people as its primary victim."[5] Alas, these activists soon found that their efforts were "met with the unexpected opposition of working-class people."[6] Disillusioned, one leader of the "class ecology" approach concluded that the workers were unable to adapt to environmental politics. The leader claimed the workers did not realize that "to have a healthy environment, it is necessary to sacrifice something." Given these efforts emerged in the 1970s, the turn to a politics of less is unsurprising.

While most continue to assume environmental interests will emerge from direct *concrete experience* of environmental problems themselves, working-class survival is most imperiled by the *abstract domination* of the market and access to money and commodities.[7] Gunn-Wright's and my wager is a working-class interest in ecology will emerge not from the *experience* of environmental threats, but from a profound *separation* from nature and the means of

3 Rudolph Bahro, *Socialism and Survival* (London: Heretic Books, 1982), 65.

4 Bue Rübner Hansen, "The interest of breathing: Towards a theory of ecological interest formation," *Crisis and Critique*, Vol. 7, No. 3 (2020): 109–37; 134, 135.

5 Stefania Barca, "Laboring the Earth: Transnational reflections on the environmental history of work," *Environmental History*, Vol. 19, No. 1 (2014): 3–27; 13.

6 Ibid., 14.

7 Moishe Postone, *Time, Labor and Social Domination: A Reinterpretation of Marx's Critical Theory* (Cambridge, UK: Cambridge University Press, 1993).

subsistence. I will show that the very classical definition of the proletariat is a class of people dispossessed of the means of production and forced to survive via the market.

This definition implies that the working class is alienated from the natural conditions of life itself. The fact that the working class must secure its life via the market creates high levels of stress and insecurity. I will argue that this terrain of life, which is by definition ecological, is the proper field through which to construct *ecological interests* that aim to simultaneously deliver more secure access to the basics of survival and restructure production to ensure the survival of all life on the planet. Unlike the politics of less reviewed in Chapter 4, I argue that we should appeal to a working-class interest in *more*—specifically, more access to the elements of a secure life.

Who Is the Working Class?

A thorny question overhanging this entire book is, of course, *who is the working class?* It is important not to get into a classificatory or locational scheme based purely on occupational status. Class is a *relationship* of ownership and power. As Michael Zweig points out, a plumber who owns their own business is in an entirely different class than a waged plumber working for a larger company.[8] I rely on Marx's definition neatly summarized by Kim Moody: "As they possess no means of production, must sell their labor power, work more hours than covers their wages, and work under the rule of capital, they are working class."[9]

The key reason not to include the professional class in this definition is their relative autonomy at the workplace. Although Moody points out many professional occupations are proletarianizing, it is not at all clear whether we can describe lawyers, doctors, or college professors as working "under the rule of capital." And, as stated earlier,

---

8   Michael Zweig, *The Working Class Majority: America's Best Kept Secret* (Ithaca, NY: Cornell University Press, 2011), 29.

9   Kim Moody, *On New Terrain: How Capital Is Reshaping the Battleground of the Class War* (Chicago: Haymarket, 2017), 21.

Moody's definition includes not only 63 percent of the employed population in the United States, but also the "nonworking spouses, dependents, relatives, [and] the unemployed" who rely on the money flowing from waged work and social services paid out of capital.[10] In the end, Moody suggests that this class encompasses "three-quarters of the population—the overwhelming majority."[11]

What kinds of employed workers compose the 63 percent, according to Moody? He draws from Hal Draper's concentric-ring model of the working class, with the core (34 percent) in industrial and manual forms of work: material production, transport, construction, and maintenance.[12] This includes everything from bakers and butchers to roofers and factory workers; construction workers and laundry workers; auto mechanics and farmers. The next ring comprises "service" workers (28 percent), which includes everything from line cooks, security guards, building maintenance workers, and child-care workers. The final and largest ring comprises "sales and office" workers (38 percent): retail workers, advertising agents, office secretaries and clerks, bank tellers, and call-center workers.

As we have seen, in modern capitalism education plays a central role in establishing stark divides in the labor market. Moody's "objective" definition is important, but the divide between professional and working class is largely subjective. Ralph Miliband argued that the working class should be seen both "at the lower ends of the income scale, and also at the lower ends of what might be called the 'scale of regard.'"[13] We cannot understate the role of higher education in these more cultural, subjective, and increasingly *political* divisions. The latest data in the United States shows that of the population over 25 years of age, 10 percent lacks a high school degree and 28 percent has only a high school degree.

---

10   Ibid., 41.

11   Ibid.

12   Stats are from Moody's table on p. 40. Hal Draper, *Karl Marx's Theory of Revolution, Vol. 3: The Politics of Social Classes* (New York: Monthly Review Press, 1978), 35–8.

13   Ralph Miliband, *Marxism and Politics* (Oxford, UK: Oxford University Press, 1977), 24.

Perhaps the most telling number: 15.7 percent of the population have "some college but no degree."[14] This group of 34.7 million Americans tried to navigate the competitive cultural milieu of higher education and either failed or gave up. Add the 10 percent with associate's degrees—a shorter and often more technical type of post–high school degree—and we reach Moody's 63 percent calculation for the working class almost exactly.[15]

These educational divisions create real barriers to working-class life in the labor market, but they also play out in everyday life. This goes to the core of what Barbara and John Ehrenreich identified as a real "antagonism" between the professional-managerial class (PMC) and the working class:

> We should add, at this point, that the antagonism between the PMC and the working class does not exist only in the abstract realm of "objective" relations, of course. Real-life contacts between the two classes express directly, if sometimes benignly, the relation of control which is at the heart of the PMC–working class relation: teacher and student (or parent), manager and workers, social worker and client, etc. The subjective dimension of these contacts is a complex mixture of hostility and deference on the part of working-class people, contempt and paternalism on the part of the PMC.[16]

To the extent that some social workers and teachers might subjectively show contempt for their working-class clients and students, the working class also has good reason to return it with equal vigor. Going back to the 15 percent of the population who tried but failed to get a college degree, this antagonism is visible directly between these individuals and their professors submitting failing grades. The way in which the

---

14   Accessed at, United States Census Bureau. "Educational Attainment in the United States: 2019." census.gov.

15   There is no perfect overlap between the non–college educated population and the working class—only a rough estimate of the *vast majority* of society regardless of how you count them.

16   Barbara Ehrenreich and John Ehrenreich, "The professional-managerial class," in Pat Walker (ed.), *Between Labor and Capital* (Boston: South End Press, 1979), 5–45; 17.

right wing has been able to equate the professional class with a coastal, snobby "liberal elite" is one of the primary means by which it won over some sections of the working class to the conservative side.[17]

More important for the ecological understanding of the working class is that it faces material struggles to meet the basic needs of life. Many believed that the short, and exceptional, period of rising working-class wages and social democratic redistributive policies in the postwar era disproved Marx's so called "immiseration" thesis.[18] This period is clearly over, especially in the United States. A recent study by the Brookings Institution found that 44 percent of the US labor force ages 18–64 are "low-wage" workers.[19] The Brookings analysis calculates that these nearly 53 million people "earn median hourly wages of $10.22 and median annual earnings of $17,950."[20] Almost unimaginably, 30 percent of low-wage workers live below 150 percent of the official poverty line.

The Brookings figures roughly correspond to a heavily circulated 2018 Federal Reserve study that showed 40 percent of Americans did not have savings to cover a $400 emergency expense.[21] (This was actually the best finding in years—it had been 50 percent in 2013.) But even the 40 percent overall figure conceals deep inequalities within the working class: the number is 58 percent for black and 48 percent for Hispanic Americans with a high school education or less.[22]

The bulk of these workers live "paycheck to paycheck"—one 2017 study found that figure to be an astonishing 78 percent.[23] Another

17   Steve Fraser, *The Limousine Liberal: How an Incendiary Image United the Right and Fractured America* (New York: Basic Books, 2016).

18   See, Aaron Benanav and John Clegg, "Crisis and Immiseration: Critical Theory Today," in Beverley Best, Werner Bonefeld, and Chris O'Kane (eds.), *The SAGE Handbook of Frankfurt School Critical Theory* (Thousand Oaks, CA: SAGE, 2018), 1629–48.

19   Martha Ross and Nicole Bateman, *Meet the Low-Wage Workforce* (Washington, DC: Brookings Institution, 2019).

20   Ibid., 9.

21   Federal Reserve, "Report on the Economic Well-Being of US Households in 2018—May 2019." federalreserve.gov.

22   Ibid.

23   CareerBuilder.com, "Living Paycheck to Paycheck is a Way of Life for Majority of US Workers, According to New CareerBuilder Survey." press.careerbuilder.com. Last accessed June 8, 2020.

study, conducted in 2019, found this number at 59 percent—still remarkably high and roughly correspondent to Moody's 63 percent of workers that constitute the working class.[24]

At the time of this writing, these alarming trends on economic insecurity have only worsened given the Covid-19 pandemic and the ensuing collapse of the labor market. As of October 2021, the US unemployment rate is at 4.8 percent after peaking at 14.4 percent in April 2020.[25] Concealed in this apparently rosy figure is the fact that over 3 million people have simply dropped out of the workforce since February 2020.[26] A recent Marketplace-Edison Research Survey on economic security reports that 44 percent of Americans over 18 are worried they will not be able to afford food and groceries.[27] As markets collapsed for basic food commodities, farmers across the country dumped milk down the drain or plowed under perfectly good, harvestable crops.[28]

Meanwhile, one of the starkest images of the pandemic is the thousands of individuals or cars lined up at food banks across the country. In May 2020, the *Financial Times* reported that food banks across the United States showed a 70 percent increase in demand, with some regions hit even harder.[29] In Florida, crushed by the collapse of tourism and restaurant and hospitality services, requests for food aid were up "400–500 percent."[30] Despite the abundance on farms, charities are running out of food to distribute to the poor. It is clear at a very basic level that the working class is a class that struggles to live.

24   Charles Schwab, "Modern Wealth Survey" (May 2019). schwab.com. Last accessed June 8, 2020.

25   US Bureau of Labor Statistics, data.bls.gov/timeseries/LNS14000000.

26   US Bureau of Labor Statistics. bls.gov/charts/employment-situation/civilian-employment.htm.

27   Janet Nguyen, "Here's how the Covid-19 pandemic has affected Americans' paychecks and working hours," marketplace.org. Last accessed June 8, 2020.

28   Matt Huber, "Covid-19 shows why we must socialize the food system," *Jacobin*, April 17, 2020.

29   Courtney Weaver, "America's hungry turn to food banks as unemployment rises," *Financial Times*, May 16, 2020.

30   Ibid.

The Ecology of Working-Class Formation

As reviewed in Chapter 1, there is actually little discussion in ecological Marxism on the centrality of the working class to politics. Because theorists like André Gorz and Ted Benton assumed ecological politics was distinct from class politics, the question of the working class could be set aside. Nevertheless, Marx's theory of the working class is inherently ecological; ecology is, after all, the study of *life* in all its relationships. The key ecological equation for any species is how that species survives through its consumption of energy and production of wastes.

Marx and Engels also define the working class in terms of what it must do to live or survive. Engels described it as "the class of modern wage-laborers who, having no means of production of their own, are reduced to selling their labor power in order to live."[31] While most equate the "means of production" with tools and machines, the most important means of production is and has always been land. As Marx explained, the commodification of labor power required displacing the producers from the land: "The immediate producer, the worker, could dispose of his own person only after he had ceased to be bound to the soil."[32] Marx's theory of primitive accumulation is a violent story of dispossessing the masses from the land through the privatization of property and the enclosure of the commons: "the great feudal lords . . . created an incomparably larger proletariat by forcibly driving the peasantry from the land . . . and by usurpation of the common lands."[33] Only by divorcing the working class from the land, or what Barca describes as "turning commoners into proletarians," is the working class forced to sell labor power for access to the means of subsistence.[34]

---

31 Karl Marx and Frederick Engels, *The Communist Manifesto* (London: Pluto, 2008), 33.

32 Marx, *Capital*, Vol. 1, 875.

33 Ibid., 878.

34 Stefania Barca, *Forces of Reproduction: Notes for a Counter-Hegemonic Anthropocene* (Cambridge, UK: Cambridge University Press, 2020), 42.

We are so fully subsumed in capitalist logics that we do not stop to reflect on the historical novelty of this arrangement. For the first time in human history, increasing masses of the population gain their living not from the land, but from money and access to commodities—the market. This is what I call *proletarian ecology*.[35] This basic fact of survival means that a defining feature of proletarian life under capitalism is profound alienation from the ecological conditions of life itself. Even the most oppressed classes throughout human history typically gained at least part of their living from the land.[36] It is different for the proletarian masses. Paul Burkett explains how money fundamentally abstracts from the differential qualities of the natural world: "Since money is the social form of people-nature relations, its dequalification of nature also tends to denaturalize human individuality in an alienating (externalized) fashion."[37] Moreover, since the working class is what Marx called the "immense majority" of the population, this also means we live in a society where most people have no connection to or knowledge of the ecological conditions of life.[38] I want to emphasize that we cannot confine this ecological definition of the working class—as *separated* from the conditions of life—to only "wage workers," let alone industrial factory workers. It refers to the masses who rely on the market to survive.[39] For example, Mike Davis provocatively argues that we must characterize late-twentieth

35   There is increasing focus on working-class environmentalism, but the focus on *proletarian* retains a definitional focus on separation from the means of production (most importantly the land). See, Stefania Barca and Emanuele Leonardi, "Working-class ecology and union politics: a conceptual topology," *Globalizations*, Vol 15, No. 4 (2018): 487–503; Karen Bell, *Working-Class Environmentalism: An Agenda for a Just and Fair Transition to Sustainability* (Cham, Switzerland: Palgrave Macmillan, 2020); and Daniel Aldana Cohen, "The big picture: Working-class environmentalism," *Public Books*, November 16, 2017.

36   Ellen Meiksins Wood highlights the *market dependence* of both capitalists and labor alike as the defining characteristic of capitalism. *The Origin of Capitalism: A Longer View* (London: Verso, 2002).

37   Paul Burkett, "Value, capital and nature: Some ecological implications of Marx's critique of political economy." *Science and Society*, Vol. 60, No. 3 (1996): 332–59; 343.

38   Marx and Engels, *Communist Manifesto*, 50.

39   This would mean even we professionals are *ecologically* working class. As I reviewed in Chapter 4, it is anxiety over their relative *bounty* of privatized provisioning through the market that yields professional carbon guilt.

and early-twenty-first-century capitalism as consisting not of primarily the waged proletariat, but primarily the "informal proletariat"—the millions of small petty producers and traders that make up the "planet of slums."[40] Nevertheless, whether formally employed or not, these masses are *also* severed from the means of production and rely on the market to survive.

It is not only that the working class is alienated from its life conditions; it also lacks control over the means of life. Following Ellen Meiksins Wood, both capitalists and wage workers rely on the market for their reproduction, and they are both alienated from nature in significant ways.[41] But, the difference is one of power. As Michael Zweig clearly lays out, class is ultimately about *power*: "A relative handful of people have great power to organize and direct production, while a much larger number have almost no authority."[42]

When thinking about ecology, the working class experiences this lack of power in two ways. First, working-class life is a struggle for the basics of existence. All individuals, including workers, are ecological beings that require food, housing, health care, and more to survive. Under capitalism, nothing guarantees these basic aspects of life. The earliest forms of Marxist thought insist that capitalism creates *insecurity* for the mass of people. In the classic Marxist "Erfurt Program" of the Social Democratic Party of Germany, this stood at the core of their understanding of the working class: "For the proletariat and the sinking middle class—petty bourgeoisie and farmers—it means an increase in the insecurity of their existence, of misery, of pressure, of oppression, of degradation, of exploitation."[43] It is remarkable, and depressing, that this remains the case—only today, the "sinking middle class" is not farmers, but the college-educated debtor class.

---

40 Mike Davis, *Old Gods, New Enigmas: Marx's Lost Theory* (London: Verso, 2018), xvii.

41 Meiksins Wood, *The Origin of Capitalism*.

42 Zweig, *The Working Class Majority*, 3.

43 The Erfurt Program 1891. marxists.org/history/international/social-democracy/ 1891/erfurt-program.htm.

Second, the working class not only lacks control over what it needs as individuals, but also over the larger socioecological "metabolism."[44] This lack of control over material production itself is what leads to the specific experience of powerlessness over the ecological crisis today, of watching an unfolding disaster caused by seemingly distant and uncontrollable forces. Whether we see these as abstract "market" forces or the corporate elite, the lack of *control* over the processes of ecological degradation creates feelings of helplessness in the face of planetary crisis.

To summarize: we can define working-class life under capitalism as alienation from and lack of control over the ecological conditions of existence. While the working class experiences its lack of control over its own lived needs on an immediate experiential level, its lack of control over the entire socioecological metabolism is not necessarily apparent. The typical professional-class approach to climate politics is to take this second problem as the reason why knowledge and education are central to the struggle. But what if we tried to forge a politics that connected these two issues on the terrain of a "politics of life"?

An Ecological Theory of Material Interests Under Capitalism

It used to be relatively uncontroversial in Marxist thought to see capitalism as structured through a core set of conflicting and objective material interests between capitalists and the working class. Marx asserts that "even the most favorable situation for the working class . . . does not abolish the antagonism between his interests and the interests of the capitalist."[45] In his theoretical outline of Marxist politics, Karl Kautsky declared in sweeping terms, "In all lands where capitalist production prevails the interests of the working-class are identical."[46]

---

44 See, John Bellamy Foster, Brett Clark, and Richard York, *The Ecological Rift: Capitalism's War on the Earth* (New York: Monthly Review Press, 2010).

45 Karl Marx, *Wage Labor and Capital* (Cabin John, MD: Wildside Press, 2008), 39.

46 Karl Kautsky, *The Class Struggle (Erfurt Program)* (Chicago: Charles H. Kerr and Co., 1910), 159.

These interests emerge directly from the relations of production under capitalism; workers not only face exploitation in the process of production, they also lack secure access to the basics of life. This want of access forces them back to the site of exploitation on a daily basis.

In the same period, capital mounted an offensive against the working class, many social theorists of the 1970s and '80s decided that this theory of objective interests was problematic. In the most influential articulation of this argument, Ernesto Laclau and Chantal Mouffe claimed the very notion of "objective interests . . . lacks any theoretical basis whatsoever, and involves little more than an arbitrary attribution of interests."[47] They even go so far as to suggest that such a formulation leads to authoritarianism: "A vanguard that continues to identify with the 'objective interests of the working class' . . . gives rise . . . to an increasingly authoritarian practice of politics."[48] They contend that any political movement that presumes to know the "real" interests of the working class will subvert the masses' "democratically" articulated interests.

This critique takes us back to the debates over whether or not it makes sense to distinguish between a "class in itself" versus a "class for itself," or between objective class location and subjective experience of class. Adam Przeworski also finds a notion of objective class interests wanting in that it ignores that class formation itself is an "outcome of ideological and political struggles."[49] He asserts, "Classes are not prior to political and ideological practice."[50] Following Poulantzas and Gramsci, Przeworski outlines a "class struggle" theory that internalizes subjective political and ideological factors into the "objective" determinants of class.

This is attractive because it makes class politics more applicable to actual "real" political articulations of class interests. Yet, it leaves hanging how to think about *material* interests in light of this revision. Is the

47 Ernesto Laclau and Chantal Mouffe, *Hegemony and Socialist Strategy* (London: Verso, 1985), 83.
48 Ibid., 56.
49 Adam Przeworski, *Capitalism and Social Democracy* (Cambridge, UK: Cambridge University Press, 1985), 69.
50 Ibid., 70.

"material" subsumed in the "political and ideological" factors Przeworski seeks to fold into the objective determinants of class? Ellen Meiksins Wood, something of a voice in the wilderness in the neoliberal 1980s, strongly defended the idea of objective material interests as necessary to a Marxist, i.e., *materialist* approach: "If the proposition that 'interests' do not exist independently of their modes of representation . . . we are in the realm of absolute idealism, where nothing exists but Idea."[51] It seems that the entire project of historical materialism rests on a grounding of class analysis in the material structure of production, apart from the political and ideological consciousness of it. As Raju Das puts it, "Relative independence of class structure from class consciousness is foundational for a materialist theory of class."[52] A materialist analysis of capitalism does not guarantee a mass working-class movement. It seems quite understandable that in a moment of profound working-class defeat, a chorus of academics concluded that the very notion of Marxist class politics was the problem.

Marx and Engels's classic articulation of the materialist approach says it clearly: "Life involves before everything else eating and drinking, a habitation, clothing and many other things. The first historical act is thus the production of the means to satisfy these needs, the production of material life itself."[53] Again, ecology is also the study of "life itself." Thus, one could argue that when we say " 'materialist' approach to history" we actually suggest an *ecological* approach that understands human society as inextricably bound to the reproduction of the human species.[54] In fact, later in the *German Ideology*, Marx and Engels accuse the German idealists of lacking an "*earthly* basis for history."[55]

---

51 Ellen Meiksins Wood, *The Retreat from Class: A New 'True' Socialism* (London: Verso, 1986), 95.

52 Raju Das, "From labor geography to class geography: Reasserting the Marxist theory of class," *Human Geography*, Vol. 5. No. 1 (2012): 19–35; 25.

53 Karl Marx and Frederick Engels, *The German Ideology* (New York: International, 1970), 48.

54 Ted Benton makes this same point. "Marxism and natural limits: An ecological critique and reconstruction. *New Left Review* I/178 (November/December 1989): 51–86; 54.

55 Ibid., 49.

Insofar as these material needs are biological, they are unavoidable—they are *objective*. This does not mean that social needs are objective. Marx and others have always insisted that needs are socially and culturally constituted.[56] Yet we must meet some base material needs if society is to reproduce itself. It is this material base—what Engels described as "the production and reproduction of immediate life"[57]—that a materialist perspective believes is primary if not determinative over a cultural and ideological superstructure in any analysis.[58]

Moreover, we can also posit that the material social relations of control and power over the means of life are similarly objective. I may wish for free access to available food—like any other species can. Indeed, analysis shows repeatedly that there is "objectively" an abundance of food in the world, more than enough to feed approximately 1.5 times the 7.8 billion people living on the planet.[59] Yet, there are also very real material barriers to this access rooted in the relations of production, property, and social power: securitized stores, police, and a dispersed network of privatized farms producing for profit. Materially objective systems of power also control the provision of energy, housing, transportation, and all the other basics of life, restricting access with the goal of generating returns for private owners.

These systems of control and restricted access are a kind of human ecology, as real as ecological barriers for all kinds of species. For example, warming waters have allowed for the spread of an oyster-killing pathogen, *Perkinsus marinus*, that has decimated oyster

---

56   See Agnes Heller, *The Theory of Need in Marx* (London: Verso, 1974).

57   Frederick Engels "Engels to J. Bloch in Königsberg," (September 21, 1890). marxists.org. Last accessed June 9, 2020.

58   I also think it is a mistake to confuse this material base with "the economic" under capitalism. As Engels's formulation suggests, and as many Marxist feminists have confirmed, the *reproduction* of life under capitalism contains many social processes not contained in the pure realm of the economic (i.e., markets).

59   Eric Holt-Gimenez, "We already grow enough food for 10 billion people -- and still can't end hunger" *Huffington Post*, May 2, 2012.

fisheries.[60] As oysters face the material constraints of a deadly pathogen, so humans face a severe scarcity of food in daily life (as many as 30 million in the United States, according to the Census Bureau).[61] Both kinds of material constraints can be lethal to the organisms involved.

Under capitalism, the vast majority of the population faces restricted access to the necessities of life. Thus it should not be controversial to say that the working class has an objective material interest in expanding access to them—indeed, that the working class has an interest in disrupting or even dismantling the material systems of power the capitalist class wields over sectors like food, housing, energy, and transportation. For good reason, Marxists tend to locate working-class interests at the point of production, where capital so clearly exploits and dominates.

Yet the ecology of working-class life is more about the means of *reproduction*—the ways in which workers reproduce their lives as biological beings outside the workplace.[62] And, because the working class must rely on the market to provision their needs, life is beset by various forms of stress, anxiety, and unfreedom wholly contingent upon their financial situation. We also need to build working-class power at the point of production (as reviewed in the next two chapters), but working-class ecological interests are about social reproduction outside the workplace (or the ecological realm of 'life' as opposed to 'work').

Debates over environmental politics rarely discuss "interests" in this way. Most importantly, as discussed in Chapter 1, most thinkers put environmental "interests" in opposition to working-class interests. This is because environmental movements often oppose various kinds of industrial development that employ workers. Thus, environmentalism can be portrayed as a threat to *some* working-class lives.

---

60   Newsweek, "A hot zone for disease" *Newsweek* July 2, 2002.

61   Dakin Andone, "Nearly 30 million Americans told the Census Bureau they did not have enough to eat last week," CNN, July 31, 2020.

62   See, Nancy Fraser, "Behind Marx's hidden abode," *New Left Review* 86 (March–April 2014): 55–72, and Barca, *Forces of Reproduction*.

Secondly, as reviewed in Part II, professional-class environmental politics so often advocates a "politics of less": of limits, increased taxes, less consumption, etc. For a working-class person struggling to meet the basic needs of life, this kind of politics can seem preposterous.

Thirdly, environmentalism itself is its own single-issue form of "interest group" politics, embodied in the nonprofit industrial complex of environmental advocacy organizations. These interest groups tend to be composed of highly educated professional-class knowledge workers. They tend to view politics as a battle over knowledge and policy, as discussed in Part II. More radical approaches adopt what I have elsewhere called "livelihood environmentalism,"[63] which assumes that because the vast majority of society is *alienated* from nature vis-à-vis the market, real environmental interests are those where communities face a clear "environmental" threat to their livelihood. This could be everything from threats to land and water among indigenous or peasant communities, to direct bodily threats of pollution in (post)industrial landscapes, like birth defects caused by chemical discharges. Barca and Leonardi assume a working-class ecological politics will emerge from these concrete "environmental" factors:

> As living beings that reproduce in particular biophysical environments, working-class people are intrinsically ecological subjects, whose existence is dependent upon that of a healthy ecosystem—including air, water, soil, the food chain, and local bio-geo-chemical cycles. We thus define *working-class ecology* as the web of systemic relations between working-class people and their living and working habitats.

This definition ignores one key reality: that the main barrier to survival for working-class people has nothing do with their

---

63   See, Matt Huber, "Ecological politics for the working class," *Catalyst*, Vol. 3, No. 1 (Spring 2019): 7–46.

immediate habitat. Of course, when communities resist threats to their livelihood, they are in fact working-class struggles over the basic conditions of life like clean air and water. But this framing tends to only see environmental interests among those facing concrete environmental threats. Under capitalism, the vast majority face *daily* threats to their livelihood via the more abstract forces of the market— what Marx called "the silent compulsion of economic relations."[64]

These threats are as "real" as pollution or land dispossession—and including them as part of all environmental interests has the capacity to build a much broader coalition. Rather than defending concrete landscapes or even people's bodies from the ravages of the market, a proletarian ecology would seek to extricate working-class needs from the market itself through a program based on *decommodification*.

Another alternative vision of "environmental interests" is the notion that the planetary crisis threatens all of us as one human species. Rudolf Bahro of the German Green Party argued that the left should shift from thinking in terms of working-class interests to "species interest": "We must go beyond Marx's own concept and direct ourselves to a more general subject than the Western working-class of today . . . we must again take the species interest as our fundamental point of reference."[65]

But it is not true that all of humanity has such an interest. As Andrew Dobson points out, this understanding is at the core of a class approach to environmental politics:

> It is simply untrue to say that, given present conditions, it is in everybody's interests to bring about a sustainable and egalitarian society. A significant and influential portion of society, for example, has material interest in prolonging the environmental crisis because there is money to be made from managing it.[66]

64   Marx, *Capital*, Vol. 1, 899.
65   Bahro, *Socialism and Survival*, 65.
66   Andrew Dobson, *Green Political Thought* (London: Routledge, 2000), 146.

You can open up the newspaper just about every day and see this objective class reality: fossil fuel companies, private utilities, and others doing everything in their power to *prevent* an energy transition away from fossil fuels. Why? Because it is in their objective, material interests to do so.

Of course, the masses of the working class might not be conscious of their shared material interests embedded in the relations of production. In 1883, Georgi Plekhanov explained that oppressed classes "wage a hard struggle for their daily subsistence without even thinking which aspects of the social organization they owe their wretched condition to."[67] Przeworski is right: it is up to *class struggle* to build working-class consciousness of the often hidden and obscure, but objective, material systems of power that are responsible for their own daily struggles. Raising class consciousness is ecological consciousness because there is a class of people who seek to maintain restricted access to the basics of life: the capitalists who control our food, energy, housing, and transport. Thus, by virtue of their lack of means of production, the working class has an objective material interest in securing more secure access to the ecological means of life.

From Material Interests to Climate Consciousness

This ecological focus on *life* at least conceptually connects to a larger ecological concern with *all* of life on the planet. There is indeed a species interest in maintaining a livable planet. With 4 to 8 degrees F of warming, even the wealthiest will not escape the terror of a heating world (even those who try to flee to outer space).[68] A class strategy for climate change means that in order to stop the destruction of most life, we need to appeal to the vast majority of society whose own ecological lives are so precarious. As it happens, the working-class struggle for a decent life and the planetary struggle for all life face a common enemy: capital. Here we see how the working-class interest

---

67 Quoted in Raju Das, *Marxist Class Theory for a Skeptical World* (Chicago: Haymarket, 2017), 428.

68 David Wallace-Wells, *The Uninhabitable Earth: Life After Warming* (New York: Tim Duggan Books, 2019).

in disrupting capital's control over the means of life coincides with our "species interest" for a livable planet.

How could we possibly conjoin working-class with ecological interests? Admittedly, it is not at all clear how ordinary working people will see their own material lives as connected to such abstract notions of ecological life as the biodiversity crisis, let alone the complex, time-delayed process of anthropogenic climate change. This is where there must be some role for political organizations in building a class politics through struggle and political education. Such organizations traditionally organize around a *political program*, and I will explain below how the Green New Deal can serve this role. But first, I want to sketch how a theory of climate class-consciousness might emerge at a more general level.

While most assume that political consciousness around climate will emerge from educating the public on the scientific reality of the dangers we face, or through experiencing climate disasters like flood, fires, and heat waves, my main contention is that *neither* of these can build a mass, popular politics around the necessity of climate action. The highly educated and the climate-disrupted are communities too small to form a mass base.

The working-class strategy would link direct, material improvements in people's lives to climate action. People would intuitively understand jobs, free electricity, or public housing as beneficial, but it would be up to political organizers to *name* those improvements as measures taken to address the climate crisis. From this basis, masses of working people might begin to see climate change not as a "cost" to bear or adjust to, but as a crisis requiring fundamental social and political transformations that improve their lives. In the United States, much is made of how so many "deny" the basic science of anthropogenic climate change: a depressing 43 percent. But at the same time there is a sizable majority (72 percent) who acknowledge that "global warming is happening," and a still sizable 63 percent who say they are worried about it.[69] Honestly, as

---

69   See, "Yale Climate Opinion Maps 2020," September 2, 2020. climatecommunication. yale.edu/visualizations-data/ycom-us.

of this writing (October 2021), it is impossible to deny the escalating heat waves and extreme weather visible everywhere. The working-class strategy seeks to build on these unscientific hunches that climate change is a problem and create mass, popular support for climate action by appealing to direct material interests.

The education or experiential paths to climate awareness necessarily focus on the negative: future dangers, disastrous presents, or traumatic pasts. In contrast, this strategy submits that positive and easy-to-understand material gains are the only path to mass, *popular* support for climate action. You do not win by scaring people, and, in a society like the United States, with no guaranteed public higher education, you do not win by making complex scientific understanding the basis for climate action.

Some might call this strategy "manipulative"; by tossing free goodies at the working class, we trick them into supporting action. But that objection ignores how our material lives are in fact directly connected to the climate crisis. It is not as if we would try to "distract" the working class by offering material gains in "non-climate" issues like energy, food, housing, and transportation. We know we must transform all of these sectors to address the decarbonization challenge. It is the professional-class technocrats who always assume these material changes must involve costs, sacrifice, scaling down, "less." Such an approach is obviously unpopular . . . but it also allows the capitalists who control those sectors to mobilize working-class opposition to any climate action. Approaching the crisis differently, as something that can make life better for everyone by transforming those sectors that touch working-class lives daily—*that* is a winning strategy for creating climate consciousness.

Working-Class Electoral Struggles in a Time of Climate Crisis

We have established that the working class lacks secure access to the material conditions of life and so has a *material interest* in reducing the power of capital to obtain more secure access to them. But that's not all: the general Marxist argument suggests that the working class possesses what Mike Davis calls "proletarian agency" with the *capacity* to overthrow the capitalist class and usher in a new mode of production.[70]

The first thing to emphasize is that working-class agency is only a theory of its *potential*. It is not a guarantee. There are many elements in that potential, but one of the most important is that the working class has the numbers: it represents the vast majority of the population—between two-thirds and three-quarters in a country like the United States. And even if the bulk of the population in the developing world are *not* wage workers and definitely do not work in factories, the vast majority are defined by a proletarian separation from the land and the means of survival it provides.

There are many ways to posit how these "numbers" can turn into power. In the socialist tradition, it is often imagined as a revolutionary insurrection organized by a mass socialist party that takes state power: the Bolsheviks' alliance of workers and peasants summed up as "Peace, Land, and Bread" toppled a reactionary authoritarian Tsarist regime. But in advanced capitalist societies, the working class faces a far more thoroughly armed state, in both military and ideological terms. As Eric Blanc asserts, "democratically elected governments [have] too much legitimacy among working people and too much armed strength for an insurrectionary approach to be realistic."[71]

But in the context of parliamentary systems based on universal suffrage, the working-class masses possess potential *electoral* power, as masses of votes. This is why Marx claimed British universal suffrage would result in "the political supremacy of the working class."[72] Late in his life, Engels declared that electoral realities would lead the proletariat in Germany to emerge as "the decisive power in the land before which all other powers will have to bow, whether they like it or not."[73]

70   Davis, *Old Gods, New Enigmas*, xvii.

71   Eric Blanc, "Why Kautsky was right (and why you should care)," *Jacobin*, April 2, 2019.

72   Karl Marx, "Free trade and the Chartists," *New-York Daily Tribune*, August 25, 1852.

73   Frederick Engels, "Introduction to Marx's Class Struggles in France," quoted in

These ideas influenced the Second International, as Karl Kautsky put in his commentary on the "Erfurt program": "Besides freedom of the press and the right to organize, the universal ballot is to be regarded as one of the conditions prerequisite to a sound development of the proletariat."[74] He goes on to argue:

> The proletariat is most favorably situated with regard to parliamentary activity . . . It is the most powerful lever that can be utilized to raise the proletariat out of its economic, social and moral degradation.[75]

There are heated debates about what a working-class party could do once it gains power, as well as many examples of how the capitalist class can fight back through capital strikes or even the overthrow of socialist governments in military coups.[76]

I do not wish to delve into these debates. Rather, I have a simple assertion: if we wish to avoid the worst consequences of climate change, we cannot ignore state power . . . and building a working-class majoritarian politics is the necessary, if difficult, route to taking that state power. In explaining his concept of ecological Leninism, Andreas Malm correctly observes, "It is incredibly difficult to see how anything other than state power could accomplish the transition required, given that it will be necessary to exert coercive authority against those who want to maintain the status quo."[77]

Nevertheless, for decades, the left has largely ignored the issue of

---

Miliband, *Marxism and Politics*, 80. Miliband explains how Engels's text was edited in a way that Engels complained would make him "appear as a 'peaceful worshipper of legality quand même.'" Yet, Miliband insists there is little doubt that the unedited version "shows a major shift of emphasis from earlier pronouncements of Marx and Engels on the question of suffrage and its uses." (80).

74 Kautsky, *The Class Struggle*, 188.

75 Ibid.

76 A good overview is Mike McCarthy, "Our first 100 days could be a nightmare," *Jacobin* No. 36 (Winter 2020): 66–79.

77 Dominic Mealy interview with Andreas Malm, "To halt climate change, we need an ecological Leninism," *Jacobin*, June 15, 2020.

the state. As Stephen Maher, Sam Gindin, and Leo Panitch put it, the socialist left is in the habit of "leaving to the side the matter of how to enter the state to change what it does, let alone to change what it is."[78] Christian Parenti rightly deems it outlandish to expect a revolutionary overthrow of capitalism in time to deal with climate change: "Given the state of the left globally . . . achieving socialism will take a very long time indeed. Thus, the struggle for climate mitigation and adaptation cannot wait for revolution."[79]

Parenti persuasively argues that few institutions besides the state have the *power* to achieve the kind of massive transformation on the time scale needed. How massive? Two important aspects of state power are at stake.

First, in Parenti's terms, the state possesses the coercive and legal power to "euthanize" the fossil fuel industry. It is actually instructive to view the climate struggle as part of a long history of state-led *popular expropriation,* one that stretches back to the Emancipation Proclamation and the wave of twentieth-century postcolonial governments that nationalized their oil or other resources.[80] In most of these cases, popular majoritarian movements seized state power.

Second, the state, especially the US federal state, has the *fiscal capacity* to engage in a massive *public investment* program aimed at building a new energy system. In its most radical variants, this kind of state program would widen the "democratic control over investment" and "fight to extend social control over production."[81] To repeat: leaving climate mitigation to the anarchy of market signals is unsound strategy. Rather, the state can implement large-scale economic

---

78   Stephen Maher, Sam Gindin, and Leo Panitch, "Class politics, socialist politics, capitalist constraints," in Leo Panitch and Greg Albo (eds.), *Socialist Register 2020: Beyond Market Dystopia: New Ways of Living* (London: Merlin, 2019), 1–29; 1.

79   Christian Parenti, "Climate change: What role for reform?" *Monthly Review*, April 1, 2014.

80   See, Matt Karp, "The mass politics of antislavery," *Catalyst*, Vol. 3, No. 2 (2019): 131–80, Christopher R. W. Dietrich, *Oil Revolution: Anticolonial Elites, Sovereign Rights, and the Economic Culture of Decolonization* (Cambridge, UK: Cambridge University Press, 2017).

81   Maher, Gindin, and Panitch, "Class politics, socialist politics, capitalist constraints," 14.

planning to build the infrastructure changes we need. (More on this in relation to electricity in the next chapter.)

Of course, the state under neoliberalism will never deploy this power against fossil capital. So this is where the working class comes in. By its sheer numbers, there is a possibility to stitch together a mass, working-class electoral coalition to win state power through campaigns powered not only by masses of working-class votes, but also by small donations that free up candidates from the more typical wealthy donors. Without mass, popular support for insurgent candidates willing to refuse corporate support and directly confront capital, we have little chance to implement a climate program on the scale needed. Of course, winning elections will not on its own be enough to enact a large-scale climate mitigation program (more on leveraging the mass action of workers in the workplace in Chapter 6), but it can be one element of a larger working-class strategy on climate.

Interestingly, in *Carbon Democracy*, Timothy Mitchell argued it was coal, and the militant power of coal workers who could halt the flow of carbon energy, that inaugurated the first era of mass democracy and universal suffrage in the West.[82] What we need now is an *anti-carbon democracy*[83]—a way to get the majority of the population behind an electoral program based on carbon mitigation. It is striking to consider that the longstanding policy toolkit of the climate movement has barely considered the *popularity* of their proposals. They have been more concerned with economistic language of "efficiency" and "cost-benefit analysis" without even asking how it might appeal to the masses. The experience of the "Yellow Vest" revolts to climate policy in France shows the perils of popular backlash to climate technocracy that does not address entrenched inequality.[84] In the midst of

82 Timothy Mitchell, *Carbon Democracy: Political Power in the Age of Oil* (London: Verso, 2011).

83 I started using this term in 2018 in unpublished public talks, but Kate Aronoff's new book draws on Mitchell to make a similar argument under the banner of a smarter term: postcarbon democracy. See, Kate Aronoff, *Overheated: How Capitalism Broke the Planet—and How We Fight Back* (New York: Bold Type Books, 2021), 246–7.

84 Andreas Malm, "A lesson in how not to mitigate climate change," *Verso Books Blog*, December 7, 2018.

writing this book, this political and electoral program has emerged under the banner of the Green New Deal.

The Green New Deal as a Working-Class Environmental Program

> I believe that in a modern, moral, and wealthy society, no person in America should be too poor to live.
>
> —Alexandria Ocasio-Cortez's definition
> of "democratic socialism"

The resurgence of socialist politics in the United States is oriented around the very innocuous premise that people should have a right to *live*. In his speech outlining his vision of democratic socialism, Bernie Sanders framed the struggle to extend human rights beyond just the political realm of free speech and religion: "We must recognize that in the twenty-first century, in the wealthiest country in the history of the world, economic rights are human rights."[85]

After decades of wealth flowing to the richest and the masses seeing nothing but debt and wage stagnation, it is increasingly clear that capitalism cannot guarantee everyone a decent and dignified life. The challenge of building a proletarian ecology is connecting this vision of life to a broader ecological vision of life and planetary climate action.

The Green New Deal program—not a set policy but an evolving program—tries to do exactly this. It proposes a ten-year national mobilization aimed at restructuring the power grid toward zero-carbon energy sources, investing in green public housing, and vastly expanding public transit, among other goals.[86] The Green New Deal idea first arose in the days preceding the financial crash of 2008 and

---

85   Tara Golshan, "Read: Bernie Sanders defines his vision for democratic socialism in the United States," *Vox*, June 12, 2019.

86   House Resolution 109, 116th Congress (2019-2020): "Recognizing the Duty of the Federal Government to Create a Green New Deal" (February 12, 2019). www.congress.gov. Last accessed June 10, 2020.

re-emerged in response to the 2018 Intergovernmental Panel on Climate Change report, which starkly claimed that preventing catastrophic warming required "rapid, far-reaching and unprecedented changes in all aspects of society."[87] The urgency of this report led a climate activism group, the Sunrise Movement, to occupy the office of Nancy Pelosi. Meanwhile, Ocasio-Cortez called on the government to enact a Green New Deal that offered solutions "on the scale of the crises we [face]."[88] Some visions of the program include a federal job guarantee that has the potential to deliver material gains to impoverished communities across the country—a recognition that, under capitalism, proletarian life is only possible through secure access to an income.

Unlike other climate policies that claim to be purely about carbon, the Green New Deal aims to tackle the twin crises of inequality and climate change. The nonbinding resolution on the Green New Deal introduced by Ocasio-Cortez and Senator Ed Markey puts human survival up front: "A changing climate is causing sea levels to rise and an increase in wildfires, severe storms, droughts, and other extreme weather events that threaten human life, healthy communities, and critical infrastructure."[89] Yet it is careful not to frame this purely in terms of environmental protection; it also decries "the greatest income inequality since the 1920s."[90] It aims to address these problems not through austerity, but through the main source of livelihood under capitalism—jobs: "To create millions of good, high-wage jobs and ensure prosperity."[91] Beyond jobs, this focus on *economic security* is about securing a better life for the vast majority via "adequate family and medical leave, paid vacations, and retirement security to all people of the United

87 Intergovernmental Panel on Climate Change, "Summary for Policymakers of IPCC Special Report on Global Warming of 1.5°C approved by governments," October 8, 2018.
88 "A Message From the Future With Alexandria Ocasio-Cortez," YouTube.com.
89 House Resolution 109.
90 Ibid.
91 Ibid.

States."[92] Finally, the resolution even aims to increase the power of the working class vis-à-vis capital, "strengthening and protecting the right of all workers to organize, unionize, and collectively bargain free of coercion, intimidation, and harassment."[93]

The nonbinding resolution was what it sounded like: nonbinding and ultimately aspirational. By introducing it in early 2019, advocates hoped the 2020 presidential race would revolve around the program—and it did. In 2020, all Democratic presidential candidates proposed competing ambitious climate plans. And in the wake of intensifying wildfires in California and other disasters, climate change skyrocketed to the number one issue among Democratic primary voters in a national poll taken in April 2019.[94] While several candidates flouted ambitious climate plans (most notably Governor Jay Inslee of Washington, who made climate his signature issue), only Bernie Sanders's campaign had the energy of the youth climate movement behind him and a fleshed-out program that scientists agreed matched the crisis or, in the words of the plan, proposed a "wholesale transformation of our society."[95]

Sanders backed the Green New Deal to decarbonize the energy system . . . and upped the ante by proposing the creation of 20 million new jobs in the process.[96] There was a lot of detail in the plan, but one item focused specifically on the proletarian concern with survival via money and commodities. The plan laid out the goal of "saving American families money by weatherizing homes and lowering energy bills, building affordable and high-quality, modern public transportation."[97] More importantly, and rectifying a glaring weakness in Ocasio-Cortez's original resolution, Sanders pledged to take on the fossil fuel industry, putting the necessity of *class struggle* at the

---

92   Ibid.

93   Ibid.

94   Miranda Green, "Poll: Climate change is top issue for registered Democrats," *The Hill*, April 30, 2019.

95   Bernie Sanders, "The Green New Deal." berniesanders.com/issues/green-new-deal. Last accessed June 10, 2020. See also Branko Marcetic, "Climate advocates are nearly unanimous: Bernie's Green New Deal is best," *Jacobin*, September 9, 2019.

96   Sanders, "The Green New Deal."

97   Ibid.

core of his plan—and repeating similar language in countless media interviews and campaign rallies:

> We need a president who has the courage, the vision, and the record to face down the greed of fossil fuel executives and the billionaire class who stand in the way of climate action. We need a president who welcomes their hatred.[98]

Still more radical versions of the Green New Deal propose a fundamentally new relation to life. The Democratic Socialists of America's Green New Deal principles include a push to "decommodify survival," "guaranteeing living wages, healthcare, childcare, housing, food, water, energy, public transit, a healthy environment, and other necessities for all."[99] Perhaps the most concrete attempt at this more radical vision took place in the spring of 2021. After hundreds died in an enormous, winter storm–induced power outage in Texas, socialist congressional members Cori Bush and Jamaal Bowman introduced a "public power" resolution asserting that

> the United States must establish electricity as a basic human right and public good, and eradicate the reliance on monopolized, profit-driven utility corporations and providers and the flawed regulatory regime that has failed to regulate these utilities in the public interest.[100]

This is what a working-class climate politics would look like. It departs from the standard professional-class calls for taxes and fees and less consumption, and from the kind of "livelihood environmentalism" that assumes environmental interests are only those with a direct stake in access to resources like land, water, and air.[101] This new

---

98 Ibid.

99 Democratic Socialists of America, Ecosocialist Working Group, "An Ecosocialist Green New Deal: Guiding Principles" (February 28, 2019). ecosocialists.dsausa .org/2019/02/28/gnd-principles. Last accessed June 11, 2020.

100 Rep. Cori Bush, "Bush Public Power Resolution." bush.house.gov.

101 Huber, "Ecological politics for the working class."

politics recognizes the working-class dependence on the market as a key source of insecurity and exploitation, and addresses it.

A Green New Deal–style decommodification program not only aims to appeal to workers' interests; it could also have tremendous ecological effects. Free public housing could integrate green building practices that provide cheaper heating and electricity bills for residents.[102] Free public transportation could fundamentally shift away from overreliance on automobiles and other privatized modes of transport.[103] And while it is easy to agree that "health care is a human right," it is ethically imperative that we also recognize food and energy as human rights too. The combination of the Green New Deal's job guarantee with the decommodification of social needs could also include the traditional left-labor demand for a shorter workweek.[104]

In sum, a Green New Deal based on decommodification is also about shifting power and control over society's resources. The most ecologically beneficial part of this program is that it aims to transfer key industries from private to public ownership so that environmental goals can predominate over profits. The very sectors we aim to decommodify require confronting industries that are the central culprits in the ecological crisis.

Challenges to the Electoral Road to Power:
The Case of Bernie Sanders

> If there is going to be class warfare in this country, it's about time the working class won that war.
> —Bernie Sanders, Twitter, August 21, 2019

The capacity of the working class to deliver electoral power is only a potential that has to be organized. On the night of February 22, 2020, Bernie Sanders won the Nevada primary by a wide margin. It was the

102   Daniel Aldana Cohen, "A Green New Deal for Housing," *Jacobin*, February 8, 2019.
103   James Wilt, "Free transit is just the beginning," *Briarpatch Magazine*, November 29, 2019.
104   Kate Aronoff, "Could a Green New Deal make us happier people?" *The Intercept*, April 7, 2019.

third straight victory for Sanders. His victory speech took a confident tone: "In Nevada we have just brought together a multigenerational, multiracial coalition which is not only going to win in Nevada, it's going to sweep this country."[105] As his above tweet indicates, Sanders was the first serious candidate in decades who foregrounded class struggle and working-class power at the core of his political strategy. And he was the only viable candidate who proposed a climate program on the scale of the crisis we face.[106] Yet as most readers will undoubtedly know, the campaign did not "sweep the country." A mere ten days later on "Super Tuesday," the centrist Joe Biden crushed the Sanders movement by winning 10 of 14 states. A 16.5-percentage-point loss in Michigan on March 10, a state Sanders won in 2016, effectively ended his campaign, and one month later Sanders dropped out of the race in the midst of the global Covid-19 pandemic.

In the wake of the loss, many professional-class media pundits pronounced Sanders's working class electoral strategy dead on arrival. In *Vox*, Zach Beauchamp explained the Sanders campaign deployed a "Marxist political strategy" with "the explicit aim of building a new, working-class electorate."[107] Specifically, Sanders's plan was to turn out *new* working-class voters disillusioned with politics in general. In Beauchamp's estimation, this was an abject failure: "Sanders's defeat is a hammer blow to the left's class-based theory of winning political power."[108] In one sense, it is remarkable that mainstream political commentators were even seriously discussing a "Marxist political strategy" with a *chance* of winning, but on the other hand the results of the 2020 election force us to reckon with the ambiguities of organizing the objective existence of a working-class majority into a concrete reality of electoral victories.

105   Associated Press, "Sanders cements Democratic front-runner status with resounding Nevada caucuses win," February 22, 2019.

106   In many ways this came about thanks to the climate movement itself. Sanders's 2016 climate policy was rather vague and included everyone's favorite policy, carbon taxes, as the main plank.

107   Zach Beauchamp, "Why Bernie Sanders failed," *Vox*, April 10, 2020.

108   Ibid.

So, what happened? First, Sanders *did* have a significant base in the working class. In particular, analyses of his army of small donors skewed remarkably to the lower end of the income scale, with teachers and Walmart and Amazon workers among his top donors.[109] His success with Latino and working-class communities in California and Nevada exemplified the working-class strategy for electoral power. Although the media often claimed Biden won all the white working-class voters Bernie had won against Hilary Clinton in 2016, he actually beat Biden in states like Nevada, Texas, and Colorado among non-college educated white voters.[110] Sanders also won among *all* young voters, and thus working-class voters, ages 18-45.[111]

But beyond this success, Sanders *lost* huge chunks of the working-class majority. Combined exit polls in all the Super Tuesday states showed Biden winning among voters without a college education (38 percent to 33 percent).[112] And just as in 2016, the Sanders campaign dramatically failed to win over huge proportions of working-class black voters in Southern states. The crushing defeat in Michigan was even more alarming, as Sanders ended up losing many of the same rural, white working-class districts he had won in 2016.[113] In retrospect, it appeared that Sanders's victories of 2016 might have been as

---

109   See, Daniel Waldron, "Bartenders for Bernie?" (September 12, 2019). waldrn. com/candidate-support-by-occupation-in-the-2020-democratic-primary. Last accessed June 11, 2020, and Karl Evers-Hillstrom, "Sanders or Warren: Who gets more support from working-class donors?" The Center for Responsive Politics (September 12, 2019): opensecrets.org. Last accessed June 11, 2020.

110   Matt Karp, "Bernie Sanders's Five-Year War," *Jacobin*, No. 38 (Summer 2020): 55–72; 64.

111   Connor Kilpatrick, "We Lost the Battle, but We'll Win the War," *Jacobin*, April 8, 2020.

112   Brittany Renee Mayes, Leslie Shapiro, Kevin Schaul, Kevin Uhrmacher, Emily Guskin, Scott Clement, and Dan Keating, "Exit polls from the 2020 Democratic Super Tuesday contests," *Washington Post*, March 30, 2020.

113   The victory of Biden in rural areas obscures the Democratic Party's overall "continued decline in rural areas" participating in primaries. Rural working-class areas are increasingly going to the Republican Party. David Weigel, "The Trailer: The suburbs, young voters, the Trump base and more of what mattered in Tuesday's primaries," *Washington Post*, March 11, 2020. Much more work needs to be done on the concept of the rural "white working class." My suspicion is that rural areas skew more toward petty bourgeois small-business owners and professionals than is often acknowledged.

much about anti-Clinton sentiment as pro-socialist working-class policies. And his 40-point loss among Michigan's black voters also demonstrated that his lack of resonance with the black working class was not merely a Southern pattern.[114] Most alarmingly, exit polls showed Biden winning union households in Michigan by a margin of 20 percentage points (56 to 36).[115] Sanders could take some solace from his 7-point advantage among those making less than \$50,000 a year (for obvious reasons these tend to *not* be union households),[116] but still, for him Michigan was a grim result.

There are many explanations to consider. First, it is worth noting that primary elections in the United States have a shockingly low voter turnout—and, unsurprisingly, working-class voters are more likely to stay home. In 2016, a mere 14.4 percent of eligible voters turned out in the Democratic primaries.[117] This has to do with the incredibly regressive and undemocratic electoral system: most elections fall on a working day (Tuesday), and caucuses are held in a narrow two- or three-hour span on specific days.[118] In fact, by the time Biden sealed his win on Super Tuesday, only 18 of 50 states had even voted. This very process is not amendable to propelling the working-class majority into power.

Second, and most importantly, many commentators puzzled at exit polls showing that the Sanders policy platform—most notably the single-payer national health care plan Medicare for All—polled much higher than Sanders's share of the vote itself.[119] Many on the left comforted themselves that we had won the war of ideas, but there's another problem innate in that belief: it shows that many in the

114 Mayes, et al., "Exit polls."
115 CNN, "Michigan Exit Polls." cnn.com/election/2020/entrance-and-exit-polls/michigan/democratic. Last accessed June 11, 2020.
116 Karp, "Bernie Sanders's Five-Year War," 66.
117 Drew Desilver, "Turnout was high in the 2016 primary season, but just short of 2008 record," *Pew Research Center*, June 10, 2016.
118 Ankita Rao, Pat Dillon, Kim Kelly, and Zak Bennett, "Is America a democracy? If so, why does it deny millions the vote?" *Guardian*, November 7, 2019.
119 Ian Millhiser, "Joe Biden is winning, even though most Democrats support Medicare-for-all," *Vox*, March 18, 2020.

working class believe in the Sanders platform—they just don't think it can win. This reflects what Mark Fisher called the "reflexive impotence" of the working class under conditions of neoliberal "capitalist realism." He describes the sentiment precisely: "They know things are bad, but more than that, they know they can't do anything about it."[120]

It is not hard to imagine why most working-class people do not believe things like Medicare for All and a Green New Deal are possible. Over the last four decades, the rich and wealthy have effectively colonized state power. One famous study in 2014 by Martin Gilens and Benjamin Page found that economic elites and business groups have the most impact on state policy, while the majority of people (that is, the working class) have next to none.[121] The Sanders campaign was asking the working class to believe his program was possible before they had any evidence whatsoever that elected officials have the *capacity* to deliver material gains. It is a tough chicken-or-egg dilemma, but it proves that a potential working-class road to electoral power cannot be conjured from thin air.

Jane McAlevey argues there are "no shortcuts" to building working-class power.[122] The socialist left should honestly acknowledge that the Sanders campaign was always a shortcut aiming to skip the more difficult work of organizing workers in their workplaces and communities. As Adam Przeworski put it, "Class shapes political behavior of individuals only as long as people who are workers are organized politically as workers."[123] On that front, the record of the US labor movement remains dismal. Although there has been a notable uptick in strike activity, union density has been declining every year for decades.[124]

120   Mark Fisher, *Capitalist Realism: Is There No Alternative?* (Hants, UK: Zero Books, 2009), 21.

121   Martin Gilens and Benjamin Page, "Testing theories of American politics: Elites, interest groups, and average citizens," *Perspectives on Politics*, Vol. 12, No. 3 (2014): 564–81; 576–7.

122   Jane McAlevey, *No Shortcuts: Organizing for Power in the New Gilded Age* (Oxford, UK: Oxford University Press, 2016).

123   Przeworski, *Capitalism and Social Democracy*, 27.

124   Kate Gibson, "Union membership in the US slid to record low in 2019," CBS News, January 22, 2020.

The other uncomfortable fact was this: while Joe Biden swept many lower-income districts in the South, Michigan, and elsewhere, it is now clear that Bernie Sanders was uniquely popular among the same professional-class people who drive climate politics. In an article "Why Americans Don't Vote Their Class Anymore," Eric Levitz explains:

> Sanders performs about as poorly with non-college-educated white voters as any other Democrat. In a recent survey from Quinnipiac University, such voters disapproved of Sanders by a 56 to 30 percent margin, which was two points worse than Biden's showing with that same demographic. By contrast, a recent survey from Grinnell College found that "suburban women" approve of the democratic socialist by a margin of 54 to 32 percent. In fact, in virtually every survey of registered voters, college-educated whites evince more sympathy for Sanders than non-college-educated ones (since nonwhite voters lean heavily Democratic regardless of class or education, the debate over whether the class basis of the Democratic coalition can be changed has centered on divisions within the white electorate).[125]

Levitz goes on to explain how some of the most progressive members of Congress won in relatively wealthy, highly educated districts. Cheekily, he concludes, in agreement with a mainstay of right-wing ideology, that "colleges really are vehicles for left-wing indoctrination."[126] Thus, working-class politics is perhaps currently most appealing to professional-class voters who, through education, have learned about the horrors of poverty and inequality. Their support for the program is not purely about material interests, but about *knowing* the truth of our gilded-age oligarchy.

That said, this movement does appeal to the material interests of a rapidly expanding stratum among the professional class facing

125   Eric Levitz, "Why Americans don't vote their class anymore," *New York Magazine: Intelligencer.*
126   Ibid.

proletarianization and increasingly barren job prospects. As one article put it, socialism is now distinctly appealing to the "well-educated and downwardly mobile millennials."[127] A political thinker on the right, Julius Krein, put it more bluntly: "the group [Sanders] primarily attracts are the most radicalized elements of the professional class (the young, academics, underemployed college graduates, and so forth)."[128]

In the end, the liberal left in the United States has framed a struggle within the Democratic Party between the liberal professional elite and the working class, but it might be more accurate to say the clash is *within* the increasingly professional-class base of the party itself—between well-educated liberals and well-educated radicals. Thomas Piketty has identified the shift of liberal-left parties to highly educated populations, or what he calls the "Brahmin Left": "the former workers' party became the party of the winners of the educational system and gradually moved away from the disadvantaged classes."[129] Of course, it is now clear that education does not make you a "winner" in an increasingly unequal capitalist system. The Brahmin Left is increasingly radical as a result.

It appears that the election of the reality television ignoramus Donald Trump—who infamously exclaimed during the 2016 campaign, "I love the poorly educated"[130]—only intensified these political dynamics. Trump's relentless lying, disdain for facts, and outright hostility toward professionalized institutions like the media and state bureaucracies have made him uniquely repugnant to the educated professional classes. Thus, we should not be surprised that in the midterm elections of 2018 it was not Bernie Sanders–style

127 Charlotte Alter, "How the well-educated and downwardly mobile found socialism," *Literary Hub*, February 19, 2020.

128 Julius Krein, "The real class war," *American Affairs Journal*, Vol. 3, No. 4 (Winter 2019). americanaff airsjournal.org/2019/11/the-real-class-war. Last accessed June 12, 2020.

129 Thomas Piketty, *Capital and Ideology* (Cambridge, MA: Harvard University Press, 2020), 756.

130 Josh Hafner, "Donald Trump loves the 'poorly educated'—and they love him," *USA Today*, February 24, 2016.

working-class candidates who won the most races, but liberal anti-Trump resistance fighters in the suburbs. Matt Karp explains, "the congressional districts where they concentrated their resources and won decisive victories . . . were almost exclusively the same affluent, educated suburbs that Clinton sought to woo in 2016."[131] He reports further:

> the twenty richest House districts in the United States, measured by median income: every single one of them now has a Democratic representative. Of the wealthiest forty districts, thirty-five of them just elected a Democrat; of the wealthiest fifty, that number is forty-two.[132]

Meanwhile, Donald Trump's Republican Party is increasingly burrowing into the formerly working-class base of the Democratic Party.[133] Similar to right-wing parties in Europe and beyond, Trump appeals to a more nationalist form of working-class rage—directing anger toward "globalist" threats from immigration to corporate offshoring. Between 2012 and 2016, exit polls indicate that with Trump as its candidate, the Republican Party's share of the vote increased by 16 points among those making less than $30,000 a year.[134] Trump also won handily among those without high school and college degrees. Even if Clinton still won the lower-income brackets, her party's biggest gains from 2012 were among voters making over $100,000 a year (a 9-point swing).[135] A fine-grained analysis by the *New York Times* found that "the Republican share of the vote has increased across the nation's most economically disadvantaged counties, while the most successful counties have moved toward the Democrats."[136] They interview a former union member at a General Motors plant in Ohio that shut down: "In a way Mr. Hoskins

131   Matt Karp, "51 percent losers," *Jacobin*, November 14, 2018.
132   Ibid.
133   Eduardo Porter, "How the G.O.P. Became the Party of the Left Behind," *New York Times*, January 27, 2020.
134   Jon Huang, Samuel Jacoby, Michael Strickland, and K.K. Rebecca Lai, "Election 2016: Exit Polls," *New York Times*, November 8, 2016.
135   Ibid.
136   Porter, "G.O.P."

feels betrayed: In the face of economic insecurity, his loyalty to the union and the Democratic Party did not protect him."[137] The article quotes him as saying, "when it came time for the doors to shut at GM, the Democrats weren't looking out for me."[138]

The 2020 presidential election demonstrated that Trumpism is not only appealing to non-college educated whites, but also, to a certain limited extent, among Latinos and other nonwhite communities. While turnout overall was at historic highs, Trump increased his vote share among Latinos by 10 percent, from 28 to 38 percent.[139] Contradicting the commonly accepted view of political geography and the urban-rural divide, the *New York Times* published an analysis showing Trump making dramatic gains in urban districts among large numbers of immigrants.[140]

In sum, the working-class road to electoral power cannot succeed without organized working-class power in the first place—the kind of power that can *force* politicians to deliver policies in line with working-class material interests. Bernie Sanders in fact said this throughout his campaign:

> The truth is that the powers that be . . . are so powerful, they have so much money, that no one person, not the best president in the world, can take them on alone. The only way we transform America is when millions of people together stand up and fight back.[141]

It was perhaps wishful thinking to imagine that Sanders could win as long as the working class itself is atomized and disorganized. The

137   Ibid.
138   Ibid.
139   These numbers are based on validated voter data. It appears some exit poll data showing gains among Black men was inaccurate. William Gaston, "New 2020 voter data: How Biden won, how Trump kept the race close, and what it tells us about the future," *Brookings Institution*, July 6, 2021.
140   Weiyi Cai and Ford Fessenden, "Immigrant Neighborhoods Shifted Red as the Country Chose Blue," *New York Times*, December 20, 2020.
141   Quoted in Meagan Day, "Bernie Sanders wants you to fight," *Jacobin*, March 12, 2019.

Sanders movement gambled that a campaign itself might *activate* the working-class masses into a political force. It did not work.

If the climate movement sees the Green New Deal as a potentially appealing mass popular program, it is worth revisiting the social forces that enacted the *original* New Deal. As Jane McAlevey explains, "The unions in 1934 understood they had to create a crisis to stand a chance to win the ability to live a decent life up against the titans of the corporate class."[142] It was not electing an enlightened Franklin Roosevelt that made the New Deal, but massive working-class revolt. As labor historian Irving Bernstein describes: "In 1934 labor erupted. There were 1,856 work stoppages involving 1,470,000 workers, by far the highest count . . . in many years."[143] Strikes shut down auto factories in Toledo; longshoremen and teamsters organized a four-day general strike in San Francisco effectively shutting down the city.[144] As Frances Fox Piven and Richard Cloward detail, "unemployed councils" used disruptive action to demand improvements in poor relief, eventually leading to the modern welfare state.[145] It is not just the New Deal. From abolition to the civil rights movement, most popular gains against entrenched power require not electoral victories but what Adaner Usmani calls "disruptive capacity."[146] As we will discuss in the next two chapters, labor strikes are uniquely disruptive to capitalist power.

Bernie Sanders was hoping he could activate such capacities from the Oval Office, but that remains unclear. What is clear is that activating a working-class majority into electoral power has happened

---

142 Jane McAlevey, *A Collective Bargain: Unions, Organizing and the Fight for Democracy* (New York: Ecco, 2020), 50.

143 Irving Bernstein, *The Turbulent Years: A History of the American Worker, 1933–1941* (Chicago: Haymarket, 1969), 217.

144 For a bracing account, see Jeremy Brecher, *Strike!* (Oakland, CA: PM Press, 2014).

145 Frances Fox Piven and Richard Cloward, *Poor People's Movements: Why They Succeed, How They Fail* (New York: Vintage, 1977).

146 Adaner Usmani, "Democracy and Class Struggle," *American Journal of Sociology*, Vol. 124, No. 3 (2018): 664–704. See also Kevin A. Young, Michael Schwartz, and Tarun Banerjee, *Levers of Power: How the 1% Rules and What the 99% Can Do About It* (London: Verso, 2020).

perhaps only once in this country's history. After passing wide-ranging labor reforms, a tax policy labeled "soak the rich," and a gigantic public jobs program, FDR delivered the famous October 1936 campaign speech in which he "welcomed" the hatred of the capitalist class.[147] Unsurprisingly, middle-class and wealthy elites abandoned the New Deal and Democratic Party in droves. Yet FDR still achieved a landslide victory in 1936 based on what Mike Davis described as a "powerful electoral bulwark that the surge of four million workers into the [Congress of Industrial Unions] during 1935-1937 offered."[148] Davis goes on to suggest that the 1936 landslide represented the "tendential political unity of working-class constituencies previously fragmented by religious and racial division."[149] The election represented an ephemeral, class-based realignment of US electoral politics based on "clear polarization of workers and capitalists between the Democratic and Republican parties."[150] The point is, this activation of a working-class electoral majority happened *after*, not before, a mass outbreak of independent and militant working-class actions in the form of strikes and unionization.

Conclusion: Materializing Ecological Interests

In this chapter, I sought to recuperate the Marxist theory that the working class under capitalism has objective material interests. On a basic level, these material interests are ecological interests, rooted in the alienation from the ecological means of life: food, housing, energy, and more. The politics of the Green New Deal seeks to conjoin working-class and ecological interests into one, under the umbrella of a politics of *life*—a platform asserting that in order to save the broad

---

147   Franklin D. Roosevelt, Campaign Address at Madison Square Garden (October 31, 1936), in Samuel I. Rosenman (ed.), *The Public Papers and Addresses of Franklin D. Roosevelt* (New York: Random House, 1938), 5: 566–73. Roy G. Blakey and Gladys C. Blakey, "The Revenue Act of 1935," *The American Economic Review*, Vol. 25, No. 4 (1935): 673–90.

148   Davis, *Prisoners of the American Dream*, 63.

149   Ibid.

150   Ibid., 65.

spectrum of life on the planet, we need to appeal to the working-class masses' needs for secure access to the basics of life. I argued that when working-class people begin to associate climate action with real, material improvements in their life conditions, political support for climate action will follow.

Yet, as we have seen, these "objective" material interests only translate into political power if the working class *believes* winning a dignified life is possible under the atomizing forces of capitalism. The only way working-class people will believe such power is possible is if they start *winning* power and see the results in their lives. Put simply, the working class needs to build *confidence* in their power.

Nevertheless, the history of capitalism shows that it takes actual working-class institutions embedded in everyday life, like unions, political parties, and the concrete processes of struggle in the workplace, to build power. It is through material struggles over the workplace that the working class experiences political conflict and learns what it takes to win and build power. It is this kind of power—the disruptive power of workers whose own labor guarantees the profits flowing to capital—which has the capacity to "create a crisis" for capital and force capitalists into the kind of concessions a Green New Deal represents.

Yet we have so little time to act on the climate crisis. A workplace organizing approach to climate action needs a clear and targeted strategy.

6

Electrifying the Climate Movement: The Case for Electricity as a Strategic Sector

Introduction: From School Strikes to Labor Strikes

On August 20, 2018, 15-year-old Greta Thunberg decided to skip school and instead protest the Swedish parliament for its lack of action on climate change. She argued later, "Why should any young person be made to study for a future when no one is doing enough to save that future?"[1] Her action inspired many others in Sweden to join her school strike, and that September, she decided to continue the practice every Friday. Thunberg comes from a professional-class context—her mother is an opera singer, her father an actor.[2] Given our analysis in Part II, it should come as no surprise that Thunberg's demands center on a politics of knowledge. In her testimony to the US Congress, she demanded: "I want you to listen to the scientists. And I want you to unite behind the science. And then I want you to take action."[3]

Apart from these professional-class narratives, Thunberg fore-grounded a decidedly working class tactic: the strike. Her school strikes spurred the development of the global "Fridays for the Future" movement that sparked climate strikes across the world. According to the organization's website, the goal of the Friday strikes is to "put

---

1   Greta Thunberg, "I'm striking from school to protest inaction on climate change—you should too," *Guardian*, November 26, 2018.

2   Her mother writes in the *Guardian*, "Greta's father, Svante, and I are what is known in Sweden as 'cultural workers'—trained in opera, music and theatre with half a career of work in those fields behind us." Malena Ernman, "Malena Ernman on daughter Greta Thunberg: 'She was slowly disappearing into some kind of darkness' " *Guardian*, February 23, 2020.

3   The Hill, "READ: Teen activist Greta Thunberg's 8-sentence testimony to Congress," *The Hill*, September 17, 2019.

moral pressure on policymakers, to make them listen to the scientists, and then to take forceful action to limit global warming."[4] Although the politics of knowledge remains, the tactics have become more militant.

Fridays for the Future evolved into a coordinated movement toward the weeklong global climate strike that took place in September 2019, from the twentieth to the twenty-seventh. Prominent climate activists like Naomi Klein and Bill McKibben joined forces with Thunberg and other youth activists in calling for the strike. McKibben's article, "This Climate Strike Is Part of the Disruption We Need," forcefully argued, "Our job is precisely to disrupt business as usual" because "business as usual is what's doing us in."[5]

The global climate strike was by all accounts a resounding success. On the first day, an estimated 4 million took to the streets across the world.[6] A week later, an estimated half million turned out in Montreal alone.[7] This kind of mass action in the streets certainly achieves the goal of "moral pressure." The movement was inspiring because it indicated a new *historical agent of change* had emerged to tackle the climate crisis: youth. And youth was deploying the tactic most successful for the "agent" discussed in the last chapter: the working class.

But is that enough? After all, the strikes have not led to a large-scale implementation of climate policies across the world. The goals of some of the strikers seem more aligned with the professional-class strategy of simply spreading "awareness." Historically, the most effective aspect of the strike tactic is not its capacity for "moral pressure," but rather the structural pressure it brings to bear on capital's profits and the reproduction of society as a whole. For example, take the

4   fridaysforfuture.org/what-we-do/who-we-are.

5   Bill McKibben, "This climate strike is part of the disruption we need," *Yes Magazine*, September 3, 2019.

6   Eliza Barclay and Brian Resnick, "How big was the global climate strike? 4 million people, activists estimate," *Vox*, September 22, 2019.

7   CBC News, "Get a unique view inside (and above) Montreal's half-million climate march," September 28, 2019.

immensely successful West Virginia teachers' strike in spring 2018.[8] By organizing illegal strike participation among the majority of teachers, and building support and solidarity among parents and community members, the teachers shut down schools across West Virginia, creating an immediate crisis. They did not need to lobby the right-wing state legislature for incremental policy change. Within a couple weeks, they won their demands. This is how strikes can build power and win.

Jane McAlevey calls the climate strike goals "brilliant and . . . uncompromising" but contends that "to halt and reverse the carbon economy . . . requires far more power and a serious strategy."[9] The Fridays for the Future movement and the global climate strike never proposed to *shut down* society in any significant way. Striking was always a *choice* among student climate activists, and there were never enough students to actually shut down the schools themselves. The very decision to do it only on Fridays allowed schools mostly to function normally. The global climate strike tried to bring adult workers in for a symbolic one-day work stoppage in solidarity, but in the call to action, activists seemed to admit the strike lacked any teeth: "We are well aware that, by itself, this strike and a week of international climate action won't change the course of events."[10] More importantly, advocates advertised the strike as purely a choice:

> We know not everyone can join us. On a grossly unequal planet, some people literally can't do without a single day's pay, or they work for bosses who would fire them if they dared try. And some jobs simply can't stop: emergency room doctors should keep at their tasks.[11]

8   For a detailed account, see Eric Blanc, *Red State Revolt: The Teachers' Strike Wave and Working-Class Politics* (London: Verso, 2019).

9   Jane McAlevey, *A Collective Bargain: Unions, Organizing, and the Fight for Democracy* (New York: HarperCollins, 2020), 105.

10   Naomi Klein, et al., "We're stepping up—join us for a day to halt this climate crisis," *Guardian*, May 24, 2019.

11   Ibid.

McAlevey argues that specifically *labor strikes* have the capacity to build power for the working class against capital. But in order to be effective, she suggests that workers organize what she calls "supermajorities," where "80 percent or more" of the workforce participates in the strikes.[12] She explains, "Supermajority strikes (not symbolic strikes, and certainly not minority strikes) are unique because they forge unbreakable solidarity and build organization among a real 99 percent."[13] But, she admits, "supermajority strikes are hard."[14]

Indeed, building the kind of power that can take on fossil capital is going to be incredibly hard. But historically, working-class disruption has the proven capacity to effectively pressure capital and political elites. As Trish Kahle avows: "Workers have power if they act collectively. Just as they can stop oil production . . . they can halt capitalism's assault on the planet."[15] The difference between an optional school strike and working-class strikes is the basic Marxist insight that workers' strategic location at the "point of production" gives them the power to disrupt capital's profits, right at their source.[16] Moreover, the West Virginia teachers' power shut down a key site of social reproduction and forced the political class to concede to their demands.

In this chapter, before the climate movement can even entertain climate labor strikes, I maintain that a working-class strategy focused on production needs a clear sectoral strategy. I contend that electric power is the strategic sector we seek, not only for its central role in any decarbonization efforts, but also because it is already highly organized in terms of union organization. I review common left approaches to social change in the electricity sector—particularly the struggle for public power—and suggest they are too focused on technology and less aware of what sectors contain reservoirs of existing working-class organization.

---

12 McAlevey, *A Collective Bargain*, 157.
13 Jane McAelvey, "The Strike as the Ultimate Structure Test," *Catalyst*, Vol. 2, No. 3 (2018): 123–35; 133–4.
14 Ibid., 134.
15 Kahle, "The seeds of an alternative," *Jacobin*, February 19, 2015.
16 Vivek Chibber, "Why the working class?" *Jacobin*, March 13, 2016.

I also question the tendency to imagine energy transition as a "democratic" process of local and community control over distributed renewable energy at the expense of any larger-scale vision of the rapid and transformative changes needed. Such a voluntarist and localist vision is at odds with the large-scale global challenge we face. First, I review the broader framework in which most imagine combining labor and climate politics: a "just transition" to a clean energy economy.

Who Has the Power to Win a 'Just Transition'?

When analysts speak of workers in relation to climate change, the conversation quickly shifts to the concept of a "just transition." The broad idea is that the transition to carbon-free energy will necessarily involve job losses in the fossil fuel and other polluting sectors of the economy. Most important for this chapter is the fact that we must shut down many fossil fuel–powered electric power plants if decarbonization is going to be in line with what science says is necessary. A "just transition" seeks to protect those workers displaced and give the social supports to transition to a new energy economy.

This concept originated in an article by Tony Mazzocchi, a former vice president of the Oil, Chemical and Atomic Workers Union, titled "A Superfund for Workers?"[17] Mazzocchi argued that workers deserved the same protections from the shutdown of polluting industries as the land does. Referring to the robust Superfund law that requires remediation and cleanup of contaminated land, he asked sarcastically, "Why do we treat dirt better than we treat workers?"[18] Mazzocchi proposed a robust set of benefits for transitioning workers, modeled off the GI Bill for World War II veterans transitioning to private-sector jobs.[19] Notably such a program would require a drastic

---

17 Tony Mazzocchi, "A superfund for workers?" *Earth Island Journal*, Vol. 9, No. 1 (Winter 1993–1994): 40–1.

18 Ibid., 40.

19 Mazzocchi had enjoyed the benefits of the GI program himself. Les Leopold, *The*

expansion of the welfare state, reaffirming the central importance of
state power to a true working-class climate policy.

Although Mazzocchi was rightly trying to build working-class
power in the context of environmental transition, the underlying
assumption focuses on worker protection in a jobs-versus-environ-
ment zero-sum game. As he put it, "This debate over jobs and the
environment should be framed by those of us who are most victimized by current policy."[20] Fast forward more than twenty years, and
Jeremy Brecher, cofounder of the Labor Network for Sustainability,
also frames the just transition as focused on vulnerability and victim-
hood.[21] He describes the just transition as "a strategy [that] has been
emerging to protect workers and communities whose livelihoods may
be threatened by climate protection policies."[22] Thus, as Stefania Barca
astutely notes, "The [just transition] and climate jobs strategies, in
fact, see workers not as the political subjects of an ecological revolution, but as potential victims of climate policies."[23] In other words, this
framework envisions workers as lacking power rather than as sources
of power to deliver the gains a just transition involves. Environmental
scholars have cast a wider net of justice to include the "vulnerabilities
of the world's poorest people."[24] The "just transition" must not only
include workers whose jobs are lost, but also a wider set of marginalized communities living near polluting factories, suffering through
energy poverty, and dealing with the direct costs of climate change
like sea-level rise or drought. The larger framework seems to fore-
ground marginalized victims in need of redress rather than view them
as social forces that can actually win.

Man Who Hated Work and Loved Labor: The Life and Times of Tony Mazzocchi (White River
Junction, VT: Chelsea Green, 2007).

20   Ibid., 41.
21   Jeremy Brecher, "A Superfund for Workers," *Dollars and Sense*, Nov.–Dec. 2015:
20–4.
22   Ibid., 20.
23   Stefania Barca, "Labour and the ecological crisis: The eco-modernist dilemma in
western Marxism(s) (1970s–2000s)" *Geoforum*, Vol. 98 (2019): 226–35; 233.
24   Peter Newell and Dustin Mulvaney, "The political economy of the 'just transition',"
Geographical Journal, Vol. 179, No. 2 (2013): 132–40; 133.

Both concepts within the "just transition" (justice and transition) deserve scrutiny. First, *justice* has emerged as the core idea uniting radical environmental politics for the last generation. Although the variants of climate and energy justice are most relevant here, they all emerged under the broad umbrella of the environmental justice movement. With its roots in the Civil Rights movement, environmental justice emerged to tackle the uneven distribution of toxic pollution dumped in communities of color throughout the United States. In 1983, the Black residents of Warren County, North Carolina, used tactics of civil disobedience to fight the siting of a PCB toxic waste dump.[25] In 1987, the United Church of Christ Commission on Racial Justice released a report, *Toxic Waste and Race in the United States*, detailing the statistical overlaps between marginalized racial groups and toxic waste and other environmental hazards.[26] In 1991, Indigenous peoples, Black leaders, and others staged the First National People of Color Environmental Leadership Summit, declaring, "to begin to build a national and international movement of all peoples of color to fight the destruction and taking of our lands and communities, [we] do hereby re-establish our spiritual interdependence to the sacredness of our Mother Earth."[27] In February 1994, President Bill Clinton passed an executive order "to address environmental justice in minority populations and low-income populations."[28]

This historical narrative seeks to recount the rise to prominence of the environmental justice movement. Yet despite lots of attention, many insider scholar-activists have questioned its success. In the year after Clinton's historic executive order, Benjamin Goldman, a data analyst for the famous 1987 *Toxic Waste and Race* report, argued that the actual power of the environmental justice movement was akin to

25   Eileen McGurty, *Transforming Environmentalism: Warren County, PCBs, and the Origins of Environmental Justice* (New Bruinswick, NJ: Rutgers University Press, 2009).

26   United Church of Christ, Commission for Racial Justice, *Toxic Wastes and Race in the United States* (New York: United Church of Christ, 1987).

27   Delegates to the First National People of Color Environmental Leadership Summit, "Principles of Environmental Justice." ejnet.org/ej/principles.html.

28   "Summary of Executive Order 12898—Federal Actions to Address Environmental Justice in Minority Populations and Low-Income Populations." epa.gov.

"a gnat on the elephant's behind" and paled in comparison to the power of capital:

> As progressives have applauded the emergence of the environmental justice movement, we have witnessed a period of the most awesome intensification in inequality, and, ultimately, a historically significant triumph for the rulers of transnational capital who have further consolidated their power, fortunes, and global freedoms.[29]

He updated the data from the 1987 report to show that "Despite the increased attention to the issue, people of color in the United States are now even more likely than whites to live in communities with commercial hazardous waste facilities than they were a decade ago."[30] Twenty-five years later, Laura Pulido, Ellen Kohl, and Nicole-Marie Cotton came to a similar conclusion and cautiously called out the "failure" of environmental justice: "poor communities and communities of color are still overexposed to environmental harms."[31]

What are the limits of the justice framework? Marxists point out that the movement ultimately "speaks fundamentally to a liberal and, hence, distributional perspective on justice, in which justice is seen as Rawlsian fairness and associated with the allocation dynamics of environmental externalities."[32] In some variants, this language of distribution and "equity" yields some not so attractive principles. For instance, the Partnership for Southern Equity asserts its goal of "energy equity" as the "fair distribution of benefits and burdens from energy production and consumption."[33] Is our goal simply to equally

29   Benjamin Goldman, "What is the future of environmental justice?" *Antipode* 28, No. 2 (1995): 122–41; 130.

30   Given this was published after the Newt Gingrich Republican wave in 1994, I can only assume the metaphor was a conscious choice. Ibid., 127.

31   Laura Pulido, Ellen Kohl, and Nicole-Marie Cotton, "State regulation and environmental justice: The need for strategy reassessment," *Capitalism, Nature, Socialism*, Vol. 27, No. 2 (2016): 12–31; 12.

32   Erik Swyngedouw and Nik Heynen, "Urban political ecology, justice and the politics of scale," *Antipode*, Vol. 35, No. 5 (2003): 898–918; 910.

33   Partnership for Southern Equity, "Just Energy." psequity.org.

distribute noxious pollution or to establish "pollution prevention measures that prohibit whole families of dangerous pollutants from being produced in the first place"?[34] Indeed, the political goals of so-called "justice-centered" approaches now so popular in NGO and academic circles are not always clear. As Velicu and Barca put it, "The sense of injury called upon by justice scholarship is a usually moral rather than political one, lamenting the exclusion (of the 'poor') from the benefits of a liberal community which is supposedly benign if only more inclusive."[35]

Many justice-centered approaches lack a theory of power that explains how groups most affected by toxic pollution could build a coalition able to reverse these trends. Indeed, the justice framework has always focused on centering the most marginalized and vulnerable communities—or, to use Tony Mazzocchi's words above, the most victimized populations. The climate movement's version of this is the notion of "frontline communities" most impacted by climate change, like coastal fishing communities or drought-stricken peasant farmers. While this project certainly is morally important, and these struggles over livelihood are working-class struggles, these populations are defined by their social weakness. It does not present a vision of a social actor—whether the youth or the working class—with the *power* to win justice. The justice framework centers more on rectifying harms and eschews what Jane McAlevey calls a "credible plan to win."[36] Such a plan must also include a social force with what Velicu and Barca call "epoch-changing agency" with the capacity to force elites to respond to the radical demands of environmental and climate justice.[37]

This brings us to the second concept: *transition*. One problem with the "just transition" framework is that it *assumes* the transition

---

34 Daniel Faber, *Capitalizing on Environmental Injustice: The Polluter-Industrial Complex in the Age of Globalization* (Lanham, MD: Rowman and Littlefield, 2008), 121.

35 Irinia Velicu and Stefania Barca, "The just transition and its work of inequality," *Sustainability: Science, Practice and Policy*, Vol. 16, No. 1 (2020): 263–73; 265.

36 McAlevey, *A Collective Bargain*, 106.

37 Velicu and Barca, "The just transition and its work of inequality," 270.

is already happening—and that the only challenge is to take care of those "victimized" in its wake. But, as covered above, this is decidedly not the case.[38] Our global capitalist economy is still stubbornly dependent on fossil fuels. It has declined in recent years in the United States but still stands at 82 percent.[39] While renewable energy generation has definitely increased markedly in recent years, it has barely kept pace with overall energy demand. The 2019 International Energy Agency report says, "The gap between expectations of fast, renewables-driven energy transitions and the reality of today's energy systems in which reliance on fossil fuels remains stubbornly high."[40]

Thus, the very notion of a just transition needs first to ignite the transition itself. This means we cannot only center the most marginal and the most vulnerable, but also explain a key social actor with the strategic capacity to build the kind of power needed to force the transition. The student strike movement assumes this social actor is youth, but historically, the working class demonstrates more of a record of forcing major concessions from the capitalist class.

Workers possess a unique *structural power* at the point of production to withhold their labor and cut off capital's profits at the source. Workers would be at the core of a wider politics of disruption meant to create a crisis and demand a response.[41] Environmentalists have long understood the power of disruption, but usually deployed it *outside* the workplace in ways that appear antagonistic to workers. Edward Abbey's *The Monkey Wrench Gang* fictionally depicts activists putting their bodies in the way of mines and other infrastructure and using

38   Sean Sweeney and John Treat, "Trade unions and just transition: The search for a transformative politics," *Trade Unions for Energy Democracy: Working Paper No. 11*. (2018): rosalux-nyc.org, 1-2.

39   The World Bank, "Fossil fuel energy consumption (% of total (United States))." data.worldbank.org.

40   International Energy Agency, *World Energy Outlook 2019* (Paris: IEA, 2020), 23.

41   Frances Fox Piven and Richard Cloward, *Poor People's Movements: Why They Succeed, How They Fail* (New York: Vintage, 1977). Kevin A. Young, Michael Schwartz, and Tarun Banerjee, *Levers of Power: How the 1% Rules and What the 99% Can Do About It* (London: Verso, 2020).

tools to dismantle the machines of ecological destruction.[42] In real life, *Earth First!* developed the tactic of "tree sitting" to block the logging of old-growth forests. Today, what Naomi Klein calls "Blockadia" describes the many activists blocking pipeline expansion and other fossil fuel infrastructure like coal-fired power plants.[43] A modern-day "monkey wrench gang" includes the "valve turners" who use bolt cutters and other tools to shut down pipeline operations, or those activists of "Extinction Rebellion," which has blocked highways and even, controversially, working-class commuters.[44] These militants recognize the power of mass disruption in winning political demands. Yet the current army of direct-action eco-activists possess only limited disruptive capacity. They succeed in blocking a pipeline here, an oil train there, but fail to put much of a dent in the mass fossil fuel complex at the center of the reproduction of capitalism. The most inspiring and in many ways successful upsurge was the 2016 Indigenous uprising #NoDAPL at Standing Rock, which aimed to block the Dakota Access Pipeline. But President Donald Trump signed an order in 2017 authorizing completion of the pipeline, and now it carries, and indeed sometimes spills, fracked crude from the Bakken.[45] Although he shut down the Keystone Pipeline, President Joe Biden appears unwilling to shut down the Dakota Access.[46] There was a recent substantial struggle to physically block construction of a new pipeline, "Line 3," through ancestral unceded Indigenous territory in Minnesota near the White Earth Ojibwe reservation.[47] Illustrating the difficulty of building the

---

42   Edward Abbey, *The Monkey Wrench Gang* (Salt Lake City: Dream Garden Press, 1985).

43   Naomi Klein, *This Changes Everything*, Chapter 9, 293–336.

44   Eric Holthaus, "Valve turners try to shut off Minnesota pipelines, say 'politicians won't act'," *Grist*, Feburary 5, 2019. Matteo Moschella and Matthew Green, "Climate-change protesters disrupt London rush hour," *Reuters* October 17, 2019. For an excellent critique of the anti-politics of ER, see Marie Smith "Common Nonsense," *Jacobin*, No. 36 (Winter 2020): 58–65.

45   A court ordered the pipeline to shut down in the Summer of 2020. Reuters, "Dakota Access pipeline can keep running amid legal fight: US court," July 14, 2020.

46   Jordan Blum, "Dakota Access Pipeline will remain open after long legal fight, judge rules," *S&P Global Platts*, May 21, 2021.

47   Alleen Brown, "Corporate counterinsurgency: Indigenous water protectors face off with an oil company and police over a Minnesota pipeline," *The Intercept*, July 7, 2021.

power necessary to confront fossil capital, the pipeline began operation on October 1, 2021 (as protests continued in Washington DC).[48]

Workers possess unique power to disrupt capital from the inside, but striking workers rely on resources from unions like strike funds. Thus, a "credible plan to win" should not just include the working class, but more specifically the *organized* working class in the trade union movement. This means we need to start building what Sean Sweeney, the cofounder of Trade Unions for Energy Democracy, calls "ecological unionism."[49] In an article written with John Treat, Sweeney argues for moving from a "just transition" strategy focused on "social dialogue"—patient, polite negotiations with management or "social partners"—to one of "social power," "guided by the belief that current power relations must be challenged and changed."[50] A social power approach will "fight for solutions to the social and ecological crisis that are commensurate to the severity of that crisis, and [this] will entail the expansion of public ownership of key economic sectors and institutions."[51] Sweeney and Treat call upon a number of already existing militant union fights, from transit workers' and nurses' unions calling for climate action to South Korean workers in a coal-fired power plant *welcoming* its closure to usher in a transition to clean energy. Similarly, Dimitris Stevis and Romain Felli articulate a just transition strategy that is not only "reactive" but "proactive," or a "radical interpretation of just transition by relating it to the balance of power in society."[52] They go on to assert: "it will not be enough to recognize workers' voices or to understand that workers have less power . . . A more equitable transition will require reorganization of the relations between state, capital and labor."[53]

---

48   Alexander Panetta, "Line 3 did something rare for a pipeline that exports Canadian crude: It got built" *CBC News*, October 11, 2021.

49   Sean Sweeney, "Earth to labor: Economic growth is no salvation," *New Labor Forum*, Vol. 21, No. 1 (2012): 10–13.

50   Sean Sweeney and John Treat, "Trade unions and just transition," 5.

51   Ibid., 6.

52   Dimitris Stevis and Romain Felli, "Global labour unions and just transition to a green economy," *International Environmental Agreements*, Vol. 15 (2015): 29–43; 32, 38.

53   Ibid., 39.

Nevertheless, the trade union movement for "energy democracy" currently appears a bit scattered. The rhetorical commitment to social power does not guarantee building it: "The challenges facing both workers and workers' organizations are formidable, even immense, and using more forceful language is of little help on its own."[54] Simply gesturing for an economy-wide need for increased union organizing is too broad. Frankly, the climate crisis is dire and in need of rapid action, and the labor movement overall is so weak, we need a short-term and targeted strategy in a specific sector.

Jane McAlevey argues that historic wins for the labor movement always applied such a targeted strategy: "The brilliant organizers of the CIO understood that some sectors of the industrial economy, such as coal and steel, were key; they mattered more than others."[55] She maintains that health care, education, and logistics are the key sectors for union activists to focus on today.[56] These are good choices, but as Meagan Day and Micah Uetricht point out, "Defining what's strategic is as much an art as a science and varies depending on context."[57] The specific context of the climate crisis requires a different sectoral approach that strategically lays out the key node in the climate struggle.[58] Clearly, that node is the electric power sector.

Why the Electric Power Sector Is Strategic for the Climate Movement

While much of the debate over climate politics and energy policy focuses on the fossil fuel extractive industry, many energy scholars have pointed out that the electric power sector is the "linchpin" of any decarbonization strategy.[59] Much consternation over any union

---

54 Sweeny and Treat, "Trade unions and just transition," 31.

55 McAlevey, No Shortcuts, 203.

56 McAlevey "The Strike as the Ultimate Structure Test," 134.

57 Meagan Day and Micah Uetricht, Bigger Than Bernie: How We Go From the Sanders Campaign to Democratic Socialism (London: Verso, 2020), 185.

58 Ibid.

59 Jesse D. Jenkins, Max Luke, and Samuel Thernstrom, "Getting to Zero Carbon Emissions in the Electric Power Sector," Joule, Vol. 2 (2018): 2498–510; 2498.

strategy on climate will focus on those workers in the extractive industry dead set on maintaining the fossil fuel economy. But in contrast, the electric sector represents a neutral technological system that currently generates electricity not solely via fossil fuels, but via other sources as well, many of them relatively clean. A climate politics that only focuses on the negative program of destroying the fossil fuel industry needs also a positive politics of cleaning up electricity.

In many ways, decarbonizing the economy is one of the most complex challenges in human history. As stated above, the IPCC warns it will entail "unprecedented changes in all aspects of society." On the other hand, decarbonization is deceptively simple. This linchpin has coalesced around one slogan: *electrify everything.*[60] Our energy system is currently bifurcated between those things that run on electricity (lighting, appliances, industrial motors, electronics) and that that run on other forms of energy, like liquid fuels for transport, residential and commercial heating (mainly natural gas furnaces), and industrial energy uses (for example, heat energy for chemical processes like the production of hydrogen reviewed in Chapter 2). Theoretically, many of these non-electric energy applications can be electrified, moving them for example, from gasoline to battery-powered automobiles, from natural-gas furnaces to electric heat pumps, and from combustion-based industrial heat to electric heat to replace such processes as steam reforming for hydrogen with electrolysis.[61]

The basis of the electrify-everything strategy is first to clean up the existing electric power sector, and second to greatly expand clean electricity production to absorb the new demand from the transport,

---

60   See, David Roberts, "The key to tackling climate change: electrify everything," *Vox*, October 27, 2017.

61   It should be noted there are certain energy applications that are very hard or impossible to electrify—long-haul trucking, aviation, and marine transport come to mind. Industries like steel and cement require enormous heat energy and also rely on fossil fuels for feedstock. These are problems, but the strategy here suggests we can cross that bridge once we've electrified *everything else*. See, Adam Baylin-Stern, Asbjørn Hegelund, and Andreas Schröder, "Commentary: Frontier electric technologies in industry," *International Energy Agency*, May 29, 2019. iea.org/commentaries/frontier-electric-technologies-in-industry.

heating, and industrial sectors. What this all means is that we do not decarbonize without clean electrification. Thus, it is clear: a working-class climate strategy that targets the electric sector would make sense. Yet we cannot ground our strategy *only* in technological terms that make sense to electrical engineers but to few others. We need a broader social and political analysis. I see three reasons why the electric power sector could be a strategic organizing space for climate labor action.

First, the electric utility sector is already subject to intense public oversight and political contestation. While the electric utility sector is largely run by private or "investor-owned" utilities (investor-owned utilities service 72 percent of US electricity customers[62]), this is not a typical private-sector industry. Since the early 1900s, what historian Richard Hirsh calls the "utility consensus" arose to grant private investor-owned electric utilities exclusive monopoly control of electricity in specific territories.[63] But because of concerns with monopoly power, Public Utility Commissions (PUCs) emerged to regulate utilities at the state level. These PUCs mostly focus on making sure that utilities charge "fair and reasonable" prices to consumers, while also justifying their costs and "fair" returns or profits. But some states empower their PUCs to make sure utilities operate in ways that are "consistent with the 'public interest.'"[64] Thus, unlike much of the private sector, which many assume should be immune from politics, electric utilities are already explicitly political entities.

The main venue of political struggle is often "rate cases," where utilities argue before PUCs for rate increases. These public hearings have long been spaces where environmental activists intervene to call

62   Energy Information Administration, "Investor-owned utilities served 72% of US electricity customers in 2017," August 15, 2019. eia.gov.

63   Richard F. Hirsh, *Power Loss: The Origins of Deregulation and Restructuring of the American Utility Industry* (Cambridge, MA: MIT Press, 1999). See also Leah Stokes, *Short Circuiting Policy: Interest Groups and the Battle Over Lean Energy and Climate Policy in the American States* (Oxford, UK: Oxford University Press, 2020), 73–9.

64   Scott Strauss and Katharine Mapes, "Union power in public utilities: Defending worker and consumer health and safety," *New Labor Forum*, Vol. 21, No. 2 (2012): 87–95; 88.

attention to the environmental impacts of utilities, but they also can be sites where workers and unions can bring their concerns. As Scott Strauss and Katharine Mapes point out, "Many traditional labor union concerns—including ensuring adequate staffing levels and safe working conditions—are intimately intertwined with a utility's ability to provide adequate service."[65] From a climate standpoint, workers could link their concerns with "safety" to a wider vision of "safe" levels of emissions on a planetary scale.

Second, electrical workers possess literal *power* over the economy as a whole. The electric sector is central to the social reproduction of both everyday life and capital accumulation.[66] Traditional labor and union strategy often seeks to find specific "choke points" where shutting down a port or logistics hub could potentially create a wider crisis to ensure that demands are met.[67] Although taken for granted, electricity is at the core of almost everything we do in an increasingly digital world. When the power goes out, people notice.[68] Speaking theoretically, a strike in the electricity sector would effectively shut down society, creating the effect of a general strike, given that economic activity is impossible without electricity.[69] Not only is electricity central to virtually every economic activity, it is also immune from offshoring. McAlevey makes this same point about other strategic industries like health care and education.[70] This power is also rooted in the fact that the mass of the public relies on electricity as consumers. Since we have ceded electricity distribution mostly to private investor-owned utilities demanding high rates to support their "fair" rates of return, there is already an existing reservoir of mass working-class anger toward utility companies. As

---

65   Ibid.

66   For the social centrality of electricity, see David Nye, *Electrifying America: Social Meanings of a New Technology, 1880–1940* (Cambridge, MA: MIT Press, 1990).

67   See, Kim Moody, *On New Terrain*, 59–90.

68   See, David Nye, *When the Lights Went Out: A History of Blackouts in America* (Cambridge, MA: MIT Press, 2010).

69   We will explore the strike or disruption strategy in the electric sector in the next chapter. Obviously, it is not without pitfalls.

70   McAlevey, *No Shortcuts*, 203–4.

Tony Mazzocchi put it: "The most radical piece of literature in America reaches the home of every American each month . . . it's called the utility bill. It is escalating the indignation of the American people."[71]

Third, the electric sector is already one of the most unionized sectors in the world in general, and in the United States specifically. According to industrial relations economists Barry Hirsch and David Macpherson's union statistics database, the electric power generation, transmission and distribution sector has 24.5 percent union membership in 2020—well above the economy-wide average of 10.8 percent[72] (some electrical occupations, like electrical power-line installers and repairers, enjoy even higher union density of 45.8 percent)[73] Apart from some specific industries like postal services, education, and public administration, this is one of the most unionized sectors in the entire economy. This means there is *already* an existing base of social power within the industry itself. Although there is an urgent need to "organize the unorganized," we cannot ignore the roughly 14.3 million *existing* union members who have a unique capacity to transform the industries of which they are a part.[74] Most climate politics bemoans the ways in which existing union leadership and power structures align *against* climate action[75] but rarely raise the question of organizing unions from within to promote strategies that are both pro-worker and pro-climate.

Throughout this book, I have argued that the climate struggle is about *power*. For Jane McAlevey, to win power you need to understand who currently has power. Thus, as we have seen, every social movement must start with what she calls a "power structure analysis" that maps the relations of power preventing you from achieving your

71   Leopold, *The Man Who Hated Work and Loved Labor*, 377.

72   Barry T. Hirsch and David A. Macpherson, "Union Membership and Coverage Database From the Current Population Survey." unionstats.com.

73   Ibid.

74   Bureau of Labor Statistics, "Union Members Summary," January 22, 2021. bls.gov.

75   Matto Mildenberger, *Carbon Captured: How Business and Labor Control Climate Politics* (Cambridge, MA: MIT Press, 2020).

goals.[76] For climate struggles, our class analysis points to who has the power to direct investment over *production*. For electricity, the answer is obvious: the private investor-owned utility industry has enormous power over the "means" of electricity production, distribution, and transmission.[77]

It has also amassed significant political power. As Robert Brulle details, the industry spent $554 million in lobbying between 2000 and 2016.[78] We often pay excessive attention to the fossil fuel extraction industry, but as Leah Stokes argues, we need to pay more attention to utilities: "Utilities waged a war on environmental science, casting doubt on climate change, acid rain, and mercury pollution."[79] She describes climate politics as "organized combat" and suggests that our policies must "effectively challenge . . . electric utilities as vested interest groups."[80]

Yet, as shown in Chapter 3, the least of the problems with the private utility industry is its effect on our *knowledge* of climate science. It is clear that the utility industry actively blocks clean energy policies because such policies pose a threat to accumulation, or as Stokes describes, "guaranteed profits from their regulators."[81] For example, Arizona theoretically should be the Saudi Arabia of solar energy production in the United States. But Stokes details how the private Arizona Public Services utility used its oversized power to fund and elect regulators to the Public Utility Commission, which then

76   McAlevey, *No Shortcuts*, 4.

77   Electricity is not your ordinary commodity and is best viewed as a "production system" that includes the transmission and distribution of power. I will say that the deregulation of electricity has *weakened* the power of the utility industry over electric generation. This has laid the basis for the emergence of "independent power producers," as explained below. But even in deregulated states, utilities have a kind of "monopsony" power as the single buyers of electricity for their regulated distribution territories.

78   Cited in Stokes, *Short Circuiting Policy*, 72. Robert Brulle, "The climate lobby: A sectoral analysis of lobbying spending on climate change in the USA, 2000–2016," *Climatic Change*, Vol. 149, No. 3–4 (2018): 289–303.

79   Stokes, *Short Circuiting Policy*, 97.

80   Ibid., 25, 33.

81   Ibid., 249.

proceeded to dismantle a decade's worth of solar incentives overnight. Neither the interest groups aligned with the solar industry nor the significant number of public environmental protests were any match for the utility's power.[82]

Crucially, utilities have already existing fixed capital investments sunk in fossil fuel infrastructure, which gives them a decided interest in blocking clean energy. In Michigan, existing investments in natural-gas pipelines and coal-fired power plants have led DTE energy to pass policies making it harder for small-scale solar, wind, and hydroelectric production to feed into the grid.[83] One Michigan state senator who supports public power argues that clean energy production brings benefits to the public but poses "a threat to the companies' business model and corporate profits."[84]

So, the question is, how can we effectively challenge the power of the private utility industry over the electricity sector and rapidly create a public power system? There are two major theories at hand. First, there are many who believe in the power of *market forces* to allow small-scale energy producers to "disrupt" the power of utilities through competition, lower prices, and better service. There is some evidence that process is underway, but not at a fast enough pace. When the pace intensifies, utilities deploy their political power to block progress.[85] Second, a different vision of electricity politics sees it as a wide set of conflicting "interest groups" in a democratic society wherein state power is subject to pressure.[86] Just as the utility industry has the Edison Electric Institute and aligns with the "dark money" of the Koch brothers network of fossil capital, clean energy advocates point to environmental advocacy organizations like the Sierra Club and clean energy trade associations like the Solar Energy Industries Association. But repeatedly, it appears that these

---

82   See, ibid., 164–93.
83   Tom Perkins, "DTE and Consumers Energy are broken and dangerous. Is it time for publicly owned utilities?" *Detroit Metro Times*, November 13, 2019.
84   Ibid.
85   Stokes, *Short Circuiting Policy*.
86   Ibid., 3.

clean-energy actors are *underresourced* when compared to the power of utilities and their allies in the fossil fuel complex.[87] The "organized combat" between interest groups may yield small victories here and there, but again at nowhere near the pace needed. Stokes advises that "clean energy advocates must learn from their opponents' playbook,"[88] but what if the game is stacked against them from the start?

Both visions suggest different actors and mechanisms of building social power. One envisions entrepreneurs using the mechanism of prices to spur change, and the other focuses on political groups using organizing and advocacy. The alternative I advocate is a *class struggle* approach to changing the utility industry. I base this on the premise that utility workers themselves can leverage their unique strategic power over electricity systems to make rapid and transformative changes.

What kind of changes? The electricity system, itself an interconnected grid infrastructure, requires massive restructuring with a primary goal of decarbonization. There is one primary obstacle: only one criterion shapes needed investments in electric infrastructure like new transmission lines and generation: cost and profitability. A recent International Monetary Fund working paper posits:

> Private investment in productive capital and infrastructure faces high upfront costs and significant uncertainties that cannot always be priced. Investments for the transition to a low-carbon economy are additionally exposed to important political risks, illiquidity and uncertain returns, depending on policy approaches to mitigation as well as unpredictable technological advances.[89]

While this analysis refers to "climate mitigation" investments in

---

87 This is the main takeaway from Stokes's book.

88 Stokes, *Short Circuiting Policy*, 227.

89 Signe Krogstrup and William Oman, *Macroeconomic and Financial Policies for Climate Change Mitigation: A Review of the Literature* (Washington, DC: International Monetary Fund, 2019), 15.

general, it relates specifically to electricity in the United States. In many regional transmission organizations (RTOs), clean energy generation is currently blocked from grid interconnection because the costs are too high.[90] Solar energy is so cheap at certain times of the day it actually becomes *unprofitable* to investors.[91] Such variable energy still needs backup power when it is unavailable, but firm sources of clean power like nuclear, geothermal, or long-duration storage are "uncompetitive" in market terms. So grid systems lean on fossil fuels like methane-leaking natural gas.[92]

Rapid decarbonization would rely on two forces inimical to market systems. First, we need centralized public planning to build out new, clean energy generation of all kinds, as fast as possible. Planning is required to connect this clean energy via an upgraded and nationally integrated "supergrid" of new transmission lines. The current transmission grid is heavily balkanized by state, regional, and private interests and would require federal coordination.[93] Second, we need enormous public investment, regardless of whether it's profitable or cost-effective. Like the rural electrification system of the New Deal era, a program implemented because private utilities found it unprofitable to invest in rural areas, we need to invest in new electricity systems because of a planetary emergency, regardless of cost.

These two principles of planning and public investment coalesce along a longstanding force in electricity: *public power*. Only publicly owned electricity can invest and plan with long-term infrastructural—and planetary—goals in mind. It should be noted that public

90   Miranda Willson, "FERC complaint highlights 'structural problem' for renewables," *E&E News*, May 25, 2021.

91   James Temple, "The lurking threat to solar power's growth," *MIT Technology Review*, July 14, 2021. For a wider theoretical and empirical account of how fossil fuels generate more profits than renewables, see Brett Christophers, "Fossilised capital: Price and profit in the energy transition" *New Political Economy* (early view, 2021), 1-14.

92   David Roberts, "Long-duration storage can help clean up the electricity grid, but only if it's super cheap," *Volts*, June 9, 2021.

93   David Roberts, "Transmission week: Why we need more big power lines," *Volts*, January 25, 2021.

power does not guarantee a sensible decarbonization plan (many public power companies are notoriously dirty and even highly undemocratic);[94] it merely opens the door to broader social control over investment and production. So, for good reason, public power has emerged as a key campaign among socialists. The Democratic Socialists of America have launched several such campaigns across the country, and, as mentioned in the previous chapter, in the spring of 2021, socialist Congresswoman Cori Bush and Congressman Jamaal Bowman announced a Congressional resolution asserting, "The United States must establish electricity as a basic human right and public good."

This resolution emerged from the catastrophic failure of private utilities during the deadly winter power outage in Texas earlier in the year, as well as longstanding failures of private for-profit utilities to offer affordable electricity to poor and working-class populations; there is also a strong rationale for public power on climate grounds. But so far, such socialist organizing has not paid much attention to the heavily unionized workers at the very core of this sector.[95] The roll call of endorsements for Bush and Bowman's resolution is a laundry list of environmental NGOs and other radical left-wing groups, but it includes only one trade union, from Puerto Rico.[96]

What role could actual electrical workers play in making a large-scale public power system happen? Unfortunately, most visions of public power today do not consider workers much at all, and remain stuck in the many shibboleths of environmentalist ideology favoring small-is-beautiful, localist solutions while the larger planet burns. A class struggle for public power would necessarily look different.

---

94 Stokes, *Short Circuiting Policy*, 246.

95 Fred Stafford, "How Trump Got His Right-Wing New Deal Victory," *Jacobin*, August 17, 2020.

96 bush.house.gov.

The Road to (Public) Power

> Ever larger grow the industries, ever more and more industries are concentrated in a single land . . . So it is that the road is being prepared for the social organization of production.
>
> —Karl Kautsky, *The Road to Power*, 1909

After decades of faith in markets and a private-sector-led decarbonization policy, it turns out the most rapid decarbonization programs have been led by the public sector, in places like France and Sweden.[97] Only the public sector can utilize central planning and *socialize* the costs of building the massive new and long-term infrastructure needed to transform the grid. The question is how should we imagine a shift to public power, where the public sector can rapidly build the energy system we need?

The debate over the direction of the electricity system typically focuses on two core themes. First, there is a fervent and purely technical debate centered on the best means of electricity generation. Obviously, the fossil fuel industry organizes around maintaining systems of coal- and gas-fired power generation. But among the climate advocacy community, there are stark divisions on what is the best path to a decarbonized electric system. Some scholars and activists argue for a path based on 100 percent renewable energy (wind, solar, geothermal, and water resources).[98] Others insist that this is unattainable because of the intermittent nature of renewables like solar and wind, which can generate energy only when the sun is shining or the wind is blowing, and unrealistic assumptions about the capacities of hydropower.[99] Then the debate pivots among those who argue we can construct a "smart" supergrid where intermittent

97 Jameson McBride, "The Green New Deal and the Legacy of Public Power," *The Breakthrough Institute*, December 17, 2018.

98 See, Mark Z. Jacobson, et al., "100% clean and renewable wind, water, and sunlight all-sector energy roadmaps for 139 countries of the world," *Joule*, Vol. 1 (2018): 108–21.

99 Christopher T.M. Clack, et al., "Evaluation of a proposal for reliable low-cost grid power with 100% wind, water, and solar," *PNAS*, Vol. 114, No. 26 (2017): 6722–7.

sources can effectively balance each other out, and others who emphasize the necessity of large-scale deployment of energy storage such as
batteries and other long-term options.[100] Still others insist that one
oft-ignored zero-carbon source must complement or even supersede
renewables: nuclear power.[101] Regardless of one's position, the key
question zeroes in on *technology*, as if we are free to construct the
technological system we want.

Second, the debate often advocates a *new geography* of electricity,
based on what is called "distributed" renewable generation. The first
and most famous version of this argument is Amory Lovins's advocacy of a "soft path" energy system based on increased energy efficiency and *decentralized* power sources like residential solar, dispersed
wind farms, geothermal, and other scattered resources.[102] Lovins
contrasted this with the "hard path" based on *centralized* power
generation characteristic of the fossil fuel-powered electric utility.
Underlying this discourse is an assumption that centralized power
generation is inherently bad, despite the fact that for decades, the vast
majority of electricity has been generated in centralized power plants,
whether hydroelectric, nuclear, gas, or coal.

These debates are mostly ambivalent about the core question: what
kind of social power might achieve these transformations? The technological debates are purely technocratic in the sense that they assume
sensible democratic societies will adopt the smartest technologies.
Lovins himself has become a passionate believer in markets as rational
mechanisms to choose the cheapest source of power. In an article
attacking the high cost of nuclear energy, he lambastes what he calls
"anti-market monkeybusiness" and makes his position plain: "Citizens
who care about climate or markets or both . . . should vigorously

---

100   Recently, a team of scholars at Princeton University produced an increasingly
influential assessment of the various options. Eric Larson, et al., *Net-Zero America: Potential
Pathways, Infrastructure, and Impacts* (Princeton, NJ: Princeton University Press, 2020).
101   For a useful overview, see International Energy Agency, *Nuclear Power in a Clean
Energy System* (Paris: International Energy Agency, 2019).
102   Amory Lovins, *Soft Energy Paths: Towards a Durable Peace* (London: Penguin,
1977).

defend markets' ability to choose climate solutions that can save the most carbon per dollar and per year."[103] Other pro-renewable authors always tend to emphasize that the technical means already exist for clean energy: "While social and political barriers exist, converting to 100 percent WWS using existing technologies is technically and economically feasible."[104] It is easy to bracket these social and political barriers, even though they continue to prevent the technical transformations the technocrats propose.

The question of social power for the advocates of a new geography of electricity is more interesting. For these advocates, the outsized *power* of the centralized utility system is the problem itself. The "soft path" vision of distributed energy hinges on the idea that power itself should be "decentered," and that a multiplicity of small, scattered, and ultimately local producers would be a far more desirable system. For instance, Gretchen Bakke's brilliant and engaging investigation into the US grid system rehearses the common disdainful way of describing centralized utilities: "The business of making and delivering power was a remarkably centralized activity, run by 'natural' monopolies (the utilities) that built infrastructure according to a top-down system of command-and-control."[105] Stokes also derisively refers to utilities as "monopolistic rent-seekers."[106]

This critique of *centralized power*, so common since the 1970s, aligns with neoliberalization, or the rightward shift of politics itself over the same period. Recall Hayek's celebration of the price system in Chapter 3 as the ultimate decentered power system where all decisions are individual and local, and no central power "directs" (or *plans*) the economy "according to a top-down system of command-and-control" (to recall Bakke's words). Moreover, although we usually point out the neoliberal disdain for state power, neoliberals also abhor

---

103 Amory Lovins, "Does Nuclear Power Slow or Speed Climate Change?" *Forbes*, November 18, 2019.

104 Jacobson, et al., "100%," 119.

105 Gretchen Bakke, *The Grid: The Fraying Wires Between Americans and Our Energy Future* (New York: Bloomsbury, 2016), xvi.

106 Stokes, *Short Circuiting Policy*, 191.

monopoly power as inimical to a free and competitive market system. Milton Friedman maintained that monopoly power "inhibits effective freedom of exchange" while characteristically pointing out that "monopoly frequently if not generally arises from government support."[107] In the case of electric utilities, however, he is correct— PUCs ultimately sanction the centralized "natural monopoly" of an investor-owned utility. The most common critique of PUCs is their tendency toward "regulatory capture" by the utility industry itself. Thus it should come as no surprise that neoliberal ideology shaped the massive *deregulation* of the electric utility industry with highly uneven results, like the blackouts in California in 2000–1.[108] Ironically, the neoliberal celebration of competition and decentralization has actually ushered in an era of *increasing* corporate consolidation and monopoly power,[109] and the abhorrence of central planning has led to multinational corporate planning systems like Walmart and Amazon that dwarf the Soviet command state.[110] Furthermore, critics of any forms of centralized power increasingly characterize unions as bastions of "corruption" and "unfair practices" (as we saw in Chapter 3, since the 1970s critics have charged unions with causing inflation with their unfair "political" interventions in the economy).[111]

Moreover, the deregulation of the electric utility sector is what has enabled the growth of small-scale renewable production—production that used to be under the monopoly control of the centralized utilities. Although we imagine small homeowners with solar panels as

107   Milton Friedman, *Capitalism and Freedom* (Chicago: University of Chicago Press, 1962), 28.

108   See, Hirsh, *Power Loss*; also Stokes, *Short Circuiting Policy*, 88–93.

109   David Dayen, *Monopolized: Life in the Age of Corporate Power* (New York: The New Press, 2020).

110   Leigh Phillips and Michal Rozworski, *The People's Republic of Walmart: How the World's Largest Corporations Are Laying the Foundation for Socialism* (London: Verso, 2019).

111   Mildenberger's *Carbon Captured* lumps labor and capital together as two kinds of "carbon-dependent economic actors" (23). Noting how few pay attention to labor's role in opposing climate policy, he cites a Koch-funded think tank claiming that they find great allies in unions (19). This chapter and the next is a wager we can see unions as more open to class struggle and not as just tools of the Kochs.

the prototypical renewable producer (or "prosumer," at once a consumer and producer of electricity), rather, it is small, independent power producers now dominating the renewables industry.[112] Such power producers might include those who construct large-scale solar or wind farms on leased or owned land scattered across the countryside.[113] This has created a completely private industry that traditional Marxist class analysis would describe as the petty bourgeoisie.[114] While small renewable capital might actually build these projects, giant conglomerates like the Goldman Sachs Renewable Power Group or Big Tech firms like Google or Facebook usually finance them.[115] These companies are not only often small, their existence is often perilously dependent on state policies and programs that go into and out of effect, as in Arizona reviewed above. This ensures the clean energy transition will happen only if it is profitable, and it ensures that the industry supposedly charged with delivering this transition will be ideologically pro-market, anti–public power, and even anti-union. This is precisely *not* the kind of large-scale and coordinated transition that climate science says is required at this point.

The "soft" path to distributed energy is rooted in a dispersed vision of small-scale communities taking the grid back by developing their own renewable production and "microgrids."[116] This small-scale local vision also shapes the movement for public power. One reason is purely infrastructural: in the past, it made sense to set up municipally owned power grids servicing an entire urban territory. The movement for "municipalization" of electricity is the most common

---

112 Nina Kelsey and Jonas Meckling, "Who wins in renewable energy? Evidence from Europe and the United States," *Energy Research and Social Science*, Vol. 37 (2018): 65–73.

113 Ibid.

114 For a larger study of the 'clean tech' industry and its various pro-capitalist ideologies, see Jesse Goldstein, *Planetary Improvement: Cleantech Entrepreneurship and the Contradictions of Green Capitalism* (Cambridge, MA: MIT Press, 2018).

115 See, Sam Schechner, "Amazon and Other Tech Giants Race to Buy Up Renewable Energy," *Wall Street Journal*, June 23, 2021, and "RIC Energy to Partner With Goldman Sachs Renewable Power on the Development of 47 MW of Community Solar Projects," *Businesswire*, March 4, 2021.

116 Ivan Penn and Clifford Krauss, "More Power Lines or Rooftop Solar Panels: The Fight Over Energy's Future," *New York Times*, July 11, 2021.

geographical expression of public power, and discourse that emphasizes concepts of the "local" and "community" suffuses the public
power movement in general. The Public Power Association begins its
explainer on the benefits of public power: "Public power utilities are
community-owned, locally controlled and operated on a not-for-
profit basis."[117] The subtitle of the report is: "Local control. Local
priorities. A stronger local economy." One of the most prominent
advocates, Johanna Bozuwa of the Next System Project, also advocates "community-owned" renewable-energy utilities as an alternative to investor-owned ones. She proposes a vision of local control
and benefits: "When renewable energy is kept local, the economic
returns to the community grow apace."[118]

Few seem to acknowledge the ways in which "local" or "community"
control has long been a trope in the conservative movement to protect
highly exclusionary school districts, laws, and tax bases.[119] Indeed, there
already are locally controlled electric utilities that espouse reactionary
politics. According to Stokes, the public Salt River Project in Arizona
"resembles a feudal institution . . . only landowners vote."[120] Although a
product of the progressive New Deal era, highly exclusionary local
boards often run rural electric cooperatives in the American South.
Nathan Schneider describes Mississippi electric co-ops as institutions
ultimately oppressive to Black and poor populations characterized by,
"exorbitant bills, all-white boards in Black-majority districts, opaque
governance procedures that prevented participation."[121]

Most importantly, the localist vision of public power represents a
contradiction between the scale of the climate crisis and the imagined

117   American Public Power Association, *Public Power for Your Community: Local
Control. Local Priorities. A Stronger Local Economy* (Arlington, VA: American Public Power
Association, 2016), 12.

118   Johanna Bozuwa, "Public ownership for energy democracy," *The Next System*,
September 3, 2018. thenextsystem.org/learn/stories/public-ownership-energy-democracy.

119   See, for example, Mary C. Brennan, *Turning Right in the Sixties: The Conservative
Capture of the GOP* (Chapel Hill, NC: University of North Carolina Press, 1995), 8.

120   Stokes, *Short Circuiting Policy*, 168.

121   Nathan Scheidner, "The $164 Billion Co-ops You Don't Know About," *Nation*
(May 22–9, 2017), 26–31; 29.

scale of social change. It is nearly impossible to imagine how we can tackle climate change by creating one local community public power system at a time.[122] An uncertain and protracted legal struggle still afflicts one of the most celebrated cases of municipalization, in Boulder, Colorado.[123] Moreover, if indeed the future of energy is powered by decentralized renewable energy, energy scholars have shown that the only way this kind of energy system will work is through "a nationally integrated grid" where production in dispersed areas can make up for curtailment in others, where the sun or wind is not available.[124] This means *more*, not less central planning of local production. Another major problem with this vision of public power is if you take over private investor-owned utilities at the local or even state level, the workers and unions shift into public-sector labor law— away from the National Labor Relations Board (NLRB) that oversees private-sector works. Highly variable by state, public-sector labor law can come with disadvantages, like prohibition on strikes. If left movements for public power want to succeed, they cannot hobble the rights of the unions in those very sectors; rather, they'll need those unions on their side.[125]

Overall, public power aligned with Lovins's "soft path" vision of distributed energy is trapped in what Greg Sharzer calls an ideology of "localism" which asserts that "factories, governments, bureaucracies have grown too big."[126] And indeed, the idea of creating micro-alternatives to capitalism has suffused the "small is beautiful" mantra of environmental politics since at least the back-to-the-land movements of the 1960s. The problem with localist politics, according to Sharzer, is it

122 Stokes, *Short Circuiting Policy*, 246–7.

123 Sam Lounsberry, "Boulder, Xcel to discuss alternatives that could end city's decade-long push for a municipal utility," *The Denver Post*, May 13, 2020.

124 Clack, et al., "Evaluation of a proposal for reliable low-cost grid power with 100% wind, water, and solar," 6723.

125 C.M. Lewis, "Opinion: Public utility campaigns have a labor problem," *Strikewave*, July 29, 2021.

126 Greg Sharzer, *No Local: Why Small-Scale Alternatives Won't Change the World* (Winchester, UK: Zero Books), 8.

"assumes we can't make large-scale, collective social change."[127] The best we can do is create very small micro-alternatives to capitalism that do not fundamentally challenge the power relations shaping society as a whole (what Erik Olin Wright calls the "escaping capitalism" strategy).[128] Sharzer says community-alternative "prospects are severely limited by the power of capital."[129] Or, as Jodi Dean quipped, "Goldman Sachs doesn't care if you raise chickens." I'll put it this way: Duke Energy does not care if you set up a locally owned micro-grid.

The localist path to social change is also deeply at odds with a traditional Marxist vision of transforming social production. From Marx's perspective, capitalism produces the material basis for eman-cipation *through* the development of large-scale and ever-more centralized industry. He explained how capitalism tends to *centralize* capital through the "expropriation of many capitalists by a few."[130] But through this centralization process, production itself becomes more and more *socialized*:

> The growth of the co-operative form of the labor process, the conscious technical application of science, the planned exploitation of the soil, the transformation of the means of labor into forms in which they can only be used in common, the economizing of all means of production by their use as the means of production of combined, socialized labour.[131]

It is fundamental to Marx's vision of socialism that the working class would *expropriate* these socialized production systems to assert social, not private, control: "namely co-operation and the possession in common of the land and the means of production produced by labor itself."[132]

127   Ibid., 3.
128   Erik Olin Wright, *How to Be an Anti-Capitalist in the 21st Century* (London: Verso, 2019), 51–3.
129   Sharzer, *No Local*, 2.
130   Marx, *Capital*, Vol. 1, 929.
131   Ibid.
132   Ibid.

We love to hate big, bulky centralized electric utilities, but they are actually precisely what Marx—and Kautsky in this section's epigraph—meant by *socialized production*. In 2000, the National Academy of Engineering named the modern electric grid the greatest engineering achievement of the twentieth century.[133] Unlike most other commodities, electricity can only be produced at the same moment it will be consumed. The material necessity of balancing supply and demand means modern grids and centralized utilities are inherently *socialized planning machines* that involve measuring and predicting millions of households and businesses' electricity consumption every day. While many imagine upstart distributed energy will naturally displace these juggernauts, the vast majority of electricity users *still* get their electricity from centralized power generation—roughly 88.2 percent in the United States.[134]

The "soft path" seems to imagine a distributed energy system will slowly displace the centralized grid system over time. But rather than assuming we have to create an entirely new geography of electricity, it is more convincing to imagine social transformation through our *existing* centralized power grid. Here again, we have a major advantage: an already existing base of social power internal to that system itself—a heavily organized union workforce.

One of the most controversial forms of carbon-free energy is nuclear power. Yet while most people debate nuclear versus other energy sources on the merits of its cost or its environmental safety, we might also ask which energy forms contain bases of *working-class power*? On this front, nuclear is clearly a winner. The Utility Workers of America, for example, are champions of nuclear as key to climate solutions. In Congressional testimony, union president Lee Anderson said, "At a time when growing economies are demanding more power than ever, the need to bring large sources of reliable

---

133 Robert Bryce, *A Question of Power: Electricity and the Wealth of Nations* (New York: Public Affairs, 2020), 18.

134 Energy Information Administration, "FAQ: What is US electricity generation by energy source?" https://www.eia.gov.

power on line in a small footprint using the existing grid could not be more compelling."[135]

Meanwhile, solar and other renewable production are notorious for hiring nonunion contract labor for dangerous jobs.[136] A 2020 report on US Energy and employment found that solar electric and wind generation are among the *least* unionized sectors in the electric generation industry: 4 percent and 6 percent respectively, while nuclear generation is 12 percent (fossil-fuel facilities are also high, at 11 percent for natural gas–fired plants and 10 percent at coal-fired plants).[137] Most solar and wind jobs are scattered construction and installation jobs, but utility workers could fight for more centralized "utility scale" solar power plants that would require union jobs to build and operate. In fact, some International Brotherhood of Electrical Workers (IBEW) locals in California have done exactly that, and celebrated a union-based pathway of solar-energy production based on "grid-scale solar projects."[138] Still, this might be more the exception than the rule. A detailed *New York Times* report of labor conditions at utility-scale solar farms found "grueling work schedules, few unions, middling wages and limited benefits."[139] The director of renewable energy for the Utility Workers Union of America said: "The clean tech industry is incredibly anti-union . . . It's a lot of transient work,

135   Lee Anderson, Government Affairs Director, Utility Workers Union of America, Before the 116th Congress, House Committee on Energy and Commerce Subcommittee on Energy Role of the Power Sector in Creating a 100 Percent Clean Economy in the United States, Rayburn House Office Building, Room 2322 Wednesday, October 20, 2019.

136   Jessica Goodheart, "Have Solar Panel Companies Grown Too Quickly?" *Atlantic*, April 12, 2017. For a fascinating study of solar production's reliance on nonunion contract labor in Georgia, see Nikki Luke, "Finding the Time: Valuing the Social Reproduction of Labor in Atlanta's Electricity Politics," Ph.D. dissertation, Department of Geography, University of Georgia, 2020.

137   National Association of State Energy Officials and the Energy Futures Initiative, *2020 US Energy & Employment Report*, usenergyjobs.org.

138   "California's solar gold rush," *The Electrical Worker Online*, December 2014.

139   Noam Scheiber, "Building solar farms may not build the middle class," *New York Times*, July 16, 2021.

work that is marginal, precarious and very difficult to be able to organize."[140]

We also need to think about public power at a larger scale, and there are bigger models that go beyond the municipal or local level. The New Deal established the public, federally owned Tennessee Valley Authority in the 1930s under the slogan "electricity for all."[141] It currently serves electricity customers in Tennessee and six bordering states, and, in 2018, generated 160 billion kilowatt hours of electricity while making $11.2 billion in revenue and $1.1 billion in profit.[142] It currently manages 73 electricity production plants, comprising 41 percent nuclear, 39 percent fossil fuels, 10 percent hydro, and 10 percent solar or wind.[143] The TVA is the largest public utility in the country, and among the more heavily unionized, with "over half of its 10,000 employees represented by unions."[144] It also evades the previously mentioned regressive public-sector state-labor laws by including a unique federal labor regime exempt from NLRB jurisdiction.[145]

Rather than imagining we take over private grids one municipality at a time, the left-wing think tank Peoples' Policy Project proposes simply expanding the TVA's authority to produce zero-carbon energy across the entire United States.[146] This proposal was taken up by Bernie Sanders's 2020 presidential campaign; he planned to make use of the TVA and other "power marketing administrations" owned by

140   Ibid.

141   TVA: Electricity for All, New Deal Network, April 23, 2014, newdeal.feri.org/tva/tva01.htm.

142   Matt Bruenig, "Fighting climate change with a green Tennessee Valley Authority," *People's Policy Project*, January 23, 2019. peoplespolicyproject.org/wp-content/uploads/GreenTVA.pdf.

143   Tennessee Valley Authority, "Our Power System." tva.com/energy/our-power-system.

144   Fred Stafford, "How Trump Got His Right-Wing New Deal Victory," *Jacobin*, August 17, 2020.

145   In 1991, the US General Accounting Office recommended that the TVA come under NLRB jurisdiction, but that still has not happened. United States General Accounting Office, *Labor-Management Relations: Tennessee Valley Authority Situation Needs to Improve* (Washington, DC: Government Printing Office, 1991).

146   Bruenig, "Fighting climate change."

the federal government that already produce electricity in 33 states.[147] The goal was to create "a sort of 'public option' that would compete with the coal, natural gas, and nuclear plants owned by privately owned power generators."[148] One key objection to this plan came from Josh Freed of the capitalist-friendly "Third Way" Democratic Party think tank, who worried it "would make it very hard for the existing generators to compete."[149] But then again, using public power to drive fossil fuel generation out of business is only a "negative" from a certain vantage point.

The existing electric utility industry is a gargantuan form of socialized production with a heavily unionized workforce. This means there already exists a *potential* source of social power intrinsic to the electric system that can push for decarbonization. Rather than assuming a new energy system will magically appear through decentralized market disruption, a more plausible strategy could harness union power in the "heart of the beast." Still, as we learned in the last chapter, *potential* working-class power is not a guaranteed realization of that power.

Conclusion: Electric Socialism

"Communism is Soviet power plus the electrification of the whole country."

—Vladimir Lenin, December 22, 1920

Long forgotten, at the height of working-class and socialist political power in the early twentieth century, came also the period of mass electrification. We take it for granted now, but the world at the time viewed electricity as an almost magical technology that created the possibility for wider human liberation. The working-class and socialist movement was premised on the belief that the abundance made

---

147   Gavin Bade, "Power to the people: Bernie calls for federal takeover of electricity production," *Politico*, February 2, 2020.

148   Ibid.

149   Ibid.

possible by electrified mass production could finally, in Engels's words, "produce not only enough for the plentiful consumption of all members of society but also to leave each individual sufficient leisure."[150] Lenin's famous quote shows how the Bolsheviks saw electrification as a critical material basis of communism itself. The other key ingredient? Soviet power—or just another name for the *workers' power* the soviet workers' councils represented.

In the twenty-first century, we might say again that eco-socialism is workers' power plus electrification of the whole world. In this chapter, I argued that the strategy of "electrify everything" is central to any decarbonization plan. This, of course, entails a colossal expansion of electricity to the transport, heating, and industrial sectors. Climate change requires this mass electrification of the whole world. But what we have not even mentioned is the need to expand electrification for *human rights* reasons. Robert Bryce did some calculations to reveal his refrigerator consumes 1,000 kilowatt hours a year, which is more annual consumption than that consumed by 3.3 billion people on the planet.[151] Those who live in electrified modern environments are quick to decry the horrors of industrialism and modern technology, yet they do not consider the need to improve billions of lives through basic access to electricity. This is not just a question of giving them access to Netflix and social media apps, but also basic health services and food-storage technologies.

Underlying a movement for public power is a more fundamental slogan, particularly in areas that suffer from a lack of it: *electricity is a human right*. The National Union of Metalworkers in South Africa argued on Human Rights Day in 2016 for "the right to a job, freedom from poverty, a share in the country's wealth, the right to receive health care, education, running water, electricity and public transport, and more fundamentally, to own land."[152] Yet lack of electricity is

---

150   Frederick Engels, *The Housing Question* (1872). marxists.org/archive/marx/works/1872/housing-question.

151   Bryce, *A Question of Power*, 74.

152   National Union of Metalworkers of South Africa, "NUMSA statement on Human Rights Day 2016," March 22, 2016. numsa.org.za/article/numsa-statement-human-rights-day-2016.

not simply a problem in the Global South. In the modern United States, private for-profit utilities routinely shut off service to residents who are behind on their bills. The NAACP published a 2017 report, *Lights Out in the Cold: Reforming Utility Shut-Off Policies as if Human Rights Matter*,[153] that showed numerous instances of how utility shut-offs in poor Black communities led to suffering and even death. In Maryland, for example, a father used a generator to make up for lost power; he and his seven children died of carbon monoxide poisoning.[154] Others who lost heat froze to death. The report demands that governments assert "electricity is a human right" by guaranteeing service for all so these needless deaths could be averted. This represents yet another example of the overlap of working-class interests and climate action: the private utility sector is not only a threat to the planet; it also violates basic human rights for its own profit.

So far, investor-owned utilities find allies among their unions and their leadership, but this need not be the case. With the right conditions, unions can always become sites of working-class struggle.

---

153   NAACP Environmental and Climate Justice Program, *Lights Out in the Cold: Reforming Utility Shut-Off Policies as if Human Rights Matter* (Baltimore, MD: NAACP, 2017).

154   Ibid., vii.

7

Power in the Union: History and Strategy in the Electric Utility Unions

Introduction: Electric Strikes

In December 2019, the electric utility union in France took responsibility for making "targeted cuts" shutting off power to homes and businesses in protest of President Emmanuel Macron's plan to cut union workers' pensions. Although illegal, the power cuts resurrected a common tactic from a more militant era of working-class organization, the early to mid–twentieth century,[1] even as reporters described the tactic of strategic power disruption as the "latest innovation in French labor strikes."[2] The union even shut off electricity to labor abusers like an Amazon warehouse during the Christmas package rush. The union leader explained, "You'll understand that spitting on the public service can make some of us angry."[3] By January 2020, Macron had scrapped the plan in the face of an equally "crippling transport strike."[4]

Jane McAlevey recounts a quote from longtime New England–based union leader Jerry Brown, "The strike muscle is like any other muscle, you have to keep it in good shape or it will atrophy."[5] It has certainly atrophied in the United States, but clearly the French working class still has deep understanding of its own strategic power at the

1   Michel Rose and Bate Felix, "French strikers angry about pension reform cut power to homes, companies," *Reuters*, December 18, 2019.

2   Ephrat Livni, "A French union cut power to an Amazon facility in support of workers," *Quartz*, December 25, 2019.

3   Rose and Felix, "French strikers angry."

4   Adam Nossiter, "Macron Scraps Proposal to Raise Retirement Age in France," *New York Times*, January 11, 2020.

5   Jane McAlevey, *No Shortcuts: Organizing for Power in the New Gilded Age* (Oxford, UK: Oxford University Press, 2016).

point of production. In France's electric sector, a public-sector union is willing to use that power to defy law and decorum and force elites to concede to demands.

Efforts to integrate unions into climate politics are not new. Over a decade ago, nine unions and five environmental NGOs formed the "blue-green alliance" to align labor's concerns with climate goals.[6] But this alliance is shaky and built atop union bureaucracies and nonprofits. It does not represent an effort to focus on *one strategic sector*—the electric utility sector—as argued in the previous chapter. Moreoever, the unions in the electric sector in the United States are not nearly as militant as their French counterparts.

But this need not be permanent and unchanging. In this chapter, I lay out the history of electrical workers' unions and propose a three-pronged strategy for reviving working-class power in the electric sector: (1) the rank-and-file strategy (2) the use of union resources for mass political education campaigns (3) the strategic use of strikes and disruption at the point of production. Although the current state of these unions makes it seem difficult to imagine these changes taking place, I propose that a targeted and sectoral union strategy is more realistic in the climate time crunch, compared with the prevailing wisdom that we must change "everything" about society all at once.

A Brief History of Union Struggles in the Electricity Sector

As in other sectors, the struggle to form unions in the electric sector emerged from the nature of the labor process. As the electric system began to develop around centralized power stations—the first being the coal-fired Pearl Street Station in New York City in 1882[7]—it was necessary for workers to construct electrical transmission lines from a central station to public, commercial, residential, and industrial

6 bluegreenalliance.org/. See, Demitris Stevis, "US labour unions and green transitions: Depth, breadth, and worker agency," *Globalizations*, Vol. 15, No. 4 (2018): 454–69; 458.

7 Bryce, *A Question of Power*, 13.

properties. As labor historian Grace Palladino explains, "the linemen's practical sense of solidarity grew out of the job itself."[8] The work posed all sorts of dangers from electrocution to falls, and "the job's inherent risks produced a strong sense of mutuality."[9] In fact, one of the key founders of the International Brotherhood of Electrical Workers (IBEW), Henry Miller, died at the age of 43 after falling from a pole doing line work.[10] The labor process also requires high degrees of cooperation among the linemen to complete the tasks of erecting poles, connecting high-tension lines to transformers, and other aspects of line construction and repair.

Linemen developed "unionism [as] a way of life," but they faced early stiff resistance from utility companies.[11] As early as the 1890s, the Edison Company faced militant strikes from building trade construction workers.[12] They responded by firing union organizers and deploying "scabs . . . armed with instructions to shoot down union men doing picket duty at the building."[13] Eventually, the centralized power of electric utilities forced linemen to forge their own district councils that combined union locals together "in an attempt to centralize their own power."[14] The very specific aspects of this labor process also yielded a "specific craft experience" that was "not easily transferred to other electrical workers."[15] The IBEW was founded in 1891 (initially called the National Brotherhood of Electrical Workers); by the end of the decade it joined the American Federation of Labor and represented the "craft unionism" common within the larger organization. The early history of the IBEW was fraught with struggles between "linemen" and the "wiremen" responsible for wiring

---

8 Grace Palladino, *Dreams of Dignity, Workers of Vision: A History of the International Brotherhood of Electrical Workers* (Washington, DC: International Brotherhood of Electrical Workers, 1991), 23.

9 Ibid., 25.

10 Ibid., 18.

11 Ibid., 23.

12 Ibid., 21.

13 Ibid.

14 Ibid., 55.

15 Ibid., 25.

residential and commercial buildings and other infrastructure for electric service.[16]

The IBEW developed along this line of AFL-style craft unionism for much of the first thirty years of its existence. Nevertheless, during that period, centralized monopoly utilities prevented widespread unionization in the electric industry.[17] And while the IBEW did have some success in organizing workers, it came most often at publicly owned utilities like the Tennessee Valley Authority.[18] Private utilities were much more resistant.

In the 1930s, there was a push for a broader form of industrial unionism aiming to organize all workers in one industry regardless of specific craft. In 1935, the Congress of Industrial Unions (CIO) was founded, just a few months after a full year of widespread strike activity. The CIO was based on a more radical, militant, rank-and-file approach to mass unionism.[19] Many strikes and actions among the early CIO unions directed their anger as much at the union bureaucracy as against the bosses.[20] CIO activists were often members of the Communist Party, brought an explicit class struggle approach to organizing, and focused on militant strikes and rank-and-file action over polite transactional bargaining carried out by union leadership.[21]

One of the prime examples of this radical approach to industrial unionism in the electric sector was the United Electrical, Radio and Machine Workers of America (UE), whose members worked mainly on electrical manufacturing equipment at plants owned by General Electric and Westinghouse.[22] It did not take long for the UE to clash

---

16 Ibid., 25.

17 Ibid., 166.

18 This historical precedent might be useful for those seeking to wed climate action with "good union jobs." Ibid., 167.

19 Irving Bernstein, *Turbulent Years: A History of the American Worker, 1933–1941* (Chicago: Haymarket, 1969).

20 Jeremy Brecher, *Strike!* (Oakland, CA: PM Press, 2020).

21 A good overview is in Micah Uetricht and Barry Eidlin, "US union revitalization and the missing 'militant minority'," *Labor Studies Journal*, Vol. 44, No. 1 (2018): 36–59.

22 Ronald L. Filippelli and Mark D McColloch, *Cold War in the Working Class: The Rise and Decline of the United Electrical Workers* (Albany, NY: SUNY Press, 1995).

with the IBEW, setting up a longstanding struggle between the two unions over organizing workers in the electricity sector. In a bitter skirmish in 1937, the UE and IBEW competed over union recognition at the National Electric Products Corporation plant in Ambridge, Pennsylvania. While the IBEW tried to negotiate a contract behind closed doors, the UE organized a nearly three-week strike.[23]

Throughout the union upsurge of the 1930s, the UE and IBEW locked horns frequently, perhaps most notably over organizing utility workers at Consolidated Edison (Con Ed) in New York City.[24] As soon as union drives began, Con Ed deployed industrial spies to prevent union activity. In 1937, two years after the passage of the Wagner Act giving unions more legal rights, Con Ed finally caved and signed a contract with the IBEW. But the UE, citing a no-strike pledge and other provisions favorable to the company, charged that the IBEW was a "company union" and tried to use the Wagner Act to deem the contract illegal. It took a Supreme Court ruling for IBEW's contract to take effect in 1938.

But only two years later, the IBEW was bringing in its more privileged members to replace existing workers at Con Ed facilities. The workers called a strike, kicked out the IBEW and eventually formed their own independent union, the Brotherhood of Consolidated Edison Employees.[25]

Regardless of these local squabbles, it was evident that "utilities could not be organized successfully along craft lines," because utilities gathered many different kinds of workers into the electric system of production and distribution.[26] Industrial unionism was the future for the electric utility sector. Understanding the strategic importance of utilities as the "backbone of modern industry,"[27] the UE and the CIO

---

23 Palladino, *Dreams of Dignity*, 163.
24 The following description relies on ibid., 166–71.
25 Utility Workers Union of America, "An Informal History of the UWUA." uwua.net/history.
26 Palladino, *Dreams of Dignity*, 166.
27 Ibid., 166.

formed a utility-specific union, the Utility Workers Organizing Committee, in 1938,[28] which in 1945 became the Utility Workers Union of America.[29] The Local 1-2 union at Con Ed eventually affiliated with the UWUA as well.[30]

After World War II, the union movement was relatively entrenched in the electric utility sector, with the UWUA and IBEW representing various locals around the country (today the IBEW is far more predominant in the sector). Because PUCs strictly regulated prices, utilities sought to grow its ratepayer base by building new power plants and expanding capacity as their main accumulation strategy, and with this expansion came union jobs for construction and utility workers.[31] Like all other unions, in the postwar period these unions purged their more left-wing (or explicitly communist) members to more firmly align with corporations and the military-industrial complex.[32]

Ironically, the shift to electricity deregulation in the 1980s not only accompanied a sustained attack against unions themselves, it also led to the proliferation of independent power producers—some of them renewable producers—whose use of nonunion contract labor also undercut the power of utility unions.[33] Nevertheless, centralized utilities remain the primary electric service providers in most parts of the United States, and their unions remain powerful in the utility sector.

More recently, the IBEW leadership has sometimes complained that the main problem among members is "apathy": "It's almost impossible to get members out to a meeting to discuss things," one union leader said in 1990.[34] As such, the utility sector has calcified

---

28   Filippelli and McColloch, Cold War in the Working Class, 42.

29   It should be noted that these unions were not only for workers in electric utilities, but also for gas, water, and railroad workers.

30   Utility Workers of America, "An Informal History of the UWUA."

31   Stokes, Short Circuiting Policy, 79–82; Bakke, The Grid.

32   Palladino, Dreams of Dignity, 222–3; Filippelli and McColloch, Cold War in the Working Class, 113–66.

33   Stokes, Short Circuiting Policy, 83–105; Kelsey and Meckling, "Who wins in renewable energy?"

34   Palladino, Dreams of Dignity, 269.

into a bureaucratic style of "business unionism." The IBEW is a staunch ally of the more centrist establishment in the Democratic Party; it endorsed Joe Biden in 2020 just after the Iowa caucuses.[35] Moreover, while various locals have constructed "Net Zero" building demonstration projects and gained contracts for utility-scale solar, the union as a whole is not exactly an ally in the climate struggle.[36] In 2014, members of both the IBEW and the UWUA occupied a federal building in Pittsburgh *in protest* of Obama's Clean Power plan to decarbonize electricity, and, in 2015, the IBEW joined a lawsuit against the plan.[37]

But this need not always be the stance. In the next sections, I explore some radical strategies to revive militant working-class power and union democracy in the electric sector.

The Rank-and-File Strategy: Socialism in One Sector

Any union strategy for climate change today needs to confront two problems: the weakness of the labor movement overall, and the extremely short time frame we have to act on climate crisis. It is very unlikely we can revive working-class power to its 1930s height in the next decade or even two, not to mention abolish capitalism. Therefore, as the last chapter laid out, we need a much more specific strategy aimed at one sector: the electric utility sector. Building power in one sector is not an isolated process from larger political dynamics, but it still does require focused energy and attention.

Several radical socialist thinkers have devised such a focused strategy on building power within specific unions: the rank-and-file

---

35 This endorsement paid off, as the IBEW president, Lonnie Stephenson, was named a key energy/climate adviser to Joe Biden's transition team in the fall of 2020. "IBEW Endorses Joe Biden for President." ibew.org.

36 Kathleen MacClay, "California solar boom makes the state a national leader and prepares new generation of workers, report says," IBEW 569, November 10, 2014. See, Stevis, "US labour unions and green transitions," 461.

37 Matto Mildenberger, *Carbon Captured: How Business and Labor Control Climate Politics* (Cambridge, MA: MIT Press, 2020), 1; Stevis, "US labour unions and green transitions," 461.

strategy (RFS).[38] Beyond being a strategy meant to produce greater
union power, it is a strategy for attaining *socialism itself*, rooted in
Marx's own political vision "that the emancipation of the working
classes must be conquered by the working classes themselves."[39] The
RFS asserts that this process can begin only if workers learn their own
power through direct confrontations with capital. Moreover, the RFS
is explicitly against "business unionism," or unions controlled by
bureaucrats and more aligned with capital. Since, as Kim Moody puts
it, union leaders are "negotiators and mediators between the members
who work for capital and the capitalists or their representatives," they
often seek *stability* and avoid the conflict that results from militant
worker action.[40]

Since we are not likely to achieve socialism any time soon, a more
modest goal is the socialization of the electricity sector—taking it
under public ownership so that decarbonization can take precedence
over private profits. Somewhat cheekily, I suggest we call this *socialism in one sector*. The RFS suggests that building worker/union power
in one sector will no doubt lead to militancy and the organization of
working-class union power elsewhere too, but the immediate goal
must be to socialize electricity as fast as possible. And as it is clear that
the utility-sector unions themselves are currently very much
entrenched in "business unionism," our only hope is to radicalize
such unions from the membership on the inside.

The RFS aims to build working-class power in the strategic site of
the workplace where workers themselves can disrupt capital's profits.
Although the strike is perhaps the most important tool of rank-and-
file action, developing class-struggle consciousness among the workers could also include a "prolonged workplace campaign, or union
reform caucus."[41] Furthermore, it asserts that unions themselves are
already existing institutions—or "schools of socialism," as Marx called

38 The classic pamphlet is by Kim Moody, *The Rank and File Strategy* (Solidarity, 2000).
39 Karl Marx, "Address and Provisional Rules of the Working Men's International
Association," London, October 1864.
40 Moody, "The Rank and File Strategy," 10.
41 Ibid., 6.

them[42]—for workers to discover and organize their own power through militant organized action. Thus, in contrast to the very important tactic of organizing unorganized workers, the RFS aims to intensify organizing within existing unions.[43] Again, even in the nearly deunionized United States, there are still 14.3 million union members throughout the country, many of whom are not especially involved in their unions. And the electricity sector is more unionized than most other sectors.

The RFS also has some advantages if we seek relatively fast radicalization of unions. For one, the RFS does not require a majority of workers to radicalize; rather, it needs only a small cadre of militant activists—what David Montgomery called the "militant minority"—to lead union radicalization, as has been the case historically.[44] As Kim Moody explains, the militant minority is an "activist layer of the organized working class."[45] Charles Post describes them as "politically heterogeneous and comprised of shop stewards and other workplace leaders who have led shop-floor struggles and promoted radical politics."[46] As Micah Uetricht and Barry Eidlin explain, the militant minority organizers "were the hardest fighters, the most dedicated organizers, and the ones that most actively built unions' cultures of solidarity. This group was key not only in leading upsurges but in consolidating their gains."[47] So if winning over the entirety of the hundreds of thousands of unionized electric utility workers seems like a daunting task, what the strategy actually proposes is *starting* with a very small group of militant activists.

---

42 Quoted in Miliband, *Marxism and Politics*, 132.

43 "Unions give workers a platform to wage class struggle in a coordinated and sustained way, in the process developing the capacities necessary for future fights. That's why many socialists rightly spend a lot of time thinking about and actively working to strengthen unions." From Barry Eidlin, "What Is the Rank-and-File Strategy, and Why Does It Matter?" *Jacobin*, March 26, 2019.

44 David Montgomery, *Fall of the House of Labor* (Cambridge, UK: Cambridge University Press, 1987), 2.

45 Moody, "The Rank and File Strategy," 31.

46 Charles Post, "The forgotten militants," *Jacobin*, August 8, 2016.

47 Uetricht and Eidlin, "US union revitalization and the missing 'militant minority'," 37.

The Democratic Socialists of America (DSA) is already embarking on the RFS. They circulated a pamphlet, "Why Socialists Should Become Teachers," that encourages DSA activists to build working-class power within strategic sectors.[48] This idea of education as strategic not only flows from organizations like Labor Notes and thinkers like Jane McAlevey, but also from the *experience* of struggle itself. As Eric Blanc details, a militant minority of DSA and other activists radicalized by the 2016 Bernie Sanders campaign organized the hugely successful 2018 West Virginia teachers strikes.[49]

So, one climate strategy could be that socialist and other radical climate activists get jobs in the electric utility sector. A current IBEW member, Ryan Pollack, has already advocated exactly the same rank-and-file strategy for winning support for a Green New Deal in his own union.[50] Still, the RFS does not assume radical workers can simply enter the workplace and convert their fellow workers to Marxism in short order. Rather, the hard work consists of what Jane McAlevey describes as "organic leader identification."[51] Such workplace leaders may actually be completely apolitical and certainly not on the left, but have deep relationships with, and respect among, fellow workers and union members. If a militant activist can identify such leaders and learn from other workers their primary concerns, they can start to build energy for change. But make no mistake, this work takes place on the shop floor, and it is involved: "Key to that day-to-day presence were dense shop steward systems that provided links between rank-and-file workers and union leadership, while also checking management's authority."[52]

I also want to make clear what I am *not* advocating. We cannot base an RFS climate strategy on converting electricity workers to the

---

48   Democratic Socialists of America, "Why Socialists Should Become Teachers." teachers.dsausa.org.

49   Eric Blanc, *Red State Revolt: The Teachers' Strike Wave and Working-Class Politics* (London: Verso, 2019).

50   Ryan Pollack, "The Case for an Ecosocialist Rank & File Strategy in the Building Trades," *The Trouble*, November 28, 2019.

51   McAlevey, *No Shortcuts*, 34.

52   Uetricht and Eidlin, "US union revitalization and the missing 'militant minority,'" 48.

"truth" of climate science and the severity of the crisis we face, like the failed professional-class focus on science and knowledge. A rank-and-file strategy must start with the more practical workplace concerns of the workers themselves. When observing the history of struggles in the electricity sector, there is one common concern that unites most worker struggles: worker safety and adequate staffing levels to deal with an increasingly strained grid.

I have already described the inherent risks involved with electrical line work such as electrocution and falling, but electrical power plant workers face a host of other dangers. Jane Latour's study of union militancy over health and safety in the Utility Workers Union of America Local 1-2 in in the 1960s and '70s in New York City is instructive in this regard.[53] One of the shop stewards, Richard Ostrowski, described the job this way: "You walk into a powerhouse and it's like an accident waiting to happen." His fellow workers said: "You're expected to die on the job. Whatever happens, happens."[54] Ostrowski first became alarmed when bosses asked workers to work in containment zones of the Indian Point nuclear plant. The bosses offered little training and threatened workers with dismissal if they refused. "They're going through scrubbings and people were walking out of containment hot, irradiated."[55] Ostrowski and other activists organized informational sessions with experts from the Union of Concerned Scientists to learn more about the dangers of radiation exposure. Eventually they formed Concerned Employees Against Radiation Exposure (CEARE).

Latour also covers struggles against asbestos poisoning for workers using "acetylene torches on the boilers" that were likely insulated with asbestos material at a power plant in Astoria, Queens. When union activists brought in a scientific expert to explain the risks of asbestos exposure and to test workers for diseases, a union activist asked a company business manager at the plant if the asbestos could be

---

53 Jane Latour, "The uncompensated costs of electricity" *WorkingUSA* Vol. 5, no. 4 (2002): 41-70.

54 Ibid., 55.

55 Ibid., 56.

removed or if workers could get proper training to work on the material. The manager replied: "Oh, the company would never do anything like that. What are you trying to do, close the powerhouses? Lose jobs?"[56]

Although these struggles came at a time of union decline and worker disempowerment, Latour describes a small cadre of militant activists attempting to mobilize members around safety issues. She is describing a kind of RFS. More than anything, she explains how even one single activist leader can build both antagonism and member participation. She explains how one activist, James Geoghegan, literally changed the whole culture of union meetings by developing a culture of opposition: "The union meetings were always very raucous. They were a lot of fun. Chairs would be flying and they were very vocal, very active union meetings . . . there was always controversy."[57] The article ends with a summation of the crucial role of this small group of rank-and-file activists: "The opposition educates the rank-and-file. When there's no opposition, there are no issues . . . and they [the rank-and-file] look for the opposition. They look for leadership."[58]

An RFS in the electric sector should start from these kinds of practical and immediate safety issues facing workers on the shop floor and on the lines to build union democracy and worker power. But there is no reason why working-class struggle could not connect these visceral issues of worker safety to the issue of climate change, or *planetary safety*. This kind of conceptual connection, however, requires another strategy also particularly suited to unions.

Political Education and Union Campaigns

The RFS tends to assume business unionism afflicts all union leadership, but this is not always the case. Unions can not only be radicalized from the inside by militant activists; they also still today can

---

56   Ibid., 62.
57   Ibid., 53.
58   Ibid., 68.

deploy significant resources and institutional networks in radical campaigns of political education (the kind that might conjoin a politics of worker and planetary safety cited above). Union dues often go straight into the trade union bureaucracy and increasingly fruitless advocacy for the Democratic Party, but in conjunction with a more radical rank-and-file activism, union leadership could shift toward building a mass base for pro-worker campaigns. On this front, it is worth revisiting the legacy of Tony Mazzocchi, a national union staffer and eventually vice president of the Oil, Chemical and Atomic Workers (OCAW), and originator of the "just transition" framework explained above.

As discussed in Chapter 1, Mazzocchi's breakthrough was to understand that *industrial production* is the source of much of the pollution so concerning to environmental activists. Although many in the labor movement dismissed environmental politics as middle class, Mazzocchi saw "radical potential" through engaging with the rank-and-file themselves: "It was the workers ... who taught me systematic conflict between [industry's] profits and health."[59] He eventually realized that a union strategy against chemical pollution could stop toxics at the source. As he put it, "When you start to interfere with the forces of production, you're going to the heart of the beast, right?"[60]

Upon becoming a national union staffer in 1965, Mazzocchi devised a plan for a national political education campaign that toured OCAW locals with teams of scientists and experts on the health risks of toxic substances to educate workers about the hazards they faced every day. It is instructive how Mazzocchi harnessed science and professional knowledge not primarily in terms of societal "awareness," but as a process of *worker self-education* in connecting their workplace with direct risks to their lives. In devising this campaign, Mazzocchi contrasted his tactics with the more typical union strategy of lobbying Congress. As he said: "We had enough union lobbyists

59   Leopold, *The Man Who Hated Work and Loved Labor*, 229.
60   Ibid.

around town. I wanted to build a mass base."[61] Fundamentally, Mazzocchi aimed to mobilize both rank-and-file workers and the public at large to support extensive regulatory reform of dirty industrial production. As his biographer Les Leopold recounts: "Rank and file evidence from Mazzocchi's road shows flooded Congressional offices. The media was picking up the issue."[62] By launching a national tour around the risks of the industrial environment, Mazzocchi started building a pressure campaign in Congress for what eventually became the Occupational Health and Safety Act of 1970. He organized union events, helped set up worker testimony in Congressional hearings, and worked alongside environmentalists to organize the first Earth Day in 1970.[63] His goal was to mobilize the wider public to connect a safe environment with a safe workplace. His political education and union campaign strategy shows what unions can do with the right radical leadership in place. If the RFS builds a radical culture within electric unions, the next step is to win leadership and transform union activities.

Just as the OCAW membership once faced the existential threat of toxic pollution and death, so today do electric utility union workers face dire threats to their livelihoods. The explosion of cheap renewable energy generation—in some cases because of state mandates—has created the basis for the construction of a largely non-union "distributed" electricity generation system, replete with new generation sites, material-intensive battery storage, and new transmission lines. Private clean-tech developers hostile to unions could be firmly in control of all this new construction and installation. If the electrical unions today are not thinking long term and strategically, a form of renewable green capitalism could rapidly destroy the industries they took decades to organize.

If private capital controls the energy transition, it will likely be a transition hostile to unions and worker power. The IBEW and

---

61 Ibid.
62 Ibid., 273.
63 Ibid., 272.

UWUA *could* launch a political education tour similar to the OCAW's that attempts to educate their members on three fronts: (a) to teach workers about the strategic centrality of electricity to the *scientific necessity* of a mass decarbonization program; (b) to help workers better understand their own objective power at the point of production to *shape* the nature of this transition; and (c) to make them aware that if they do not use this power proactively, their industries and unions face ruin in a capitalist-led transition to renewable energy.

It will take a broader legislative framework to *mandate* that the jobs of the clean energy transition are good, well-paying union jobs. Although politicians, President Joe Biden included, like to say that climate action will create good union jobs, we will actually need concrete policies that require all the jobs of constructing and installing new energy systems are unionized. This kind of legal mandate will only be the result of *pressure* from the kind of "mass base" that Mazzocchi aimed to mobilize with the worker safety campaign that led to OSHA. The utility unions could mobilize a similar kind of base, which will fight for a Green New Deal that requires union contracts for new public works projects.

It would be one thing if the OCAW campaign was the only example of this kind of broader union political education initiative, but we actually do not have to look far to find a historical example within electricity itself. In 1992, Congress passed the Energy Policy Act, which "proposed competition in power generation at the wholesale level . . . With these changes, independent power producers would be able to operate more broadly."[64] The unions representing electric utility workers saw this as a threat through which unregulated production could undercut production and union jobs in the "regulated" utility sector.

The 1992 act delegated deregulation to the states. Thus, unions fought the struggle against electricity deregulation on a state-by-state level. Even so, the IBEW launched a *national* strategy, with the

64 Stokes, *Short Circuiting Policy*, 90.

formation of the union's Committee on Electric Power Industry
Restructuring.[65] The initiative delegated power to specific union
districts and utility-centered locals, which then elected two local
members to the committee to shape organizing strategies. The
national/international office provided the material resources and
support. One such example was a gargantuan three-ring binder titled
*Electric Power Deregulation: Understanding the Issues, Shaping
Opinions and Influencing Policy Makers—A Reference Guide for
Presenting the Issues.* The binder included countless tools for union
members in making the case against deregulation: a presentation
guide, a media relations guide, a mobilization guide (including
template letters to the editor and speech tips), data, and policy
summaries.

The binder also included an introductory letter from IBEW
President J.J. Barry that is worth quoting at length, because it sounds
like it comes directly from the Tony Mazzocchi playbook of public
mobilization:

> There is a strong movement underway by powerful interests to dereg-
> ulate and restructure the electric power industry . . . There is a serious
> need to raise the level of public debate and awareness of what is at
> stake. We cannot afford to sit on the sidelines and watch a few greedy
> leaders of business dismantle the laws enacted to ensure a fair proper
> balance of interests within the electric power industry. As union lead-
> ers, it is incumbent upon all of us to speak out on behalf of our
> members and play a visible role in influencing public opinion on this
> issue . . . I trust you will find these to be high-quality tools that will
> inspire you to lead the fight to protect our members' interests in this
> effort.[66]

The union campaign was not only about mobilizing the rank and file.

---

65   I'm thankful to IBEW Local 2304 President Emeritus Dave Poklinkoski for alerting
me to this history and providing some documents from the campaign.

66   John Barry, "A Message From President Barry," January 1997, 1–1 (included in
binder mentioned above).

It was also about mobilizing the wider public against deregulation. More specifically, the campaign centered electricity consumers who could see higher rates and increasing blackouts due to deregulation. A pamphlet developed by the campaign, "Will deregulation short-circuit North America's electric power supply?" showed how deregulation could adversely affect "consumers, utility workers, business and investors."[67] In other words, the literature called upon a mass base to oppose deregulation. The pamphlet outlined how deregulation represented broad threats to the public as a whole: "There's a battle being waged right now that could jeopardize your electric service and drastically impact your quality of life."[68] The message moved deregulation beyond being an issue for workers alone, into an issue threatening everyone who relied upon electricity.

The campaign had some impact toward halting runaway deregulation, a trend that seemed unstoppable at the high point of 1990s free-market neoliberalism. In 2000, nineteen states were exploring deregulation through public PUC or legislative investigative processes[69]—but ten years later, none of them had passed deregulation restructuring. To be sure, this was partly, or even primarily, because of the total debacle of electricity deregulation in California and its rolling blackouts of 2000–1.

But unions were making their voices heard *before* that crisis. The former president of IBEW Local 2304 in Wisconsin told me that the Public Service Commission's Advisory Committee on Electric Utility Restructuring was so inundated with union worker participation, feedback, and objections, it ensured that the deregulation process would simply be too complicated to enact. The IBEW local did not act alone; it also called upon working-class ratepayers, helping set up a coalition called "Customers First," which still functions today. It describes itself on its website as "a coalition to preserve Wisconsin's

67 Committee on Electric Power Industry Restructuring, International Brotherhood of Electrical Workers, "Will Deregulation Short-Circuit North America's Electric Power Supply?" n.d., cover page.

68 Ibid., inside flap, front cover.

69 Stokes, *Short Circuiting Policy*, 92–3.

affordable and reliable electricity."[70] This draws on a basic objective working-class interest in cheap electricity reviewed in Chapter 5. When it came time to try implementing deregulation in Wisconsin in 1996, officials proposed a wildly complicated 32-step plan.[71] The union coalition's objections had the desired effect, and the effort was shut down. Long after the union-driven blockages hamstrung the drive to deregulate, the California crisis killed deregulation for good.

Building a "militant minority" activist layer within the IBEW, the UWUA and other electric utility unions could create the conditions to marshal union leadership, resources, money, and organizational power into a national Green New Deal or clean-energy-transition political-education campaign. If there is no "mass base" behind the necessity of ensuring that the clean energy transition is a pro-union program, it will probably continue to be a process dominated by private capital. One might argue this is fine as long as private capital delivers the transition we need, but experience shows that capital's inherent risk-averse nature and narrow focus on profit is not likely to accomplish the task.

Strikes and Disruption at the Point of Production

As stated in the previous chapter, electric utility workers have literal power over the economy. As soon as unions developed legal rights to collective bargaining and "the right to strike," legal scholars raised questions on what the limits should be in the name of the "public interest." At the outset of a many-decades attack on labor, one legal scholar warned, "A break in the continuity of the services they render could conceivably paralyze all human activity within a short space of time and cause endless damage to organized society."[72] Naturally, they

---

70   customersfirst.org.

71   Jeffrey M. Fang and Paul S. Galen, "Electric industry restructuring and environmental issues," *National Renewable Energy Laboratory* (Golden, Colorado, 1996), 29.

72   O.S.B., "Public utility labor problems. Strikes 'affected with a public interest,'" *University of Pennsylvania Law Review*, Vol. 97, No. 3 (1949): 410–21; 411.

went on to raise a further concern, asking rhetorically, "the question arises whether the community would be wise in imposing community control over labor's right to strike in public utilities."[73] Regardless if this vague "community control" were imposed, any strike that shut down electrical service to masses of people might generate mass public backlash.

This all said, workers in the utility sector still go on strike surprisingly often. An online database tracking strike activity for the last couple of decades found the IBEW involved in 1,019 strikes, with 331 classified as strikes against "utilities."[74] The much smaller UWUA has been involved in 43 strikes.[75] Any particular strike at a power-generation facility faces efforts by transmission and distribution companies to lease power from other producers (especially in deregulated states with lots of "independent power producers.") Thus, strikes among utility workers on the distribution and transmission side often have *more* ability to actually shut off power. Nevertheless, power shutdowns have long been a nonexistent tactic in the United States, ever since the 1919 Seattle General Strike, when union threats to shut off power to the entire city, including hospitals, generated strong backlash and were never carried out.[76]

On the other hand, utility workers have used militant action to *make visible* the centrality of their labor to keeping the essential service of electricity running. In 2012, 8,500 members of UWUA 1-2 threatened to strike, but were locked out of Con Ed's utility operations.[77] The workers responded by taking to the picket line under the slogan "When We Go Out, the Lights Go Out,"[78] as managers replaced

---

73 Ibid., 412.

74 unionfacts.com/strikes/International_Brotherhood_of_Electrical_Workers. There is no way to disaggregate electric utilities from water, gas, and others in this list. However, all of these would involve "essential" services like electricity.

75 unionfacts.com/strikes/Utility_Workers.

76 Nicholas Greenwood, "Electrical Workers' Unions and the Seattle General Strike." depts.washington.edu/labhist/strike/electrical_workers.shtml.

77 Matthew Cunningham-Cook, " 'When we go out, the lights go out': workers locked out at Con Ed," *Nation*, July 5, 2012.

78 Ibid.

union workers at the controls. A UWUA mechanic, Chris Spadafore, called out Con Ed's haphazard labor-replacement scheme as dangerous to public safety:

> They've called in 5,000 managers to do 8,500 people's jobs. They can't do our jobs. We can . . . Even if the managers came out of the union, they're still out of practice. One little screw-up and they're dead. To me this shows that Con Ed doesn't care about their people, that they're willing to put them in harm's way.[79]

After what the union described as "the largest lockout of workers in US labor history by a private corporation," the union agreed to a contract it described as a "fair, equitable and decent return on the fruits of our labor."[80] The use of picket lines and militant language on the centrality of utility workers to the electrical system also mobilized support from elected officials and the larger public.

Globally, electrical workers demonstrate much more militancy. In Nigeria recently electrical workers shut down power until the state met their demands.[81] As mentioned above, French electrical workers have strategically shut off power to protest national rollbacks of labor laws.[82] But power cuts and labor strikes are on the far end of what we might call a spectrum of disruption. Electrical workers can employ other tactics besides strikes, like "work to rule" campaigns that employ slowdowns and shirking to force management to listen to demands.[83] Since strikes and power cuts are particularly risky, the IBEW Local 2304 president from Wisconsin mentioned above found "work to rule" the more successful way to harness working-class power in electric power plants. A union document recommends: "The strike should be a weapon of last

---

79   Ibid.
80   "UWUA Local 1-2 Update Tentative Agreement." uwua1-2.org.
81   Jude Egbas, "Nigeria's electricity workers suspend strike," *Pulse.Ng*, December 12, 2019.
82   Angela Charlton and Nicolas Garriga, "Power blackout as French workers strike over labor bill," Associated Press, June 2, 2016.
83   Samantha Winslow, "Hawaii teachers unleash work-to-rule campaign," *Labor Notes*, November 30, 2012.

resort . . . Workers have a lot more power than simply withholding their labor."[84] A later document on "in-plant strategies" emphasized the importance of democratic rank-and-file involvement: "Internal organization puts the union in a position to be able to credibly threaten the employer . . . threatening to do it . . . is usually more effective than actually doing it."[85] The document asserts a philosophy of working-class power where employers will not do what is good for workers (or the planet for that matter), until they face real pressure. Marx also recognized this philosophy: "Capital . . . takes no account of the health and the length of life of the worker, unless society forces it to do so."[86]

Building Solidarity in the Broader Labor Movement

While I advocate focusing on one strategic sector, there is no doubt a need to build wider solidarity and power within the labor movement as a whole. If unions within the electric sector were able to build power and militancy within their own unions, they would absolutely need support and solidarity from allies in the broader labor movement. Much is made of the current anti-environmentalism within building trade unions and those sectors wrapped up in the fossil fuel industrial complex. Yet some building trade leaders realize what a Green New Deal could mean for their sector. In Philadelphia, the president of Local 3012 of the Brotherhood of Maintenance of Way Employees Division of the International Brotherhood of the Teamsters said, "Even if you don't care about climate change, even if you have a more narrow interest, there's a ton of money in the Green New Deal for the building trades, for infrastructure."[87] While the election of 2016 centered on the mythologies of the coal worker, those workers

---

84   IBEW Local #2304, "Draft of strategy and proposals for 1987 contract negotiations," December 9, 1986. Thanks again to Dave Poklinkoski for sharing these documents.

85   IBEW Local #2304, "In-plant strategies: General lessons and principles to be learned from our past as well as our recent history," February 28, 1989.

86   Marx, *Capital*, Vol. 1, 381.

87   Mindy Isser, "The Green New Deal Just Won a Major Union Endorsement. What's Stopping the AFL-CIO?" *In These Times*, August 12, 2020.

make up an infinitesimal part of the working class, and unfortunately automation and regional production shifts have largely destroyed their union power. The most recent report on labor and energy employment claims only 853 unionized coal workers left in the mostly extraction-oriented coal fuels sector; representing a mere 1 percent of the overall workforce![88]

Jane McAlevey bemoans the often-discussed tensions between unions and environmentalists. She draws from a labor leader in New York State, Vincent Alvarez, who claimed, "rather than focusing on the 10 percent of issues that are divisive—such as the Keystone pipeline and fracking . . . it makes more sense to start with the 90 percent of issues that environmentalists and unions can easily agree on."[89] Alvarez was involved in a prime example of bringing unions to the core of climate strategy, the "Climate Jobs NY" initiative, a coalition of labor unions, the state government, and Cornell University.[90] McAlevey explains how the unions were able to win project labor agreements for offshore wind projects aiming to generate half of New York State's power by 2035.[91] She insists that this outcome did not result from unions merely being one stakeholder among many, but from unions having "the *power* to shift public subsidies—that's taxes—into a deal that enabled them to meet both scientific standards for emissions reduction and the good unionized and wage and benefit standards that members expect and are willing to fight for."[92] Unfortunately, too much climate politics ignores the latent power of unions.

Beyond the building trades, other unions fight inherently for environmental benefits, like public transit unions. The Amalgamated Transit Union has been one of the earliest and loudest supporters of a Green New Deal. Major strategic unions like the American Federation of Teachers and the Service Employees International Union have also

---

88   *2020 US Energy & Employment Report*, 19.
89   McAlevey, *A Collective Bargain*, 107.
90   climatejobsny.org.
91   McAlevey, *A Collective Bargain*, 109.
92   Ibid.

endorsed the Green New Deal.[93] More broadly, the most unionized part of the United States, public sector unions, will also inherently understand and fight for what one analyst calls "public goods unionism" and others call "bargaining for the common good."[94] Alyssa Battistoni has also argued that "reproductive" or "care" sectors of the economy like education and health care are already "low carbon" and "green jobs" from the start.[95] National Nurses United, for example, advocates for national health care and a Green New Deal.[96]

The most obvious example of bargaining for the common good was the recent militant actions taken by teachers. For example, the United Teachers of Los Angeles were not only striking for better wages and benefits, they were also concerned about the learning conditions of their students; among their demands were smaller class sizes and more mental health counselors. More to the point, they advocated for more environmental green space in the community as a critical kind of infrastructure for healthy communities as a whole.[97] In July 2019, the Massachusetts Teachers Association called for a still more radical measure: a *national* teachers' strike for a Green New Deal.[98] Of course, calling for a national teachers' strike is not the same as *organizing* one, but this kind of mass action could shut down society in ways that youth climate strikes could never do.

93   Mindy Isser, "The Green New Deal just won a major union endorsement. What's stopping the AFL-CIO?" *In These Times*, August 12, 2020.

94   Joseph A. McCartin, "Bargaining for the future: Rethinking labor's recent past and planning strategically for its future," Report for the Kalmanovitz Initiative for Labor and the Working Poor, Georgetown University, Washington, DC, June 18, 2014. See also "Bargaining for the common good": bargainingforthecommongood.org.

95   Alyssa Battistoni, "Living, not just surviving," *Jacobin*, No. 26 (Summer 2017): 65–71.

96   Trish Kahle, "Take On the Fossil Fuel Bosses," *Jacobin*, March 14, 2019.

97   Jane McAlevey, "The Los Angeles Teachers' Strike Is a Master Class in Using Unions to Secure Progressive Wins," *Stanford Social Innovation Review*, Vol. 18, No. 1 (Winter 2020): 19–21.

98   "Massachusetts Teachers Union Calls for Strike for the Green New Deal," *Labor Network for Sustainability*. labor4sustainability.org.

Conclusion: A Real Just Transition will Take Union Power

Given the entrenchment of the electrical unions within the Democratic Party and their seeming hostility to more radical demands like a Green New Deal, it may seem unrealistic to imagine we could radicalize these unions to meet the scale of the climate crisis. Yet, I would suggest radicalizing *one union sector* is a lot less daunting than the wholescale societal transformation often called for. As the climate crisis intensifies and the technical case for electrifying everything becomes clearer, a "socialism in one sector" approach could be the core of a public sector–led decarbonization program.

But first, unions must shape this decarbonization program to ensure that the transition includes unionized jobs, as opposed to the non-union workforces currently deployed by the private renewable power industry. The leadership of unions might be quite comfortable, but the rank-and-file members should know that electricity unions face a dire existential threat in capital-led decarbonization programs.

While support for public power within the unions and the labor movement is uneven, workers in the utility sector do understand that many of their problems are rooted in private, for-profit management. In fact, in 2015 the Utility Workers Union of America president, Michael Langford, expressed strong support for the report on public power produced by Trade Unions for Energy Democracy:

The Utility Workers Union of America fully supports reclaiming the utilities and the power generation sector in order to serve the public good. America's energy infrastructure—both physical and human—is in terrible condition. Methane, a potent greenhouse gas, is leaking everywhere as a result of crumbling pipes. Meanwhile, workers in coal-fired power stations are being kicked to the curb by greedy corporations. Whole communities have been left stranded. My union believes in a planned and just energy transition, and a scale-up of renewable energy under public control as a means of creating good jobs and addressing climate change. But the key issue for us is democratic control and decision-making driven by the public good and not private gain. This is a fight we are willing to wage, because our collective future depends on it.[99]

Although Langford is no longer president, his statement implies that union leadership is already aware of, and on board with, the need for transformative change of the electric utility sector. But nothing can happen without mass action from the members themselves.

My students often ask me what they can do to save the climate. I imagine they're used to hearing things about lightbulbs or electric cars. But they need to hear something different: *join a union.*

---

99 Trade Unions for Energy Democracy, "Unions welcome new report highlighting the need to 'reclaim' and democratize the energy system and to promote publicly owned renewable power," June 24, 2015. unionsforenergydemocracy.org/power-to-the-people-toward-democratic -control-of-electricity-generation.

Conclusion

Species Solidarity at the Climate Crossroads

So comrades, come rally,
And the last fight let us face.
The Internationale
Unites the human race.

These are the words of the chorus of the British version of "The Interationale," so embedded in socialist and working-class movements across the world in the nineteenth and twentieth centuries. While many might view it as old-fashioned, it takes on new meaning in the age of the climate crisis. Now it is not the international workers' movement, but rather international scientists who assert humanity must "unite" and face what could be its "last fight."[1]

A basic Marxist conviction undergirded the international socialist movement: capitalism had ushered in real historical possibilities for human emancipation. Ellen Meiksins Wood explains, "socialism was now on the historical agenda because there existed, for the first time in history, not only the forces of production to make human emancipation possible, but more particularly a class which contained a real possibility of a classless society."[2] For Marx and later socialists, these convictions were borne out through the real-world clashes between capital and the working classes. Out of these struggles grew political parties, trade unions, and other institutions that made it seem like

---

1 On the climate-labor struggle, Sean Sweeney cites the American lyrics which reference the "final conflict" for humankind. Sean Sweeney, "The final conflict? Socialism and climate change," *New Labor Forum*, Vol. 29, No. 2 (2020): 16–24. See also, Matt Huber, "5 Principles of a Socialist Climate Politics," *The Trouble*, August 16, 2018.

2 Ellen Meiksins Wood, *The Retreat From Class: A New 'True' Socialism* (London: Verso, 1986), 90.

class struggle was indeed the driving motor of history, and like the working class was the class to end classes. Meiksins Wood again insists Marxist socialist politics "implies that the working class is the only social group possessing an immediate interest in resisting capitalist exploitation but also a collective power adequate to end it."[3]

Today we live in a different context, with capital triumphant and the global working class defeated and in disarray. But as I argued in Part I, the motor of history is still driven by class struggle—though this time largely from above. The unadulterated power of the capitalist class over material production has given us a world-historical crisis of climate change. In the wake of the collapse of the Soviet Union and the supposed victory of capital, Francis Fukuyama declared the "end of history."[4] Now we might have what Sean Sweeney called the "end of history, the sequel," growing out of the very triumph of capitalism itself.[5] The resurgent capitalist world has produced nearly half of all cumulative emissions since Fukuyama uttered those words.[6]

The climate crisis requires a reevaluation of the very notion of the social potential of "proletarian agency" described in Part III. Francis Mulhern argues that this potential is "not determined by the moral and political vicissitudes of the labor movement. It is fostered by the ordinary contradictions of capitalism."[7] Clearly, the climate crisis represents a stark example of the "ordinary contradictions" of capitalism. The class-struggle environmentalist Tony Mazzocchi believed "the struggle of capital against nature was *the* irreconcilable contradiction that would force systemic change."[8] While James O'Connor theorized ecological breakdown as capitalism's "second" contradiction,

---

3 Ellen Meiksins Wood, *Democracy Against Capitalism: Renewing Historical Materialism* (London: Verso, 1995), 103.

4 Francis Fukuyama, "The end of history?" *The National Interest*, No. 16 (Summer 1989): 3–18.

5 Swenney, "The final conflict?" 18.

6 Paul Griffin, *The Carbon Majors Database: CDP Carbon Majors Report 2017* (London: Carbon Disclosure Project, 2017), 5.

7 Quoted in Wood, *The Retreat From Class*, 92.

8 Les Leopold, *The Man Who Hated Work and Loved Labor: The Life and Times of Tony Mazzocchi* (White River Junction, VT: Chelsea Green, 2007), xiv.

climate change is also an example of the first, summed up by Engels as the "contradiction between social production and capitalist appropriation."[9] While private fossil fuel companies are legally able to dig up fossil fuel, sell it as a commodity, and monopolize the profits, the effects of fossil capitalism are increasingly making the planet uninhabitable.

The climate crisis creates a *historical crossroads* for human society as such. On the one hand, fossil fuel–powered industrialization has created conditions of unprecedented labor productivity. This productivity led to the kind of proletarian ecology I describe in Chapter 5: the working class, now the vast majority of humanity, is a class *separated* from the ecological means of livelihood, most notably the land. This process was only possible insofar as agricultural productivity dramatically lessened the labor coercively bound to the land. This is, indeed, a world-historical result of capitalism: to tear the vast majority from a direct relationship between nature and livelihood. That majority must now survive through the violence and vicissitudes of the market. On the other hand, the productivity of fossil-fueled production is generating such a cascade of multifaceted ecological crisis (species collapse, global pandemics like Covid-19) that it requires a wholesale restructuring of production.

This crossroads means that reconciliation can go in one of two directions. First, the crisis itself has understandably led to a reaction among environmentalists to focus on a "return" to local land relations that predominated before the working classes were torn from it. The profound alienation from the land has led many to seek a *disalienation*, and localization of production and consumption relations to reconnect relations with the land through projects such as community gardens, food sovereignty, energy autonomy, and, as covered in Chapter 6, community-based public power movements. Moreover, much attention has been paid to struggles over environmental

---

9 James O'Connor, *Natural Causes: Essays in Ecological Marxism* (London: Guilford, 1998); Frederick Engels, *Socialism: Utopian and Scientific* (Chicago: Charles H. Kerr and Co., 1918), 110.

displacement among communities defending their actual, existing relationships with the land: indigenous struggles against extraction, peasant struggles against land dispossession, and communities' struggles against climate-based displacement.[10] This has also led to the kind of livelihood environmentalism described in Chapter 6 where locally based struggles over land, resources, or toxic pollution have shaped notions of environmental and climate justice and indigenous and peasant land sovereignty.

All these struggles are extremely important. Indeed, control over land and subsistence is perhaps the most important class struggle over the means of production. It remains a core principle of socialist politics to advocate the right of "self-determination" for all oppressed groups.[11] But all efforts to recover a rooted and localized relation to nature ignore the very basic definition of working-class proletarian ecology: the *lack* of direct connection to the ecological means of life. The question becomes: what is to be done about the masses of people *already* torn from the land?

What Ralph Leonard calls "proletarian rootlessness" was not something classical socialists thought was a problem in need of re-rootedness.[12] Conversely, it was this very rootlessness that makes the proletariat what Mike Davis refers to as the "universal class,"[13] a class whose reliance upon a wage for survival means that working-class people everywhere *share* a common struggle against exploitative bosses and for survival through the market. Proletarian revolution was always meant to be *universal emancipation*, what Hal Draper called a "revolution in humankind."[14] The Internationale *unites the human race*.

---

10   See, Elizabeth Lunstrum, Pablo Bose, and Anna Zalik, "Environmental displacement: The common ground of climate change, extraction and conservation," *Area*, Vol. 48, No. 2 (2016): 130–3.

11   Vladimir Lenin, "The right of nations to self-determination," in *Collected Works*, Vol. 20 (Moscow: Progress Publishers, 1972), 393–454.

12   Ralph Leonard, "Stop apologising for cultural appropriation," *UnHerd*, July 1, 2020.

13   Mike Davis, *Old Gods, New Enigmas: Marx's Lost Theory* (London: Verso, 2018), 7.

14   Hal Draper, *Karl Marx's Theory of Revolution Volume II: The Politics of Social Classes* (New York Monthly Review Press, 1978), 24.

Some Marxist thinkers have come up with an extremely awkward term for this: the "Proletarocene."[15] If our current geological epoch of planetary crisis is the Capitalocene—the radical corrective to the Anthropocene concept that implies all humanity is at fault—might there be a way to usher in a new era? And might the traditional antagonist of capital—the working class—have that potential? As the theorists of the proletarocene point out correctly, "the vast increase in carbon emissions since 1990, and the fall of the Soviet Union, was accompanied by a world-historic expansion of the global proletariat."[16] Given this mass expansion of the proletariat, is it possible to envision that only this universal class can deliver "systemic, planet-wide transformation"?[17]

After all, the goal of classical socialism was not to reconnect the working class to nature, but for this "immense majority" of humanity to take *social control* of production systems that were already highly socialized and global. As Neil Smith astutely argued in his argument against the *capitalist* "production of nature": "Truly human, social control over the *production* of nature . . . is the realizable dream of socialism."[18] Today we live in a world in which the everyday reproduction of the working class means subsisting off commodities produced by labor dispersed around the planet. And here again, the contradiction posed by the climate crisis is staring us in the face: a *planetary crisis* requiring global social coordination of production. Put simply, climate change means localism will not work. Global production must be socially coordinated to stave off climate catastrophe.

Thus, the second direction we can take in the climate crossroads, the direction firmly entrenched in the tradition of Marxist working-class politics, is *toward* a global reconciliation of our species-wide

15 Salvage editorial collective, "The Tragedy of the Worker: Towards the Proletarocene," *Salvage Magazine* January 31, 2020. salvage.zone/editorials/the-tragedy-of-the-worker-towards-the-proletarocene.
16 Ibid.
17 Ibid.
18 Neil Smith, *Uneven Development: Nature, Capital and the Production of Space* (Athens, GA: University of Georgia Press, [1984] 2008), 91.

relation to nature. Any global arrangement must be firmly entrenched in another core concept of working-class politics: solidarity. While international labor solidarity was deeply infused in the workers movement of the past, we need to rethink it for the age of climate crisis. We need a form of *species solidarity* recognizing that species survival is at stake.[19] But more to the point, a Marxist vision of species solidarity asserts that the working class is the agent of species emancipation, precisely because of its global outlook and rootlessness from local places. Unlike earlier socialist movements, forging species solidarity is not only about human emancipation, but also about the reconstruction of the basic metabolism between society and nature. Species solidarity must be forged across borders as workers, peasants, and indigenous peoples join together to see their shared interest in reconciling all modes of livelihood production with the conditions for a livable planet. Whereas land-based struggles seek to develop a *particular relation* between human groups and local parts of the earth, the working class's universal separation from nature itself requires a *universal* conception of what unites human beings on the planet.

Going back to Marx's earliest writings we find just this kind of universal idea: "species-being." For Marx, production is at the heart of humanity: "man [*sic*] produces even when he is free from physical need and only truly produces in freedom therefrom."[20] For Marx, it is *production* that is humanity's "active species-life."[21] Under capitalism, where capital controls the means of production and despotically directs the vast majority to produce for others, humanity's "species-nature is estranged from [itself]."[22]

---

19   I had been referring to this as "planetary solidarity." But as George Carlin pointedly put it: "The planet is fine. The people are f*cked." Even if the biodiversity and ecosystem crisis afflicts manifold species, human survival is primarily at stake. Eco-socialism might be fashioned as a project to give humanity as a whole control over production so we could better protect biodiversity and nonhuman nature more generally.

20   Karl Marx, "Estranged Labour." marxists.org/archive/marx/works/1844/manuscripts/labour.htm.

21   Ibid.

22   Ibid.

Thus, constructing a kind of species solidarity means acknowledging both that the climate crisis requires the working class to "seize the means of production," and that humanity as a whole has a deep and universal need to direct and control production. In Marx's words, capitalism creates a "social formation in which the process of production has mastery over man, instead of the opposite."[23] He described the social organization of production as guided by an "anarchic system of competition" and shaped by the vicissitudes of market forces.[24] This *lack of control* over production is what yields feelings of helplessness as the world burns.

We have spent decades pretending that the "costs" of climate change can be priced into the anarchic forces of the market, but it's increasingly clear that only conscious social control of production can guide us toward anything resembling a sustainable path. In his specific articulation of democratic socialism, Martin Hägglund argues, "For us to become truly social individuals in Marx's sense, we have to be *the subjects of* production—planning and directing it for our purposes— rather than be *subjected* to production for the sake of capital."[25]

But the planning of social production cannot be done in isolation. Here again, we see this necessity in light of the climate crisis, the need for a *planetary* form of social production "planning and directing it for our purposes." This is in fact what the scientists mean when they say we must undergo "rapid, far-reaching and unprecedented changes in all aspects of society."[26] We must take control over the very basic production of energy, housing, transportation, and food to direct and plan it toward a different priority: *decarbonization*. But just as "socialism in one country" was inconceivable to some Marxists, decarbonization in one country while others continue to spew emissions does nothing to solve the problem.

---

23 Marx, *Capital*, Vol. 1, 175.

24 Ibid., 667.

25 Martin Hägglund, *This Life: Secular Faith and Spiritual Freedom* (New York: Pantheon, 2019), 264.

26 Intergovernmental Panel on Climate Change, "Summary for Policymakers of IPCC Special Report on Global Warming of 1.5°C approved by governments," October 8, 2018.

The prospect of species solidarity means we conceive of humans as capable of managing their own relation to nature on a planetary level. While environmentalists often talk about globalization in irreducibly negative terms, we also need a positive vision of global species-wide coordination. Leigh Phillips and Michal Rozoworski describe this as "planning the good Anthropocene . . . [where] . . . we accept our role as collective sovereign of Earth and begin influencing and coordinating planetary processes with purpose and direction, ever furthering human flourishing."[27] While this might horrify some eco-centric environmentalists, the climate crisis gives us no other choice but to assert global control over our energy and emissions systems. As Holly Jean Buck argues, the emissions situation and carbon budget are so dire they require us to simultaneously resist imperialist designs to regulate global climate under the rubric of "geoengineering" and explore what options might exist for a left approach to atmospheric carbon management aligned with broader human need.[28]

Again, this vision of planetary species-wide social coordination is aligned with the classical socialist vision of human emancipation. This is exactly what Marx envisioned for the construction of a classless and ecological communist society:

> From the standpoint of a higher socio-economic formation, the private property of particular individuals in the earth will appear just as absurd as the private property of one man in other men. Even an entire society, a nation, or all simultaneously existing societies taken together, are not the owners of the earth. They are simply its possessors, its beneficiaries, and have to bequeath it in an improved state to succeeding generations as *boni patres familias*.[29]

* * *

27 Leigh Phillips and Michal Rozoworski, "Planning the Good Anthropocene," *Jacobin*, No. 26 (Summer 2017): 133–6; 136.

28 Holly Buck, *After Geoengineering: Climate Tragedy, Repair, and Restoration* (London: Verso, 2019).

29 Karl Marx, *Capital*, Vol. 3 (London: Penguin), 911.

Unfortunately, we are unlikely to abolish class and private property at the global level in time to avert climate catastrophe. Yet we must start somewhere. Given the weak position of the left and working class more broadly, I think we start by simply resuscitating the notion of *public good* over private profit.

To do so in relation to climate change must assert that the crisis itself is a *public crisis* that requires public-sector coordination and action. There are several sectors that some societies already affirm should not involve profit and market provision—education and health care, for example. Many of these public goods themselves emerged out of widespread public crisis and social struggles to carve out what is "public." For example, in the 1800s, widespread crises of water-borne illness and inadequate sanitation services led to public sewage and water-treatment systems.[30] Although the rich tried to blame the poor for their own private behavior, reformers realized that the market could not solve this particular form of urban pollution. They did not institute excrement taxes as a market fix; they invested in crucial public infrastructure that socialized costs to produce widespread public health benefits. Now it is not just cities drowning in contaminated water, but the global atmosphere overheating in contaminated air. The need for public infrastructure is the same.

Public provision at least creates the possibility of a different *logic* guiding production. Socialists often contrast production for profit versus production for social need. The stark differences between these two was recently revealed in the Covid-19 global pandemic. Governments around the world entertained nationalizing whole sectors to produce *use values* for public health needs.[31] For-profit production of ventilator machines or masks was simply not in line with what sick human beings actually needed.

Clearly, the social need in question today is the need for a decarbonized energy system. Most radical proposals for a Green New Deal

30 Martin Melosi, *The Sanitary City: Environmental Services in Urban America From Colonial Times to the Present* (Baltimore: Johns Hopkins University Press, 2000).

31 Editorial Board, "Virus lays bare the frailty of the social contract," *Financial Times*, April 3, 2020.

or other large-scale climate interventions use "public works" or "wartime emergency" as analogies, because in those contexts planning and social need guided production.[32] Yet, despite the increased intensity of climate disasters, the political class still insists that decarbonization is an emergency best handled by capital and the narrow criteria of profit.

As covered in Chapter 6, our strategy for climate change should focus (for now) on only one sector: electricity. Public power can make decarbonization the primary goal of electricity provision, replacing profits. In 2020, the publicly owned Sacramento Municipal Utility District announced an ambitious plan that sets decarbonization targets ahead of what is required in California. The district announced that the public utility "recognizes the risk of uncontrolled climate change and is committed to urgently do more."[33]

Still, some are skeptical of public power. Strangely, after an entire book detailing the corrupt predations of the private utility industry, Leah Stokes advises that the climate movement should be "focusing less on ownership."[34] While we keep waiting for clean energy to be profitable, private owners of utilities are still quite happy to profit off combusting fossil fuels to generate electricity. Policy experts like Stokes seem more confident in complex regulatory mechanisms to force utilities to behave; today excitement revolves around something called the "Clean Electricity Standard" (CES), a market-based mechanism that sets goals for the amount of clean electricity a utility must produce. But such technocratic fixes often forget a key aspect of building power: a *mass popular base* for your program.[35] Although advocates claim that CES is "popular" according to some polls, it is not clear how the measure would lead to real material gains for a working

32 A really useful proposal is found in Andrew Bossie and J.W. Mason, "The public role in economic transformation: Lessons from World War II," Roosevelt Institute, March 26, 2020.

33 "Sacramento utility aims higher than state on climate," *E&E News*, July 20, 2020.

34 Leah Stokes, *Short Circuiting Policy: Interest Groups and the Battle Over Clean Energy and Climate Policy in the American States* (Oxford, UK: Oxford University Press, 2020), 241.

35 See, Matt Huber, "The revenge of the plans," *The Trouble*, April 2, 2021.

class that needs cheaper or even free electricity—and indeed in some states with existing CES policies, advocates admit it will come with higher costs.[36]

Stokes is correct that just shifting to public ownership does not *guarantee* decarbonization. For example, the state of Nebraska's electricity system is almost entirely publicly owned by the Nebraska Power District, but still gets 55 percent of its electricity from coal.[37] The Tennessee Valley Authority, even with its high unionization, still uses coal and gas for 44 percent of its power.[38] All public power does is to grant us a democratic opening for creating a comprehensive public sector–led transformation of the electricity sector in line with what climate science says is necessary. Actual movements need to do the rest.

The question is, what kind of social force could possibly create the kind of robust public institutions that take on private capital on behalf of society as a whole? Ellen Meiksins Wood put it bluntly in 1986, "No one can seriously maintain that any other social movement has ever challenged the power of capital as has the working class."[39] Of course, despite much excitement about "new" social movements or "new" agents of transformation, no social force has emerged since she wrote this: the power of capital has only grown. One can say generally that in societies in which working-class power is organized and strong, a robust public sector thrives, serving the working class as a whole.

The peak of working-class power in the United States was the 1930s, the same decade when the welfare state, limited as it was, came into being. The New Deal was also a massive energy program aimed at expanding electricity access to rural communities and others who needed it. Its ambition was matched with results. In 1934, 11 percent

---

36   Miranda Willson, "Wash. 100% clean power rules get blowback," *E&E News*, January 12, 2021.

37   Energy Information Administration "Nebraska State Profile." eia.gov/state/?sid=NE#.

38   Tennessee Valley Authority, "Our power system," tva.com/energy/our-power-system.

39   Wood, *The Retreat From Class*, 185.

of farms had access to electricity; in 1950 it was 90 percent.[40] These robust people-centered programs did not arise automatically through the good will of Franklin Roosevelt. Mass action like unemployed councils and labor strikes pushed the administration to build more ambitious public and working-class programs.

We do not need better environmental policy ideas to solve climate change; *we need a stronger working class.* As long as we are losing the larger class struggle, we are also losing the climate struggle. It is no coincidence that the establishment of the environmental regulatory state behind the Clean Air and Water Acts and the Environmental Protection Agency—the most significant environmental victories of the twentieth century in the United States—came at a time when working-class power was still relatively strong.

While there is no sugar-coating the continued weakness of the working class and the left in general, there are also encouraging signs. While he did lose both times, the presidential candidacies of Bernie Sanders restored a long-lost language of *class struggle* to politics generally, including the sense that the masses of workers are losing because the rich "billionaire class" is winning. Sanders's politics made clear that only through confrontation with the capitalist class can our longstanding problems be solved.

On the climate front, Sanders clearly and repeatedly asserted the need to "take on the fossil fuel industry" and in so doing inspired, along with Alexandria Ocasio-Cortez, a generation of youth climate activists in the Sunrise movement and beyond who understood their task was to build what they call "people power."[41] Insofar as the working class is the vast majority of this "people," these movements are on the right track. In 2020 and 2021, Bernie Sanders-style socialists—most, if not all, endorsed by Sunrise and the Democratic Socialists of America—continued to win office all across the country.

---

40 Dianna Everett, "Rural Electrification," *The Encyclopedia of Oklahoma History and Culture* okhistory.org.
41 Sunrise Movement, "Who we are," sunrisemovement.org/about.

Moreover, after a long slumber of atomization and resignation, work stoppages and strikes have increased in the last few years. In 2017, there were a mere 25,300 workers involved in major work stoppages. In 2018 and 2019, this rose to 485,200 and 425,500 respectively, the highest numbers since 1986.[42] Although the COVID-19 pandemic lessened strike actions overall in 2020, with many staying home for public health reasons, there were still several notable strike actions among "essential workers" at Amazon warehouses, meatpacking plants, and grocery stores.[43] As this book goes to press (October 2021), there has been a significant militant upsurge of strike activity including workers in health care, film, and ten thousand workers at John Deere plants across the country.[44] It is also clear the pandemic has created a "tight" labor market, which traditionally enhances worker leverage in the labor market, as a whole.

More importantly, it seems as if the post-pandemic political economy will yield profound volatility and economic crisis. As the Federal Reserve continues to inject billions of dollars in liquidity into banks and corporations, stocks and housing are once again experiencing unrestrained bubbles.[45] Supply chains remain disjointed and, most frighteningly, climate chaos is disrupting agricultural production across the world.[46] We can state with confidence that as indifference to working-class life among the wealthy and powerful becomes more and more evident, the material conditions for increased radicalization and militancy grow ever more favorable.

We should remember that in the United States the labor movement was relatively subdued in the late 1920s and early '30s, in the wake of

42 US Bureau of Labor Statistics, "25 major work stoppages in 2019 involving 425,500 workers," February 14, 2020.

43 Bryce Covert, "The coronavirus strike wave could shift power to workers—for good," *Nation*, April 16, 2020.

44 Hamilton Nolan, "The strike wave is a big flashing sign that we need more new union organizing" *In These Times*, October 14, 2021.

45 Ashley Brown, "Economy's bubble—from stocks to real estate—could be about to pop, say UNC experts," *WRAL Tech Wire*, July 17, 2021.

46 Associated Press, "UN chief: World hunger worsened by climate change, conflict," July 26, 2021.

red scare state repression and capitalist "open shop" tactics. But it didn't take long for a mixture of overwhelming crisis, policy shifts, and above all militant upsurge from workers themselves to dramatically tilt the balance of power toward the working class between 1933 and 1936. The result was the most significant restructuring of capital-labor relations in the twentieth century, the New Deal. Of course, it was fraught with contradictions and conciliations with the capitalist class, and by 1947 the working class was once again on the retreat. But we can learn lessons from these failures if a working-class upsurge comes again in the 2020s.

If it does, the conditions for massive political change will come quickly with it. The stakes this time are not simply class relations as such, but literally the planetary conditions for all human life. This time the masses of the working class have quite a lot more to lose than their chains. We not only have a world to win, but a planet to repair from the ravages of the capitalist class. Time is growing short.

Acknowledgments

Even though I wrote part of it in the isolation of a global pandemic, this book was a collective endeavor. The National Science Foundation generously funded the research for Chapter 2 (Award # 1437248). Special thanks to Carlo Sica and Jonathan Erickson, whom the grant funded as stellar research assistants. The grant also funded my conversations with chemical engineer Jesse Bond, who explained the nuances of ammonia synthesis with excitement and good humor. I want to thank the scholars and students at a variety of institutions who listened to, asked questions, and sometimes got angry about the various iterations of the arguments made here. This includes Lund University; the State University of New York at Buffalo; Temple University; Clark University; the National Socio-Environmental Synthesis Center; Yale University; and the University of South Carolina. I also want to thank all the graduate students at Syracuse University who taught me so much from various seminars on *Capital*, racial capitalism, and the political economy of nature.

I usually say this is more a "political" than "academic" book. So, beyond academia, I've gained so much from comrades in the Democratic Socialists of America, particularly those in the various political education efforts and eco-socialist committee within the Syracuse chapter. I also want to thank comrades from the Bread and Roses Caucus who have taught me more about political organizing and strategy than anything I've learned in universities

Special thanks to Fred Stafford and everyone else in the "chat" who really shaped my thinking on how electricity systems actually work. Thanks to Jane Slaughter for putting me in touch with David Poklinkoski from IBEW local 2304 in Wisconsin. Thanks to David for sharing such fascinating materials from his local and for the illuminating correspondences on his history of labor organizing in the electric utility sector. I also learned a lot thinking with Nikki Luke for a special issue we organized on "electricity capital" for *Environment and Planning E: Nature and Space* (but I learned most from her amazing dissertation on the topic, *Finding the Time: Valuing The Social Reproduction of Labor In Atlanta's Electricity Politics*, University of Georgia, 2020).

Massive thanks to Andreas Malm and Michael Pulsford, who provided incredibly generous (and generative!) comments on a draft of this manuscript. Thanks also to Diana Ojeda whose feedback and conversation significantly shaped the revisions to the manuscript. Thanks also to all the production staff at Verso Books and my editor Sebastian Budgen for keeping me on task.

In this barbarically unequal world, I'm beyond fortunate to have had so much love and support from my parents. I'm so thankful you've escaped the fires of California to join us in Central New York. I also want to give special thanks to my parents-in-law, who are not only super great people and fun to hang out with, but also provided so much childcare—especially during the summer months when I had more time to write and Angela was growing food. Here's hoping a low-carbon world can figure out how important this care work is for all of us.

It's become a cliché, but my feelings of urgency about writing a book on climate change came with becoming a parent, and the dread of what the future holds for a now six-year-old. Loretta, I love you so much! You bring the *fire* we need in this world! I just hope we can put out the literal fires to make sure the planet is safe into old age.

Angela, I'll never forgot that when the world went to hell, we got stronger for each other. I couldn't have written this without your unending love and support. I love living and laughing with you in this little corner of earth among the hills.

Index